My prayer is that this book, written by Hanspeter Nüesch, will be a source of encouragement to all men and women in ministry, and particularly to those contemplating the call of God on their lives. I was especially pleased by the emphasis placed on my wife and ministry partner, Ruth, because without her support I could not have done the work God gave me. For whatever our ministry has accomplished, I give all the glory to the Lord because it is his doing.

Billy Graham
Montreat, North Carolina

Ruth and Billy
GRAHAM

Ruth and Billy
GRAHAM

THE LEGACY OF A COUPLE

HANSPETER NÜESCH

MONARCH
BOOKS

Oxford, UK & Grand Rapids, Michigan, USA

Published by Monarch Books
an imprint of
Lion Hudson plc
Wilkinson House, Jordan Hill Road,
Oxford OX2 8DR, England
Email: monarch@lionhudson.com
www.lionhudson.com/monarch

ISBN 978 0 85721 536 9
e-ISBN 978 0 85721 537 6

First edition 2014

Acknowledgments
Scripture quotations are from the Holy Bible, New International Version®. NIV®. Copyright © 1973, 1978, 1984, 2011 by Biblica, Inc.™ Used by permission of Zondervan. All rights reserved worldwide. www.zondervan.com

A catalogue record for this book is available from the British Library

Printed and bound in Malta, January 2014, LH28

Contents

Foreword

One morning I received a call from my son informing me that a Swiss man connected with Campus Crusade for Christ had contacted him, wanting to meet me because he was writing a book about my mother and father. Because I receive many requests similar to this, I was a bit dubious and not very enthusiastic; however, to be nice, I agreed to meet him.

Later that week, Hanspeter arrived at my home in Florida.

Minutes after the first warm handshake, I knew I had met a new yet already very dear friend.

His exuberance, his enthusiasm, his energy, his laugh, his smile, his sense of humor, his love of life were all contagious. But more than these, his love of the Lord and his sense of purpose drew me to this very special person.

Hanspeter shared with me about the project he believed God had placed upon his heart—to write a book about my parents. It was a big project, and I was not at all sure he would be able to accomplish it, but I soon learned, if Hanspeter decides to do something . . . watch out!

A few months later, while visiting Hanspeter and his family in Switzerland, I began to get a small glimpse into the seriousness of this project. Hanspeter had spent hundreds of hours researching my family. He had gathered every book and article ever written about or by my family. He had acquired any piece of information he could get his hands on—books, papers, letters, and articles I had never even seen or knew existed. At times I had to laugh because he seemed to know more about me and my family than I did. Again I was caught up in his energy and enthusiasm and, yes, now believed he would accomplish this task.

The following summer Hanspeter and his wife, Vreni, visited me in North Carolina. One day we went to my parents' home to visit with my father. During this delightful visit, Hanspeter had a difficult time containing the excitement he was experiencing. He was so full of energy and exuberance for the Lord and his work in Europe and other parts of the world that I thought it would be overwhelming for my elderly father, who has a difficult time hearing. But it didn't take long before I realized my father was also excited by all the things God was doing through this enthusiastic Swiss Christian, and he wanted to hear more. So the next day my father invited us back again for lunch.

Hanspeter's wife, Vreni, writing to me in a letter, described Hanspeter and this book project the following way: "HP is so excited to be able to put down all the good and interesting and helpful stories and messages on paper. He is so filled with them that sometimes he is like a volcano."

I chuckled, as I recalled a few short months ago, standing in the window of their lovely home just outside of Zurich, taking in the beauty surrounding their hillside home and the charming village below. Vreni was in the kitchen preparing a delicious raclette, one of my favorite meals. The aroma emitting from the preparations made it difficult to give my undivided attention to Hanspeter, who kept trying to return my full attention to his book project. Hanspeter was so full of enthusiastic energy, so focused, so dedicated, so determined, so full of thoughts and ideas that he just could not contain himself. He just had to erupt like a volcano. I knew then that until this project was complete, Hanspeter would have a one-track mind.

Hanspeter's focused enthusiasm and obedience to what he felt God called him to do have paid off. This book is the finished product.

Thank you, Hanspeter, and thank you, Vreni, for supporting your volcano. You both bless me more than I can say. You too are people "who change the world." And I am grateful and privileged to call you dear friends.

Gigi Graham

Acknowledgments

Many people have contributed to the creation of this book, but without God's sovereign oversight and leading, I would never have met several of these people. Therefore, my primary thanks go to him.

I would first like to thank my wife, Vreni, the great love of my life for the past forty years. You are a continuing source of encouragement to me and have often given me wise feedback. Thanks for the many helpful conversations concerning this book, some of which took place in the middle of the night. I would also like to thank our four children—Stephan, Gretina, Daniel, and Seraina—who not only prayed for the book project but also contributed in a practical way with little touches here and there. Gretina, together with Iris Fontana, entered hundreds of quotations into the computer for later use.

But, humanly speaking, no one was more crucial to the success of the book project than Gigi Graham, who has become a true friend to Vreni and me. She hosted us in her home and visited us several times in Switzerland. She shared her life experiences as the eldest daughter of Ruth and Billy Graham with us and allowed us to peek behind the scenes of her parents' lives. She also made it possible for us to meet her father twice in his home. Gigi opened her personal photo albums and collected many valuable documents for the book.

I cannot imagine a more genuine and helpful person than Gigi Graham. Thanks also, Gigi, for your very personal foreword to this book. Thanks also to the staff at the Billy Graham Archives of Wheaton College, who helped me find missing documents. I am also very grateful for the helpfulness of Graham's personal staff in the Montreat office. Thanks to them, I was able to obtain a number of valuable documents as well as a long-sought-after book on Graham's teenage years. Inordinate generosity was shown by Stone Table Media, who provided me with many DVDs of interviews with Ruth Graham and people close to her at no cost.

I thank my staff at Campus für Christus Switzerland and in particular my personal assistants, Felix Rechsteiner, Michelle Maeder, and Vivane Herzog. They invested hundreds of hours in this project and were often the only ones who were able to maintain an overall perspective. The book could never have been produced without their enormous dedication.

Finally, I would like to thank the staff at SCM Haenssler in Germany and mainly editor in chief Uta Mueller, who helped initiate the project, not only for her great professional competence but also for her inner commitment.

A special thanks to Henriette L. Ludwig, who translated the book into English. She spent many hours trying to understand what I really wanted to communicate and phrased it in appropriate English. Thanks also to Tracy Koenig, Jeannie Wurz, and Laura Eastman (the sister-in-law of the Beatle Paul McCartney), who meticulously proofread and polished the text.

Last but not least, I would like to thank our twelve personal prayer partners, who have supported my wife and myself in prayer for many years and specifically also prayed for the book project. Your faithfulness and commitment are an incredible testimony, so, in a way, this book is also your book.

Hanspeter Nüesch

1

Partnership—A Couple's Legacy

She was born in 1920 on the East Coast of China and grew up as the daughter of an American missionary doctor in the midst of civil war. Not a single night passed in which she did not hear gunfire and fighting. The missionaries were called foreign devils. Many of them died as martyrs. She knelt before her bed and prayed, "Lord, let me also die as a martyr for you!" Her older sister prayed at the same time, "Please don't take her prayers seriously. She's too young to understand what she's praying." As a teenager, she had only one desire: to go to Tibet as a missionary. She didn't need anything or anyone for that, not even a husband. Jesus and the Bible would be enough. Yet she was also a very lively young girl, full of fun and always up to pranks. In order to receive a proper education, she was sent to Pyongyang, the capital of present-day North Korea. Far away from her parents, she learned how to overcome loneliness and homesickness by trusting Jesus Christ and making him her confidant and friend. In long letters to her family and in poems, she tried to express her thoughts and feelings. Most important to her, however, was her time alone with God. Studying the Bible was her favorite occupation. Her calling appeared to be clear.

He was born in 1918 in Charlotte, North Carolina, in the southeast of the United States, as the son of a dairy farmer. Milking cows was part of the daily routine, aside from school. But he much preferred driving his dad's car around with a pretty girl at his side. His main interests were baseball, girls, and world history, especially the history of the American presidents. He was an avid reader of Tarzan books. Then he was converted at a revival meeting in his hometown and attended Bible college. To finance the additional education, he worked as a door-to-door Fuller Brush salesman. He later left Bible college because he felt it was too rigid and authoritarian. Signs posted in dormitories said, "Griping Not Tolerated." At his departing interview, the director of the Bible college told him that if he kept on going the way he was going, nothing special would ever become of him—at most he would be a poor country Baptist preacher out in the sticks.

He tried another Bible institute in Tampa, Florida, where he had more freedom and soon fell in love with a pretty student, who became his girlfriend. He was already making wedding plans when she broke up with him. Gently but clearly she let him know that he was a really nice guy, but she wanted to marry a man who had a clear focus in life and was going to amount to something. She didn't think he was going to make it. Billy's world fell apart. He began to seek God and his will even more intensively. One night he strolled across the golf course at the Bible institute, brooding over his life. At the eighteenth green, he fell on his knees and prayed, "All right, Lord, if you want me, you've got me. I'll be what you want me to be, I'll do what you want me to do, and I'll go where you want me to go."[1]

If he wasn't going to be a famous preacher, then at least he wanted to be a soul winner. Time and again, he paddled into the swamps and preached to the trees and the alligators. Soon, the first opportunities came to preach at various churches. He also began preaching regularly at a mobile home park, which was more promising than preaching on the street, where he often had to deal with angry shop owners.

The daughter of the medical missionary in China had to leave the country abruptly due to the civil war and was sent to study at Wheaton College near Chicago. The farm boy received a scholarship for the same college after Bible school, and there they met. The farmer's son fell in love with the missionary's daughter. She was very impressed with his faith and earnestness. "This man knows who he's talking to," she thought to herself on hearing him pray in the room next door. He invited her to go to hear Handel's *Messiah*. She accepted the invitation. Afterward, she wrote in her diary that she would consider it her greatest privilege to spend her life at this man's side.

(Years later she remarked that if she had known what that would mean, she probably would not have had the courage to write something like that.) She still dreamed of working as a missionary in Tibet. However, he felt that God had given him a different calling. After a clarifying talk together, she gave up her life's dream with a heavy heart and committed herself to supporting his calling from that point on. She wrote in her diary, "He will be increasingly burdened for lost souls and increasingly active in the Lord's work. I will slip into

Ruth and Billy Graham
at their wedding in 1943.

the background. In short, be a lost life. Lost in Bill's." On August 13, 1943, Ruth Bell and Billy Graham married and started a teamwork that would influence the lives of countless people on all continents. This book is about two people from very different backgrounds and their relationships with God and their associates, their priorities and their principles, their love for people and their partnership. It's about a married couple functioning as a true team who had a lasting effect on the world: Ruth and Billy Graham. The story of Billy Graham's worldwide ministry has been recounted from many angles. Unfortunately, the same cannot be said of the significant contribution Ruth made to his ministry. What Billy Graham stands for to this day would not have been possible without his wife, Ruth.

No one did as much as Billy Graham to share the gospel with so many people face-to-face in the second half of the twentieth century. In addition, he reached millions of people via mass media. He preached on the American television network NBC when scarcely every fourth American even owned a TV. He transmitted the gospel of Jesus Christ in many great places on this planet and challenged people to make a decision. At the closing event of his first London Crusade in 1954, Wembley Stadium couldn't hold the enormous crowd of people who wanted to hear him. The same was true for the Olympic Stadium in Berlin soon after.

Graham's evangelistic campaigns in Europe—especially in Great Britain, Finland, and Germany—remain the biggest Christian events ever to take place in those countries. The same is true for Australia and New Zealand and many other countries around the world. Only the popes, particularly John Paul II, ever preached to similar multitudes. In 1954, the German weekly *Der Spiegel* ran a cover story about Billy Graham's mission in Germany.

A year later, the *Zürcher Kirchenbote* reported after his campaign in Zurich that never had so many people heard the message of the Bible all at once: "It was a moving moment when tens of thousands

The Berlin Olympic Stadium was bursting at the seams when Billy Graham preached the gospel there in 1954.

earnestly followed the gospel of redemption in Jesus Christ."[2] Many years later, the French newspaper *Le Figaro* titled a report on his ministry "Billy Graham, la voix de Dieu" (Billy Graham, the voice of God). The newspaper described him as a nearly untouchable institution or statue, an unequaled preacher who believed totally in the truth of the Bible.

Over the years, Billy Graham reached countless people through his live sermons; TV series; his weekly radio broadcast, *The Hour of Decision*; and his daily column, "My Answer." For many, he was God's messenger par excellence. In 1972, the *Saturday Evening Post* described him as "the greatest personal phenomenon of this age" and "the best known man in the world today." The *New York Times* may have been slightly more accurate when, after his appearances at London's Trafalgar Square and New York's Times Square, it stated that Billy Graham had transformed the "crossroads in the world" into "great cathedrals." The culmination of his worldwide evangelistic ministry occurred during his Global Mission in 1995, when the sermons of the seventy-seven-year-old preacher were transmitted from Puerto Rico via a network of 30 satellites to 165 countries. Together with subsequent broadcasts, it is estimated that one billion people had heard at least one of his messages. Over the course of more than half a century, Billy Graham is believed to have spoken face-to-face with more people than anyone in history, having preached the gospel in 185 countries in over 400 missions.

Graham was not only God's ambassador for the masses; he was also a confidant of royalty and a counselor to heads of state, including no less than twelve US presidents in a row. According to the staff members who accompanied him, he regularly used the meetings with politicians from around the world to speak about key aspects of the Christian faith. He knew he was to be the ambassador of God and not of the United States. He was the first—and for a long time the only—Western preacher to preach the gospel behind the Iron Curtain during the Cold War. Between 1967 and 1988, he preached in Yugoslavia, Hungary, Poland, East Germany, Romania, Czechoslovakia, and the Soviet Union.

Billy Graham preached in all kinds of places, such as in a bullring in Caracas, Venezuela, in 1962.

He was not only an evangelist who invited many to follow Jesus but also a prophetic voice of God for the nations, first and foremost the United States. For sociology professor William Martin, author of *A Prophet with Honor*, the most comprehensive biography of Billy Graham, Graham is "an icon not just of American Christianity but of America itself."[3]

Graham was rightly called America's pastor in the second half of the twentieth century. He was regularly asked to say the prayer at presidential inaugurations or to provide comfort, as after 9/11. For many years, Billy and Ruth were "the first couple of American Christianity." In 1996, the American Congress awarded Billy and Ruth Graham the Congressional Medal of Honor for their service to humanity, the highest honor Congress can give to a US citizen. It was only the third time in history that a woman received this award. For fifty years, Billy was always at the top in US surveys naming the most respected people. *Time* magazine stated, "Moral authorities have come and gone, but Graham has endured, his honor intact despite his proximity to the shattering temptations of power."[4]

When Ruth and Billy Graham married, they had no way of imagining their later fame. After their marriage, Billy was pastor of a small Baptist church for a little while. During this time, Torrey Johnson became aware of him. He asked Graham to take over his forty-five-minute weekly radio show *Songs in the Night* on Sunday evenings. After consulting with his church, Graham agreed. He was able to convince the singer George Beverly Shea to provide the musical part. Ruth helped with writing the sermon texts. Graham's evangelistic speaking ability became increasingly evident, especially to Johnson. He was convinced that Graham's call was evangelism and that he should give up his pastoral position in favor of becoming an evangelist. He challenged the twenty-six-year-old to help found Youth for Christ and serve as the first executive vice president. Youth for Christ was a youth movement that originally focused on members of the military. Its goal was to reach young servicemen while they were on leave. Johnson, commenting on the ministry of Graham at that time, said, "He has contacted youth leaders in America, Canada, Great Britain, Scandinavia and Europe, and fired them with enthusiasm to begin Youth for Christ rallies."[5]

Graham learned how to make the gospel message attractive without compromising the content. The Youth for Christ people said to themselves, "Why not use vessels that God's enemy generally uses and use them instead to lead people

In 1996, the American Congress awarded Billy and Ruth Graham the Congressional Medal of Honor for their service to humanity, the highest honor Congress can give to a US citizen.

to Jesus?" In the book *Deconstructing Evangelicalism*, the method of evangelism at the time is described as follows: "Its leaders, a group of unknown revivalists, combined born-again faith with the 'style' and 'media' of Hollywood and radio. . . . The rally leaders were borrowing from the very dens of the Devil . . . to accomplish the Lord's purposes."[6] And hundreds of teenagers and servicemen publicly confessed their faith in Jesus Christ.

Even in later years, Graham sought to use all worldly media, particularly the mass media, to spread the world's greatest message. Even before the internet existed, he used satellite technology to broadcast the gospel to several countries simultaneously. Yet he and his team did not want to place their trust in modern communication techniques but rather in the work of the Holy Spirit. For Graham, it was always important not to compromise content when using modern mass media. He wanted to communicate the gospel of Jesus Christ clearly without diminishing its content. Therefore, prior to TV appearances, he always spent considerable time in prayer.

He wanted to do justice to the great responsibility of being God's ambassador when using the world's tools.

Graham was a sought-after guest on talk shows, primarily due to his unaffected, natural manner. Larry King, who interviewed him no less than twenty-four times on CNN, honored his work with the following words: "His ministry on radio, TV, and in every type of magazine touched millions of every color, tribe and race. From Parliaments to Presidents, from kings to common folks, each one heard the truth of God's amazing grace."[7] King called Graham a true friend and thanked him for his prayers when he was ill.

But Graham also recognized the dangers of the media circus:

> With this kind of publicity and media exposure, people have a tendency to feel that you are larger in life. Many people put me on a pedestal where I do not belong. I am not the holy, righteous prophet of God that many people think I am. I share with Wesley the constant feeling of my own inadequacy and sinfulness. I am often amazed that God can use me at all.[8]

U2 lead singer Bono, who visited the Grahams' home, said of this humble attitude, "At a time when religion seems so often to get in the way of God's work, I give thanks just for the sanity of Billy Graham, for the clear and empathetic voice."[9]

The lives of Graham and his team bore so much constant fruit over the years because their root, their relationship with God, was healthy. From each individual's relationship with God also sprang a healthy team spirit. The onstage team (Billy Graham, Cliff Barrows, and George Beverly Shea) stayed together for over sixty years and proclaimed the simple gospel in words and song on all continents. They were the ones who were the most astonished about how God used them.

The core team around Graham worked very hard to fulfill their mission. They wanted to give their best for God and others. Excellence was their standard in all areas, be it radio recordings, choir singing, or the framework of the evangelistic events. This pursuit of the best possible performance also spread to the office staff.

In the seventies, I had the opportunity to visit the headquarters of the Billy Graham Evangelistic Association (BGEA), which was located in Minneapolis at the time. What struck me most was the absolute professionalism with which everyone carried out their work. Everything was done so that the people who had responded to the proclamation of the gospel were taken care of in the best possible way and found themselves in the company of active Christians. Graham said that the best message deserved to be supported by the best possible management. Good, professional management was especially important for follow-up so that the fruits of the ministry did not rot but instead fully matured.

Today, the BGEA offices are located in Charlotte, North Carolina, not far from the place where Graham grew up. They are just as professionally organized as they were in Minneapolis. The call center, which receives incoming calls from seekers, has become smaller. But new ministries have been added, such as a Rapid Response Team, which focuses on disaster counseling, and Dare to Be a Daniel, a ministry specifically geared toward the younger generation. Graham no longer does any live preaching, but recordings of his sermons are still at the heart of evangelistic missions in which local Christians watch the films together with their neighbors and friends. Through the My Hope television projects, local believers all across a nation or a geographical region are trained to open their homes to share the gospel using filmed broadcasts of evangelistic sermons by Billy and Franklin Graham. To this day, the BGEA helps meet the urgent need for Christians to share the gospel. By 2011, they had trained more than twenty thousand people in personal evangelism through the Christian Life and Witness Course.

Billy Graham's evangelistic campaigns, many of which were broadcast nationwide, his weekly radio broadcasts, his daily newspaper columns, as well as his books, some of which became bestsellers, all had a strong revivalist influence on Christian believers as well as on people who came to faith through them. Church historians all agree that Graham's ministry contributed significantly to a revival of faith and to increasing church attendance, particularly in the postwar period in the United States and Great Britain. In the mid-fifties, three times as many Christian books were sold in the United States than the total of any other books combined. In the sixties and seventies, every second person who entered a full-time Christian ministry in Great Britain could trace their decision to Graham's evangelistic campaigns. I have personally met a number of spiritual leaders who told me that they received Christ at a Billy Graham crusade. Among them are people as diverse as George Verwer, founder of Operation Mobilisation; Norman Rentrop, initiator of the German Bibel TV; the pastor of our local Baptist Free Church; as well as the president of the local Protestant State Church.

The longer Billy Graham preached at a particular location, the more sustained were the results and the more evident the effects on

Billy Graham said, "The best message deserves the best marketing." This photo shows a particularly creative example of advertising from the mid-1950s in Germany.

society. After his missions in
Great Britain, the social cli-
mate changed in such a way
that faith and Jesus Christ
were topics of hot debate for
everyone from the workman
on the street to the executives
in top levels of management.

The effects of his three Australian evangelistic missions
were astounding. The *Sydney
Daily Mirror* reported in 1959
that the Billy Graham crusade
had reduced the crime rate in

In the early years of Billy Graham's ministry, *Life* magazine reported extensively on his campaigns. In 1950, in Columbia, South Carolina, Billy preached before a stadium packed with people.

parts of Sydney by half. The Australian Bureau of Statistics noted
a significant reduction of alcohol consumption as well as illegiti-
mate births, in addition to a falling crime rate. *Christianity Today*
stated in 2007 that the effects of the Billy Graham crusades were
still evident in the present. They "changed the course of Australian
history." The Graham crusades in Australia also affected the local
churches. Marcus Loane, archbishop of the Anglican Church at the
time, summed it up:

> The Graham Crusades . . . brought a lasting uplift into the experi-
> ence of many parish churches. During the decade which followed,
> there has been a constant stream of candidates for the ministry or
> for missionary service: men (or women) whose lives were touched by
> the Spirit of God and who could not resist the call to His service.[10]

Peter Jensen, Anglican archbishop of Sydney, who together with
his brother, Phillip Jensen, had become a believer at a Billy Graham
crusade, held a Thanksgiving celebration for Billy Graham crusades
in Australia in May 2009 on the fiftieth anniversary of the first crusade. So great was the impact of Graham's ministry in Australia!

delegations from abroad in the past but rarely by such brothers and sisters in faith who loved the Lord Jesus as they did. I visited North Korea for the first time in 1995, just one year after the death of Kim Il Sung. I must credit Graham's previous visits for the great trust we from Switzerland were granted by confessing evangelical Christians, from the lower officials all the way up to the minister level of the government.

Many missions agencies and Christian leaders testify that Billy Graham gave them a decisive push to start their ministry. For him, it was never about increasing his own organization but that the ministry of the body of Christ as a whole should grow. Time and time again, he used his good reputation to promote all kinds of evangelistic ministries and other Christian initiatives. Unlike many other evangelicals at the time, he valued representatives of the Pentecostal-charismatic movement, such as Oral Roberts and David Yonggi Cho, as blessed brothers and stood up for them publicly. In doing so, he provided an invaluable service to maintain unity within the body of Christ. His only goal was that as many people as possible could hear the gospel of Jesus Christ. All of his life, his greatest desire was to win souls. He subordinated everything else to this goal.

Together with his longtime associates, Billy Graham changed the lives of countless people in the second half of the twentieth century through his evangelistic preaching and the wide network of his ministries. It was always individuals whose lives were changed. However, because there were so many of them—estimates range in the millions—the effects were felt in countless families and even in the extended networks of these changed people. Some who were converted within the framework of Graham and his organization's ministries not only bore fiftyfold or hundredfold fruit but also helped thousands, yes, tens of thousands to hear the gospel. Quite a few of them were also called to full-time Christian service. Hundreds of workers in God's kingdom all over the world attribute their calling to Graham's ministry.

Who is the person who stood beside Billy Graham as his wife and helper throughout his life? Ruth Graham, who passed away in 2007, was definitely an extraordinary person. The authors of the book *Christian Wives*, who portray and compare the lives and ministries of seven wives of outstanding Christian figures, describe Ruth as follows: "Yet of all the seven women in this book, none is more unique than Ruth Graham. . . . Unique means one and only one, and that is the best description of Ruth Graham."[14]

The more I studied the life and ministry of Billy and Ruth Graham, the more I discovered how the partnership they lived out was decisive for Billy's world-spanning ministry. The reports from people who were personally connected to them were particularly helpful in revealing their different roles. All five of the Grahams' children agree that Billy Graham as we know him would not have existed without Ruth. She must be counted among the most influential Christian personalities of the twentieth century.

A number of character traits were symbiotically interwoven into Ruth's personality: profound faith and a global interest, sensitivity and compassion, earnestness and feistiness, sharp intellect and passionate drive, unorthodoxy coupled with courage, "a lion's courage," as her son Franklin once expressed it. One thing really stood out: her quick wit and sense of humor. Billy was also humorous, but his humor was different from his wife's. According to Ruth and Billy's children, it often happened that everyone was laughing except Daddy, who was the actual reason for the laughter. His youngest son, Ned, remarked on his father's humor, "Well, Dad has a sense of humor, but he doesn't know he's funny. He cracks people up, and then he looks around the room and wonders why everyone is laughing. He's just hilarious."[15]

Ruth saw the home as her main area of responsibility. She once said that her husband had only one project, and she had several: their children. All five kids—three daughters and two sons—followed in their parents' spiritual footsteps and serve in manifold ways, both sons, however, only after going the long way around.

For Ruth, the children always had priority, and for herself, there was no greater privilege than being a mother. In order to have time for her children, she was rarely active in public ministry. She felt that one member of the family who traveled around the world and preached was enough. Billy was often away for weeks, so it was important that at least she stayed at home. Billy's periods of absence were very hard for both of them. Billy often had to secretly wipe the tears from his eyes when he left his family for a mission in a foreign country lasting several weeks. Ruth never complained in front of the children about her husband's absences, but she did on occasion take one of Billy's jackets to bed to at least have something of his near her.

Ruth and Billy Graham with their five children. From left, the oldest child, to right, the youngest one: Gigi, Anne, Ruth, Franklin, and Ned.

It helped Ruth to write down her feelings and deal with them in poems. The following words reveal Ruth's emotional state during the times when Billy was away for longer periods:

When in the morning I make our bed,
pulling his sheets and covers tight,
I know the tears I shouldn't shed
will fall unbidden as the rain;
and I would kneel,
praying again words I mean
but cannot feel.
"Lord not my will
but Thine be done."
The doubts dissolving one by one. . . .
For I will realize as I pray,
that's why it happened
. . . and this way.[16]

Aside from her tasks as wife and mother, Ruth stood at her husband's side in many other ways. She was Billy's lifelong, wise adviser. She was educated and extraordinarily well-read, a woman with a broad horizon. She provided input and collected illustrations for his sermons. She helped him write his books and articles by pointing out appropriate Bible verses or literature on a particular topic. Thanks to her excellent Bible knowledge and wide learning, Ruth was a constant source of inspiration for her husband. Many illustrations in her husband's sermons bear her mark.

The official Billy Graham biographer, John Pollock, emphasizes that no one contributed to Billy's broad horizon as much as Ruth:

She had no need to polish his manners or graces, but she was cultured, traveled, with a love of art and literature. She saved his seriousness from degenerating into stuffy solemnity, and preserved from extinction the light touch, the slice of small boy. Moreover, Ruth and her family, loyal Presbyterians, eased Billy Graham from his unspoken

you, and the Americans would never elect a divorced person president." That set things straight once and for all.

Ruth was very wise. She had a fine sense of God's will for a particular situation. She gained this intuitive knowledge in her time alone with God and his Word. Billy accepted Ruth's counsel gratefully. He knew that God had put Ruth at his side, and he therefore needed to listen to her. In his last appearance on the *Larry King Live* show on June 16, 2005, Billy paid her a great compliment: "I don't think I could have ever married anybody that would have been more helpful to my work and ministry than she has been. And she is still very bright."[19]

Ruth went home forever on June 14, 2007, at the age of eighty-seven. Billy dedicated the following testimony to her on the occasion of her passing:

> Ruth was my life partner, and we were called by God as a team. No one else could have borne the load that she carried. She was a vital and integral part of our ministry, and my work through the years would have been impossible without her encouragement and support. . . . My wife, Ruth, was the person to whom I would go for spiritual guidance. She was the only one I completely confided in. She was a great student of the Word of God. Her life was ruled by the Bible more than any individual I have ever known.

⌒ↂ⌒

At Ruth's request, on her gravestone is written, "End of Construction—Thank you for your patience." She saw it originally at the end of roadwork.

Ruth and Billy Graham were not perfect Christians. They had strengths and weaknesses like all of us. Although she was a very sensitive person, Ruth at times could confront people very bluntly, to the point of irritating them. Billy had weaknesses in other areas. There were times when Billy confused American culture with the kingdom of God, as he himself later admitted. There were times when he was in danger of not only standing by the American presidents as a spiritual and moral counselor but also giving political advice. If Ruth hadn't repeatedly warned him, this would have happened far more often. His wife once kicked his leg under the table when they were dining with President Johnson and Billy attempted to give him political advice.

Of the twelve presidents he'd known, eleven became friends, and seven of them close ones. Often, in times when important decisions needed to be made, they were simply glad to have a friend in Billy Graham, who was nearby, whom they trusted, and with whom they could share their burdens and pray. In their book *The Preacher and the Presidents*, *Time*'s Nancy Gibbs and Michael Duffy described the personal relationship of the presidents to Billy Graham:

> They entered into an unspoken covenant of private counsel and public support. The presidents called for comfort, they asked the simplest questions: How do I know if I'll go to heaven? Eisenhower wanted to know. Do you believe in the Second Coming? Kennedy wondered. Will I see my parents when I die? Johnson asked.[20]

During my research, I discovered—with quite some surprise—that Billy Graham personally got to know most of the American presidents of his lifetime many years before they took office, with the exception of President

Billy Graham speaking to President Lyndon B. Johnson.

38

Truman and President Obama. Billy got to know Ronald Reagan, who was still an actor at the time, in 1953 on the golf course, because Nancy's mother wanted to introduce Billy to her new son-in-law. Could Billy have imagined at that time that twenty-eight years later he would say the prayer at Ronald Reagan's inauguration to the office of president of the United States? And

Former President Bill Clinton speaking at the 2005 New York Crusade. Bill Clinton, in a tribute to Billy Graham, said, "Billy Graham visited me after the pain of my private sin became public and the subject of political debate. We talked about repenting, atonement, and forgiveness. He was a source of strength, reassurance, and faith beyond my ability to relate."[21]

could he have thought that his 1959 crusade in Little Rock would stir the thirteen-year-old Bill Clinton so deeply because Graham boldly preached the message of God's love and reconciliation in the midst of exploding racial hatred? Clinton recalls that immediately after that event he began donating some of his pocket money to Graham from time to time. Years later, when Clinton was governor of Arkansas, he got to know Graham in a very personal way when they visited Clinton's pastor, who was suffering from cancer, and prayed for him together.

It seems that God arranged these meetings because he obviously wanted the American presidents and their wives to have two people like Billy and Ruth come alongside them to serve as counselors. I cannot explain this extraordinary fact in any other way. Ruth remained friends with several first ladies. She was particularly close to Lady Bird Johnson, Nancy Reagan, and Barbara Bush. Yet she always was herself, something the first ladies truly appreciated about her.

Despite the mistakes they made, there was much Ruth and Billy did well, so well, in fact, that God entrusted them with a very great responsibility. He could do this because they loved him above all else and sought solely his glory. God could fully trust that they would fulfill their commission and life purpose and pass on his Word simply and without compromise, and without placing themselves in the foreground. President George W. Bush attributes Graham's successful ministry to the fact that his humility and obvious love for God can overwhelm even a cynic. Bush described him as a magnet to people, but Graham himself would not be a magnet to Billy Graham. He would be a magnet for a higher power.[22]

It is truly remarkable how faithfully Ruth and Billy carried out their evangelistic mandate for over sixty years without letting themselves be distracted in any way. God could entrust Ruth and Billy with the responsibility of being his ambassadors because they loved their fellow men—and not just the likeable ones—with all their hearts. Ruth had a special affinity for people on the darker side of life and for those who had failed in the eyes of others. She always tried to see them through God's eyes.

Billy and Ruth's desire to live out God's mercy is certainly a reason why God never retracted his blessing on them and their team for over sixty years. When they made mistakes, they claimed God's grace and forgiveness, and in the same way, they extended mercy toward their spiritual brothers and sisters. They also stayed the course because, contrary to other spiritual leaders, they were never involved in scandals, mainly due to the guidelines they stuck to from the start of their ministry.

The Modesto Manifesto, as it is now called (discussed in detail in chapter 6), protected the couple and their co-workers from many pitfalls. Particularly the principle not to participate in criticism of spiritual brothers and sisters but instead to encourage and motivate them became a great blessing for Billy and his team. And Ruth reinforced this biblical truth because she believed that Satan trembles when he sees the weakest believer upon his knees but that he laughs without restraint when saints bash other saints. When the Grahams were attacked, they handed the matter over to God and joyfully continued their ministry to proclaim the gospel of Jesus Christ.

Billy always greatly esteemed brothers and sisters who saw their calling in other areas and who had a different theological focus. At the same time, however, he emphasized that his calling was to proclaim the key gospel truths simply and understandably and to urgently call people to follow Christ. He was convinced that the content of the message remained the same, whether he was speaking to people in America, Europe, Asia, or Africa, whether they were educated or not. The human heart and the basic problem of sin were the same everywhere. The form of the proclamation and the types of illustrations could be different but not the key content: God's unconditional love, the saving grace of Jesus Christ, and the call to repentance.

Even with all of his openness toward different expressions of faith, Billy never compromised on the content of his message. "The Bible says" became his trademark. No other person in the twentieth century made people as conscious of the fact that God speaks to us through the Bible. For Billy and Ruth, the Bible was the absolute authority and thus the guideline for faith and life because it was inspired by God. They emphasized time and again that God had laid no promises on sheer human words but only on his Word, the Bible. The Holy Spirit uses the biblical Word to show people God's love, to explain Jesus's work, and to convict them of their sins. That is why the Grahams held the conviction that the unabridged gospel message should be preached and the core content should remain intact. Early on, Billy had decided not to give a sermon without placing Christ's death on the cross at the heart of his message and to call people to make a decision—a commitment he remained true to all his life.

Billy always emphasized that following Christ has its price. Friends will turn away because we will no longer participate in their sinful behavior. The "I" must always be crucified anew, otherwise it will stand in the way of God's plan for our lives. He often quoted Jesus's exhortation in Mark 8:34: "Whoever wants to be my disciple must deny themselves and take up their cross and follow me." Ruth and Billy always spoke about Jesus Christ, whether in private, personal conversations or in front of thousands of people in a stadium. There was no proclamation of the gospel without the invitation to "love Jesus and hate sin" from now on. Their message was the fundamentally new life that Christ gives, and not a life improved by human effort. This new life is based on an entirely new source of strength, the Holy Spirit, who works in the believer when Christ has become the Lord of his or her life. Billy always emphasized that any lasting change must happen from the inside out. He attached great importance to the key role of the local church, whose job it is to deepen the faith of new believers and to anchor them in God's Word. He felt his contribution to this was very small, as the more important task was up to the local Christians. According to Graham, the commitment of local churches and fellowships was irreplaceable. Active collaboration of the local churches was the element that, in the end, proved how blessed the evangelistic meetings would be and how much long-term fruit would result.

Graham represents a type of evangelism that from beginning to end is focused on the growth of Christian churches. His closest co-worker for many years, T. W. Wilson, in the anthology *Evangelism in the Twenty-First Century*, emphasized the key importance of the local church with regard to evangelistic crusades: "I know of no other institution on earth that is better equipped to make disciples than the local church. Crusade evangelism should serve the church rather than the church serve the crusade."[23]

Ruth and Billy Graham combined truth and love in their lives. Their lives and ministry are proof that compassion and deep love for people need not be at the expense of an undiluted biblical standpoint. They connected with people through their kindness and the appreciation they showed toward others, even those who held different opinions.

They built bridges within the body of Christ and united Christians in their evangelistic assignment because they never lost sight of the center, Jesus Christ. They knew they were solely accountable to their divine Friend, whose name they wanted to glorify. It was also their hearts' desire to contribute to reconciliation of the different ethnic groups. Long before the Anti-Discrimination Act, Billy only accepted invitations to speak at integrated events. For him, all people were equal before the cross of Christ, and all prayed to the same God and Father.

Ruth and Billy had a deep trust in the power of prayer. Both spent an extraordinary amount of time in prayer. During the initial years of his ministry, Billy spent so much time on his knees in prayer that the doctor feared Billy's knees would be damaged. Ruth also cultivated an intensive prayer life and always tried to remain "online" with God throughout the day. She was convinced that prayer is the best weapon in the battle against the enemy of God and that prayer changes not only circumstances but also ourselves. Ruth said, "Satan fears prayer because God hears prayer. God has decreed to act in response to prayer. We cannot pray and remain the same." Ruth was convinced that nowhere do we grow spiritually more quickly than on our knees. She had an extraordinary trust in God's power and love and was convinced that in his sovereignty he would know what the best answer to a prayer would be. She saw as one of her primary tasks to pray regularly for God's blessings on Billy and his various ministries, as well as for their children.

Billy's great trust in the power of prayer expressed itself in the fact that he always asked for prayer for himself and his projects. In his evangelistic outreaches, great emphasis was placed on prayer and training in prayer. One woman traveled from one crusade to another to pray for Billy and his team. When the team learned about this, the woman was specially honored, and as a token of their appreciation, her photo was published alongside other photos of "VIPs" who had supported the campaign. Ruth and Billy repeatedly emphasized the very important contribution that prayer partners made to the success of the crusades. They deeply believed that only thanks to the intercession of countless people was so much spiritual fruit produced.

Billy and Ruth always vehemently fended off attempts to place them on a pedestal, which only God deserves. They emphasized that Jesus Christ was and is the only one who will never disappoint us. Precisely because they always directed the attention to God, they can serve as role models for us. If anyone was acutely aware of God's daily grace and mercy, it was them. This fact made them very gracious toward others. Their lives radiated some of God's unconditional love, and everyone felt comfortable in their presence. Ruth and Billy privately lived what Billy publicly preached.

What distinguished Billy and Ruth more than anything else was their uncommonly deep, personal relationship with God. Out of this relationship flowed humility and sincerity, which were reflected in all areas of their lives and ministry. When I asked their daughter Ruth, whom the family calls Bunny, to describe her parents with a brief phrase, she replied, "Daddy is thoroughly authentic, and Mother is just in love with Jesus."

Popular novelist Patricia Cornwell moved to Montreat, the hometown of the Grahams, at age seven following her parents' divorce. She was often in the Grahams' home. Patsy, as she was called, provides a beautiful testimony about Billy: "I dearly love Billy Graham for his ever sweet, unassuming, and gracious attention, and, most profoundly, for not disappointing me up close. You are better than your legend and bigger than your name."[24]

Many of Billy's and Ruth's typical character traits, such as their true modesty and lifelong faithfulness to God's calling, can only be understood and classified within the context of their intimate relationship with their divine Friend. Their deepest, heartfelt wish was never to disappoint their Friend. Billy's typical reply to the praise of former presidents Carter, Bush Sr., and Clinton at the official opening of the Billy Graham Library in Charlotte was, "I just wanted to please the Lord."

After the death of his wife, Ruth, my wife and I had the privilege of visiting Billy at his home in Montreat in the North Carolina mountains to share and pray with him. We experienced a man who combined a deep relationship with Jesus with an active interest in what was happening in the world. And what a modest person! In our conversations, he repeatedly pointed away from himself to Jesus Christ: "I am glad that you lift up Jesus. He deserves all the honor. If there is any fruit in my ministry, then it's all because of him."

In an interview on NBC in 2005, during his last major crusade in New York, Graham was asked how he would like to be remembered. He answered, "Well, I hope they'll say that he was faithful. That he was faithful to the message all through his life. He didn't depart. He didn't veer. And I'm thankful that I have the help of the Holy Spirit to do that."[25]

Based on his thorough studies of Graham's theology of evangelism, Thomas Paul Johnston confirms that Graham's theology and

Vreni and Hanspeter Nüesch during a visit with Billy Graham at his home in Montreat, North Carolina, shortly before his ninetieth birthday.

key message always remained the same and that he always practiced what he preached, which makes him different from many of
his contemporaries. The author summarizes Graham's legacy as an
evangelist briefly and succinctly: "His more than sixty-three years
of crusade evangelism ministry have restored honor to a profession
misunderstood by the world."

And in the quite critical anthology *The Legacy of Billy Graham:
Critical Reflections on America's Greatest Evangelist*, his legacy is
described in a similar way:

> Probably for the first time in the twentieth century, especially in the
> Church of England, a distinct form of enthusiastic, experiential, and
> revivalist conservative Christianity gained the official seal of approval.
> What had usually defined itself negatively against other competing
> versions mutated into a normal type of Christianity. . . . He has perma-
> nently influenced the preaching of many thousands of our preachers.[26]

Ruth and Billy displayed an extraordinary faithfulness to God and
his Word, the Bible. They were convinced that the biblical message
is relevant to all and did not need to be *made* relevant. Graham's
message was not improvement but rather a totally new creation. He
proclaimed a fundamentally new life with fundamentally new empowerment, with Jesus Christ at the center. To him, it was not about
people straining with all their might to lead a morally acceptable life
but instead being connected to the divine power supply that makes
a life as a Christian possible in the first place.

Ruth was a full-fledged evangelist too. While Billy proclaimed the
gospel from the podium, she shared it from person to person. Many
people have confessed that Ruth showed them the way to follow Jesus
by making God and his grace visible to them.

While I was studying Ruth and Billy Graham's lives, I was surprised time and again by how they simply do not fit any clichés. Their
dependency on the Holy Spirit was extraordinary, especially when
you take into consideration that they cannot be counted among the
Pentecostals or the charismatics in the narrow sense. Would one

have expected an evangelist to
write an extensive Bible exege-
sis on angels? His book *Angels:
God's Secret Agents*[27] became a
bestseller. Ruth stood out with
her great love of thorough and
systematic study of the Bible.
Ruth was the theologian of the
house due to the way she meticulously consulted different
translations and commentaries when she studied the Bible.
Billy never considered himself a
theologian. Contrary to Ruth,
who graduated with a degree in
theology, his major had been anthropology. He therefore found
it important to seek the help of
renowned evangelical theolo-

At Wheaton College near Chicago they first
met each other and fell in love. On August
13, 1993, Billy and Ruth returned to the place
to celebrate their fiftieth wedding anniversary.

gians. By linking up with these theological thinkers, who shared his
missional concerns, Billy became an evangelical voice heard around
the world. The combination of a passionate heart and a cool head
shaped his ministry and particularly the mission congresses he initiated. Contrary to the reasons for which people often reproach evangelists, Billy and Ruth lived and taught a holistic understanding of
missions in which words and deeds are in balance.

We do not do Ruth and Billy justice if we judge them only by
Billy's evangelistic sermons, despite their great importance. Personally, I find that their practiced partnership in all aspects of life and
ministry is their greatest legacy. Billy's and Ruth's lives and ministry
show very clearly what a great blessing lies in a togetherness in which
both partners lead a life completely focused on God and their joint

calling. Ruth and Billy have shown what a great blessing it is when both spouses contribute their talents to the whole and thus complement and enhance each other. Partnership characterized their lives. They saw ministry as teamwork. This was also true for their closest associates, Cliff Barrows, George Beverly Shea, and T. W. Wilson, with whom they worked all their lives. That is why the topics of partnership and teamwork run throughout the following chapters like a red thread. Without this lived partnership in all areas, Billy Graham as we know him today would not exist.

What can we learn from Ruth and Billy and their closest team members? What guidelines marked their lives and ministry? What character traits are evidently important in God's eyes for spiritual leaders? Where did Ruth and Billy set their priorities? How did they keep their focus throughout their lives? What mistakes did they make from which we can learn? In the following chapters, I will deal with these and other questions in more detail and try to provide answers. In doing so, I will not hide some of the weaker points of this couple because we can often learn more from mistakes than from successes. And if anyone was aware of their deficiencies and a need to depend on God's grace, it was the Grahams.

2

Authenticity—Genuine Living

Billy Graham is the same person all the time. There is no coverup or facade. Billy is Billy wherever he is, preaching to multiplied thousands, jogging on a path near his home in Montreat, riding horseback, playing golf, swimming, preparing a sermon, or eating lunch with his lovely wife, Ruth.[1]

Grady Wilson, longtime team member

Ruth refuses to be poured into a mold. She does exactly what she wants to. . . . Ruth is fiercely independent about many things; and though many people are "leaders with no followers," Ruth is a natural-born leader—yet also one of the most dedicated followers of Christ that you'll ever meet.[2]

Betty Frist, neighbor

Though the world knows and loves Billy and Ruth Graham, God has graciously allowed me to know Billy and Ruth as Daddy Bill and TaiTai. Perhaps the greatest blessing is that there is absolutely no difference between the public life of Billy and Ruth Graham and the private life of Daddy Bill and TaiTai. The authenticity of the Gospel lived out in the lives of my grandparents has been a gracious example given to me by our loving Heavenly Father.[3]

Basyle "Boz" Tchividjian, grandson

While we receive the best impression of what is going on in Ruth's heart by reading her poems, Billy's heart can best be felt by studying his messages. What he spoke from the podium characterized his life. His personality came out in his message and vice versa. When he shouted "God loves you" to the crowd three times in a row, it was not a shrewd marketing ploy for God but instead a reflection of his innermost convictions. The core of his message remained the same for over sixty years. This core marked all the facets of his life and ministry, and he passed on this message with simplicity but with great force.

In 2005, as one of his last public appearances, Billy Graham held a three-day evangelistic outreach in the city of New York. The words

In his last sermon in New York in 2005, Billy Graham pointed to Jesus Christ.

with which he ended his last sermon there are an excellent summary of what he stood for throughout his life and what filled his heart:

The Bible says all our righteousness is like filthy rags in the sight of God. All the good works that we do don't count anything toward Heaven. After you receive Christ, you want to do all the good works you can, but before that, you must repent and come to Christ by faith. When Jesus came, He didn't come just to teach us how to live. He came to die on the cross. . . .

The Bible says there is going to be a great coronation. Millions of angels, along with millions of people who have followed Christ in their life here on this Earth, are going to have a gigantic banquet called "the marriage supper of the Lamb." Jesus is the Lamb, and He is going to be crowned King of kings and Lord of lords.

What a glorious moment that's going to be! I'm looking forward to that. In fact, George Beverly Shea, whom you just heard sing so beautifully "How Great Thou Art," is ninety-six. I'm eighty-six, on my way to eighty-seven. I know that it won't be long before both of us are going to be in Heaven.

Jesus said, "Be ready." In Amos, the fourth chapter, it says, "Prepare to meet your God." Are you prepared? Have you opened your heart to Jesus? Have you repented of your sins?

You say, "What is repentance?" Repentance means you say to God, "I am a sinner. I am sorry for my sins, I'm willing to turn from my sins, but Lord, You have to help me to turn. I've tried so many times to give up things I know are wrong, but I just can't do it. I need Your help." Then by faith, you receive Christ who died on the cross for you. You open your heart and say, "Yes, Lord Jesus, come in. I'm ready to follow You." . . .

This might be the last day of your life. We never know. The Bible says that "Today is the accepted time, today is the day of salvation!" The Scripture says, quoting God, "I will not always strive with man." There comes a time when it is too late. The only way you can come to Christ is with the Holy Spirit helping you to come—and He will help you, but not always.

51

There comes a time when it will be too late for you. I'm going to ask you to come to Christ today. This may be the last opportunity you will ever have. I'm going to ask you to get up out of your seat and come in front of this platform and say tonight, "I want Jesus in my heart. And I'm going to do my best to repent of my sins and follow Him."

And if you are watching in some of the other parts of the stadium, you can come to the front of that television screen and there will be people there to talk with you and pray with you and give you some literature to help you in your Christian life. I'm going to ask you to come now and receive Christ into your heart. God bless you.[4]

With the above words, Graham finished his last evangelistic campaign in New York on June 26, 2005. Two of his friends participated in the service: Cliff Barrows, who, as always, led the choir, and George Beverly Shea, who prepared the audience musically for the sermon with his deep baritone voice. The trio had begun their evangelistic ministry together sixty years earlier, and after having brought the gospel to millions of people around the globe, they also ended their public service together. If further proof is needed

For sixty years, the stage team served together and proclaimed the gospel on all continents in word and in song. From left to right: Cliff Barrows, Billy Graham, George Beverly Shea. The photo was taken at a mission in Jacksonville, Florida, in 2000.

for the genuineness of Graham and his closest team members, this was it. You can only keep up personal passion if you don't have to keep up appearances—if you are the same person in public as you are behind closed doors.

One of the reasons why the core team stayed together for so many years was because Graham was the opposite of a prima donna. He was a brother to the rest of the team: genuine and very real. Russ Busby, the official photographer for over forty years who accompanied Graham on his national and international trips, put it this way: "I appreciate Billy personally, and if he wasn't real, I couldn't work for him this long. I would not be happy. But I have found him very real and very honest."[5]

At the press conference in New York, Graham was asked what his most frequent prayer had been in recent times. He answered with disarming honesty, "Lord, help me!" The media representatives who were present could identify with this confession, because it was a slice of real life. Even the world-famous evangelist confessed that he was just as dependent on God and his help as anyone else. Graham could openly confess his need for help, and this very fact made him so authentic and, as a result, so credible.

Charles Templeton, Graham's fellow evangelist of Youth for Christ, after having turned his back on the Christian faith in general and on evangelists in particular, described him as the only trustworthy servant of God, especially because he stood by his weaknesses. Graham had been able to tell him, "Pray for me, I'm scared to death."[6] Billy's grandson Tullian Tchividjian likewise emphasizes that this genuineness is what makes his granddad so loveable:

Daddy Bill is normal! He gets mad; he gets sad; he's fun to be around. His favorite movie is *Crocodile Dundee*. His favorite drink is orange juice, and he loves catfish. He's just another man with all of the limitations and idiosyncrasies that the rest of us have—and I love him for it!

Tullian's brother Basyle told me that as a young boy he had noticed how his grandfather, just after having spoken to the president on the phone, devoted his entire attention to the maid and asked her how she was doing. This had left on him an indelible image of Daddy Bill.

George Beverly Shea, Graham's close co-worker for over sixty years, praises Graham's authentic Christian faith, calling him a "twenty-four-hours-per-day Christian." Graham was the same in public as at home or with his close associates. Even the media noticed his genuine character. *Time* magazine described him as "almost unnaturally natural."[7] Even in the glittering world of hotels, banquets, charity drives, and popular adulation, he moved with unaffected simplicity. A female reporter writing about his first major mission in London, where he faced a pack of very negative reporters, perceived him as "completely disarming. . . . He seems to have the sincerity, ingenuousness, the sort of simple charm that is the greatest fun about Americans and the quality that makes us love Danny Kaye so."[8]

David Frost had the opportunity not only to interview Graham several times on his TV show but also to get to know him on a more personal level. He was once asked what impressed him the most about Graham. Frost said:

> Well, the very man himself, as your question implies, is so impressive because you never hear him make a cheap or rude remark about anybody, even in private. He basically lives the gospel. The Billy Graham you meet in real life is the same person he is on platform.[9]

Why is that so? Graham provided the answer himself without knowing it: "People put me on a pedestal, you know," he said, "but they don't know me. I am a sinner like everyone else. I constantly must go to God and ask forgiveness."[10]

Despite all the fuss people made about him, Graham could remain genuine because he saw himself first and foremost as a child of God, whom he wished to please with all his heart. Face-to-face with God and his Word, he was always conscious of his weaknesses and failures. He objected when people tried to make a saint out of him. Time and time again, he emphasized his weaknesses and insecurities in public, for example, when he was asked to state his goals prior to a major mission. A good example is his first major evangelistic mission in New York in 1957. He spoke of serious doubts that he would be able to reach New York City with the gospel at all. He spoke of times when he felt so afraid and terrified that he wanted to flee. "I'm prepared to go to New York to be crucified if necessary. When I leave New York, every engagement we have in the world might be canceled." Yet at the same time he also spoke of his great dreams: "We hope the whole city will become God-conscious, that religion will be a talking point in the bars, in the subways, in the barbershops."[11]

Billy asked Ruth to accompany him to the New York mission in 1957 because he felt he needed her at his side when facing one of the biggest challenges of his life.

Shortly before Billy left for New York, he happily told Ruth that he felt strong and armed for the battle, and she replied that this was the result of the many people who had been praying for him and the people of New York. Billy felt the same. Any success would be due to God's intervention in answer to the prayers of his many children. He was thus able to face New York calmly. The same God who fortified him in the North Carolina mountains was also his strength in the world's largest city at the time.

Graham was not disappointed. After the major mission, which lasted several weeks, the following was reported:

In repairing unhappy marriages and broken homes the New York campaign achieved spectacular results, especially in its television

55

ministry. Suicides were averted; clandestine sex appointments interrupted; separated mates restored; dead marriages revived. The conversion of marital partners was a nightly spectacle of the campaign.[12]

Capacity crowds of 18,500 daily in Madison Square Garden, up to 100,000 in Yankee Stadium, and an audience of more than 10 million for Saturday telecasts made Ruth's and Billy's dream come true. The home office received over 10,000 letters daily from people who had made a decision for a life with Jesus, and this continued for more than six weeks! Newspapers reported that leading members of New York's most notorious teen gangs had changed their ways and had declared the area around Madison Square Garden a neutral zone. Hundreds of youths had been converted during a special youth emphasis week. What an encouragement for Billy and Ruth after they had struggled in prayer beforehand, longer than for any other outreach, and had hesitated for a long time even to accept the invitation to New York!

In 1957, there was no more room in Madison Square Garden for several thousand people who were only able to watch a live broadcast on-screen.

Who we are when nobody is looking is who we really are. Graham's closest associates repeatedly mentioned that he took every opportunity to transmit the gospel to each individual he encountered, even those he met by chance. And this often happened in the middle of so-called important events. Two reports that appeared in 1959 during Graham's major campaign in Australia illustrate how the public and private persona of Graham were truly alike.

Enquirers came from every economic background, from every income bracket, from city, from suburb, from outback; from executives, employers, unionists, workmen, tramps; from club and prison, from shop, office and factory, from learned and unlettered—aboriginal Australians, white Australians, new Australians—churched and un-churched: there was no segment of society in which these miracles of re-creation did not occur. The very highest of high society was powerfully influenced by the preaching of Billy Graham, including some of the sophisticated elite of Melbourne's Toorak and Sydney's harbourside. Knight's ladies, parliamentarians, financial magnates, gentlemen of leisure, discovered a dimension to life many of them had not even suspected. In one state the wife of the governor, representa-tive of the Queen, stood alongside an Archbishop's wife to declare her faith in Christ, and the two of them were counseled together by the wife of a Member of Parliament. . . . There were remarkable consequences and effects among the leading personalities of Sydney's glittering, wealthy social set.[13]

The second story shows Graham's other, private side. After the long and intensive weeks of evangelistic ministry in Australia, he wanted to withdraw with his team for a few hours to the seaside. But it didn't take long before he was discovered.

As he often does, Billy Graham was reading aloud to Lee Fisher from a new book. While he was reading, a girl walked by. She was taking a dog for a walk. Lee Fisher noticed that she was staring in their di-rection. Presently she came over and, standing in front of Billy, said: "You're Dr. Billy Graham, aren't you?" Billy agreed. She had been to two of the crusade services and Billy, seizing the opportunity as a faithful evangelist, said: "Did you receive Christ?" Her eyes became moist and her inner self-assurance began to weaken. No; she had not accepted Christ. Billy said: "Wouldn't you like to receive Him?" The girl said: "Yes, I really would." On that isolated stretch of beach Billy took out his New Testament, read the promises of salvation, and explained the meaning of Christian conversion. He prayed for her, then invited her to pray. She clearly and sincerely affirmed her faith in Christ. (They later heard that she was radiantly happy in her new-found living faith.)[14]

Graham was only able to have such a strong and convincing effect in public because he never felt too great to ask Ruth and the members of his team for help. A personal experience his brother-in-law, Leighton Ford, had with Graham in Australia illustrates this fact. Ford recounts:

I have learned that a man who is great and famous can be very lonely. One afternoon recently

Even in Australia and New Zealand, Billy Graham's name alone was sufficient to draw thousands of people to the meetings.

in Australia I went up to his room. I was leaving for the United States and I wanted to tell him good-bye. His wife, Ruth, had left several days earlier. I got up several times to take my farewell but he asked me, "Please stay, don't leave." So I stayed on even though the time was coming when he had to leave shortly for the evening meeting, and when I left he asked me to pray and I put my arm around him and he laid his head on my shoulder and put his arm around me as I prayed for him.[15]

Although Billy often asked his co-workers for help, Ruth, on the other hand, did not wish to bother others with her problems. Her problem solver, with whom she discussed everything, was her God, and she could not praise his faithfulness enough. The times with her divine Friend were balm for her soul and strengthened her for her ministry. Ruth was a great encouragement to her fellow human beings. However, she could be that way only because she continuously sought strength from her divine Encourager.

Her daughter Ruth, called Bunny, told a moving story that shows how important these intimate moments with her Father in heaven were for her mother.

Her mother was very frail and bound to a wheelchair because of many surgeries and advancing arthritis in the last years of her life. When one of the caregivers checked on her late in the evening, she saw Ruth on her knees, her body leaning against the bed, her hands folded, deep in prayer.
Her daughter said:

> She was communing with God, worshiping the One she adored, totally unaware of the caregiver's presence in the doorframe. . . . Mother was in poor health, her body as vulnerable and frail as a kitten's. We recognized what kneeling must have required of her. She who had every excuse in the book not to get down on her knees, she who knew intense pain as an ever-present reality, had somehow in her frailty mustered the strength to get down from her bed to the floor in order to worship God in the same manner she had done so for most of her life.[16]

Reflecting on the situation, she then added:

> My Mother possesses tremendous inner strength and commitment. A woman who loves God more than she loves herself. Who knows and loves him intimately. Whose utmost desire is to be with him.[17]

It was obvious that despite her great pain and frailty, Ruth wanted to be at the place once more where God had spoken to her and where she had spoken to him throughout her entire life. There, on her knees, Ruth had not only cultivated her friendship with her Father in heaven but also become conscious of her authority as a child of God and wife of an evangelist. She ruled majestically from this throne at God's feet. Ruth said, "Billy needs my protection." Billy needed Ruth to cover his back, just as Ruth needed Billy to back her too. Ruth also prayed a lot for their five children: Gigi (1945), Anne (1948), Ruth (1950), Franklin (1952) and Ned (1958).

It is wonderful how God answered Ruth's prayers for both of her sons, who spent many years away from the Lord. Today, Franklin and

Ned are testimonies of God's grace, and both lead Christian ministries. Franklin is head of the Billy Graham Evangelistic Association as his father's successor as well as head of the relief organization Samaritan's Purse. Samaritan's Purse is known for its Christmas shoe box drive Operation Christmas Child, but the ministry also has a large medical aid branch.

Ned heads East Gates International, a ministry that helps the body of Christ in China, providing Chinese Christians with biblical tools they need to grow in faith and reach out to others. East Gates International has been able to print over three million Bibles and distribute them throughout China as well as to some extent in Tibet. God thus fulfilled one of Ruth's dreams, in view of the fact that she had originally intended to become a missionary to Tibet. Since her youth in China, Ruth had fostered a special love for the Chinese, and now it was her youngest son, whom she had worried over for many long nights, whom God was using to fulfill her dreams and answer her prayers.

Because Ruth maintained such a close relationship with the Lord of lords, she was not particularly impressed by the lords of this earth,

and this in turn seemed to impress them. They had probably not experienced such a lively, uncomplicated person in their entourage in a long time. Once, Richard Nixon, then vice president, was a private guest of the Grahams at what appears

Grandfather, father, son. Franklin's oldest son, Will (left), followed in the evangelistic footsteps of his father (middle) and his grandfather. Since 2006, Will Graham has held his own evangelistic rallies, which he calls celebrations.

to have been a very informal event. When she said good-bye, Ruth remarked that Nixon had better hurry so she would have enough time to tidy up the house.

Because of Ruth's priestly dependency on God, the King of kings, she displayed a kingly independence in regard to people and their opinions. She also influenced her husband with this attitude. "Let God be the judge" was her attitude whenever her husband was criticized. She once wanted to give Franklin a lesson on how he should behave when someone criti-

Ruth combined a deep faith with an adventurous spirit and a great sense of humor.

cized his father at school: "Franklin, what would be your response?" Franklin said, "It depends how tall he is." Franklin inherited much of his quick wit from his mother.

Ruth was also quite adventurous. She wanted to try out what was popular with young people. She even tried to ride a Harley Davidson once, but as she forgot to ask how to stop the motorcycle, the ride ended in a ditch. She also wanted to fly a hang glider at least once, which also ended in a fiasco.

After Ruth's passing, the true story finally came out. In 1975, Ruth had asked a student at Montreat College to teach her how to fly a hang glider. He was a bit surprised that a woman of her age wanted to learn to hang glide and felt that it might not be the safest sport for someone who—and before he could say anything unkind, Ruth tactfully interrupted him—"could be your grandmother?" At that time she was already fifty-five and actually had several grandchildren.

Finally, a flight instructor gave her the necessary training. After the basic lessons, Ruth wanted to give it a try. She ran a few steps along a hill, and the hang glider filled with air as it should so that Ruth lifted off. She enjoyed that first flight so much that in her excitement she apparently forgot how she was supposed to land properly. They had warned her that the start was optional but the landing was a must. In the thrill of the moment, she forgot to push the steering bar forward on landing.

> The ground leveled, but the wing continued gliding downward. First her feet began to drag, and then her knees, until with a shudder, the kite itself ground to a sudden stop, with its pilot hanging suspended by the airframe a few inches above the dirt. With dignity, Mrs. Graham got up and brushed off her knees. She thanked everyone, said she enjoyed her flight, but that she didn't want to try it again.[18]

When she was confronted with this rumor many years later, she replied that it was a silly thing that wasn't worth mentioning. I have mentioned it because it's an amusing story that illustrates Ruth's pioneering spirit and courage. And didn't she herself once say that it's impossible to love someone you can't laugh about?

Ruth was quite embarrassed when people praised her too much. She emphasized that the focus should always be on God and his faithfulness, not on people. Ruth had a healthy self-esteem, but it was based on her awareness of being God's co-worker in an important ministry. She considered it a great privilege to be her husband's partner in his ministry to introduce God's love and faithfulness to others. She did not have to secure her value and identity through other people or through a publicly acknowledged service. She didn't need to impress anyone. There was no discrepancy between the public Ruth, wife of the most famous evangelist of his time, and the private Ruth, mother of five very normal children. She was always herself, a clear expression of true genuineness.

Ruth had two inherent qualities: a deep spirituality and a sense of humor displayed in a zest for authenticity. She was close to God's heart yet at the same time close to people's hearts. She combined her love of adventure with her hunger for God, for example, by climbing a tree just to be alone with God. Throughout her life, she was thirsty for real life and therefore also thirsty for God. She said that her most important goal in life was to make others thirsty for God too. This adventurously unorthodox and at the same time profoundly devout woman certainly always appealed to me.

Ruth stood with her husband as a partner in his God-given mission. When somebody once remarked that Billy wasn't exactly the best preacher, Ruth replied that this was then proof of how powerful the Holy Spirit was. One time she was with a friend, watching on television how an unsympathetic interviewer tried to trap Billy with a trick question. Billy answered the question very wisely. Ruth remarked to her friend, "You and I both know Billy is not that smart. That was God." She once reacted to criticism with the remark that the critics didn't know who they were fighting against. And if things got to be too much for her and she was afraid she would react in the wrong way, she withdrew for a private audience with the King of kings.

In general, the Grahams lived a very ordinary daily life. Gigi told us how often she was amused by the idea of outsiders that they always spent their leisure time reading the Bible and praying. Like all children, the Graham kids didn't always enjoy the family devotionals, despite the fact that their parents tried to make them brief and interesting. The children loved their housekeeper Bea not least for the fact that her prayers were shorter and more concise than their father's. One Christmas, when the religious part of the program was delaying the opening of the Christmas packages, Franklin moaned, "Bethlehem has never been so miserable."

When once a child misbehaved, a visitor asked Ruth how it was possible that Billy Graham's children could do such things. Ruth replied, "They have me in them too." She and her sister Rosa were always playing pranks in their childhood and often teased each other. That's why Ruth could empathize with children like that.

On one occasion, Franklin and a friend of his were spitting at each other. The friend's mother was embarrassed by her son's behavior. She told him to apologize to Ruth, which he didn't really do. The mothers agreed that if one of the boys spit again, the other could spit back. Ruth invited the boy and his mother to dinner, put a pot of water on the table, and smilingly said, "Here's your ammunition."

Ruth always distinguished between moral misconduct, such as lying, stealing, and rudeness toward the elderly, for which she held her children accountable, and age-specific things such as long hair or loud music, which she tolerated as long as it was not bothering anyone. Since the five children's temperaments were quite different, Ruth also had to apply different methods to teach them. Anne reacted to subtle hints, whereas Franklin needed stronger medicine. When he repeatedly refused to get up and go to school, Ruth set off a firecracker outside his door.

Ruth was a feisty woman with a fighting spirit. She would go all out for things that were important to her. Her methods were often quite unorthodox. At a public gathering, she once tore a sign out of a demonstrator's hands and sat on it. He pressed charges, and Ruth had to go to the police station to explain her conduct.

Ruth could also use more subtle methods. When Franklin kept coming home

A kitchen scene with Ruth Graham and daughter Gigi in their first house in Montreat before they built the log cabin on the mountain.

64

late, she decided to
stay in the living room
until he came back and
give him a friendly wel-
come, without remark-
ing about his late re-
turn. After a while, it
got too embarrassing
for Franklin to have his
mother staying up for
him, and he decided to
get home earlier.

Ruth with a donkey at the Great Wall. Ruth felt especially close to donkeys because donkeys could be quite stubborn, not giving in too quickly.

Ruth sometimes had difficulties with her husband, mainly in the early years of their marriage, because he was not used to having a wife who had her own opinions. Once, when she hit the gas pedal instead of the brake and ended up down-hill from their home, Billy wanted to forbid her to drive again, whereupon Ruth replied, "Abraham did not take the camel away from Sara either."

Ruth loved to spend her free time rummaging around in second-hand stores and at flea markets. She often found objects nobody except she liked, and she fixed them up to be used again. Some of the furniture in their home got its finishing touches from Ruth.

Billy preferred jogging in his leisure time or playing golf whenever possible. He loved to play golf, not least because it was almost the only thing he could do in public without being disturbed. When he ate in a restaurant, his food would often get cold because so many people wanted to shake his hand and exchange a few words. His friendliness did not allow him to turn anyone away. During his time at the Bible college in Florida, when a renowned evangelist refused to give him an autograph, he vowed never to react in such an unfriendly way. He was irritated by the behavior of his spiritual role model. His own experience made him aware of how important small acts of kindness and attention in everyday life can be as a true witness of God's love and friendship.

Billy was a gentleman even at home. When Ruth brought the food from the kitchen into the dining room, he regularly stood up. When I asked Gigi about this, she said it had to do with his Southern upbringing. That was certainly part of the reason, but I think it was more than just his Southern upbringing that made him give his full attention to strangers and take time for them. He was aware that the way he behaved out of the spotlight toward an individual was just as important to God as how he behaved on the podium in front of thousands of people. And for that one person, his friendly attention could be vitally important.

My wife and I had the privilege to have lunch with John Carter Cash, the son of Johnny Cash and June Carter. John shared that his parents and the Grahams were good friends and often spent holidays together. Once, one of his step-sisters returned from the beach when her parents were eating lunch with the Grahams. When she entered the room, Billy stood up quickly. She was perplexed and asked, "Is something wrong?" Her father had to explain to her the reason for Billy's attentiveness, which made a lasting impression on the kids of Johnny Cash and June Carter.

It was also important to Ruth that Christians pay attention to the small things in life, as these things could be very important to others. Shortly before their golden wedding anniversary, she emphasized in one of her rare

Johnny Cash and his wife, June Carter, standing between Ruth and Billy Graham, were close friends of the Grahams and served several times in crusades by singing and giving a personal testimony of their faith.

interviews the value of courtesy: "Courtesy takes care of a lot of things. Courtesy for strangers, courtesy for one's superiors, courtesy for everybody—and a desire to help."[19] For Ruth and Billy, courtesy and giving attention to others were part of a life that reflects God's kindness and loving care.

Ruth and Billy had a very romantic relationship, according to them, even more so in later years than at the start of their marriage. Billy described in his last interview with Larry King in 2005 his love relationship with Ruth:

> I love her more now, and we have more romance now than we did when we were young. We can look each other through the eyes. Now, we don't have the physical love, but we have eye contact that tells you "I love you," and there is not a single day that I don't say "I love you" and I love her with all my heart.

Although in old age romance took the place of physical love, when younger they had a very relaxed attitude about sexuality, particularly when you take into account the times in which they grew up. They felt that within God's guidelines sexuality was a gift of God, given for the marriage partners' enjoyment and not only for procreation. In 1969, Billy described the role of sexuality in the following way for *Time* magazine:

> Now, sex is a gift from God. We went too far in the Victorian period. We hushed it up. It should never have been suppressed. It's something that God gave us. We should talk about it. It shouldn't be in the back alleys in the dirt and trash. Young people are getting the wrong idea about sex. Within marriage it's the most wonderful of relationships. It's more than a propagation of the race. This is where I disagree with the Pope. Sex is more than just to produce children. Sex is for enjoyment within the confines of marriage. Sex is also for the fulfillment of a couple.[20]

Billy could give Ruth a big kiss or hug her affectionately, even if other people were around. Billy's combination of sincerity and charm impressed Ruth early on. Prior to their wedding, she wrote to her parents:

> His great earnestness is what most deeply impresses those who know him. He is undoubtedly a man of one purpose, and his fearlessness in preaching the Gospel must be a joy to the Lord. . . . Despite Bill's fearlessness and sometimes sternness, he is just as thoughtful and gentle as one would want a man to be. . . . At any rate, he really makes you feel perfectly natural and looked-after without being showy or obnoxious.[21]

When Billy would finally return from a longer trip, it was time to celebrate. It was usually family time on Sundays. Thanksgiving was also a special family highlight. There was always a lot to talk about, as their daughter Anne remembers:

> But the highlight of Thanksgiving is not the food, or the televised football games, or the fun. The highlight is always the fellowship around the dining room table. As we sip our coffee and gorge on one last piece of pie, my father presides at the head of the table as each person shares what he or she is most thankful for. Most of us, including the ruggedly handsome boys who are crossing the threshold into manhood, have tears in our eyes as we listen to the testimonies of thanksgiving to God for His faithfulness and goodness throughout the previous year. As I drink in my father's love and my mother's radiance and my brother's strength and my sister-in-law's misty-eyed joy and my entire family's

Both Billy and Ruth enjoyed spending time together when Billy was at home. They especially enjoyed outdoor picnics.

68

gratitude to God, again and again I have exclaimed in my heart, "It just doesn't get any better than this!" But it will![22]

Anne's older sister, Gigi, emphasized how important it was for the development of her personal faith that her parents and grandparents were genuine Christians and full of life: "They were happy, fun-loving Christians and whetted my appetite for what they had." It was their mother's fondest wish that people would thirst for God because of their way of life. Ruth was convinced that joy was for the most part the result of a personal decision. To be joyful was "a serious matter" for her:

> Do you enjoy God? Man's chief end, as we all know, is to glorify God and enjoy Him forever. . . . Then, irrespective of the circumstances, happiness does follow. Do you delight yourself in the Lord, as we are told in Psalm 37:4: . . . "Indulge yourself with delight in the Lord." If you enjoy God, you will enjoy prayer and you will enjoy your Bible study. And it will show. You can't hide it. If you don't enjoy it, that will show too.[23]

To Ruth, a happy, loving character was the result of a decision to be a channel of God's love and kindness. Her positive attitude was the result of her continuously looking up to God and thanking him for his faithfulness, for the promises his Word contained, for fellow human beings, as well as for the love he had shown her in her personal life. She tried to look at everything from God's perspective. She was convinced that often behind difficulties lay a blessing of God, which was to be welcomed in faith. Thankfulness opened her channel to God and made her receptive to his blessing. Her stability, which greatly benefited her husband, had a lot to do with the firm decision she had made to always cultivate thankfulness, especially in difficult situations. Thankfulness keeps us steady and praise uplifts us.

Ruth was quite a character. "She was a firecracker," said a store owner in Montreat when I asked him to describe Ruth Graham. A restaurant owner of the nearby town Black Mountain remarked on her passing, "She may have been the wife of the world's most famous evangelist, but to residents and business owners, Ruth Bell Graham was like a sister or a mother."

Ruth was the same person everywhere: unaffected, natural, but also warmhearted and perceptive; pious in the positive sense, but at the same time always with a witty remark at hand, which relaxed the atmosphere around her. People felt at ease in her presence because they could just

Billy reading a Bible story to Bunny, Anne, and Gigi.

be themselves. Sally Pereira, the daughter of Billy's longtime associate T. W. Wilson, experienced Ruth as a constant encourager: "She loved beauty, flowers, books, and always encouraged me."[24] Gay Fox, who grew up with Ruth, described her as follows: "She was one of the steadiest, most creative, really kind and funny people that I've ever known. She had style in everything she did, from her home to her clothes. She had a contagious laugh, and never got uptight over anything. Ruth was a good sport, and took things in stride. She faced illness with a lot of courage. She was a tremendously strong and sensitive lady."[25]

Tremendously strong and still very sensitive—what a rare combination! Ruth gained that strength in her communion with her divine Friend and through intensely studying his Word. She loved nothing more than to read the Bible. She often sat on the porch at sunrise and read the Bible while sipping her coffee. Ruth often said that she only managed her tasks, particularly raising the children, with God's help: "I've raised my children on my knees." Because she was also very sensitive, she was often disappointed with herself and expressed her feelings of failure again and again in her poems. Sometimes she felt that she remained at the surface instead of going deeper.

At times, she simply felt washed out. In a letter to Gigi, she lamented that she was too lazy to do anything. Sometimes she felt overwhelmed by the many challenges her life as a mother of five children at the side of one of America's most prominent men brought. She told the *Charlotte Observer* about a lesson she learned in 1954 during the first large evangelistic mission in London: "Just pray for a thick skin and a tender heart. You need it when people stare coldly and call you a racketeer. Of course, there are many others who think we're just the cat's whiskers."[26] At the time, she had accompanied her husband during the first weeks of the mission in England, working as a counselor and ironing Billy's shirts. They were often attacked by individuals and by members of the media who were not on their side. Forty years later in 1991, in an interview with CBN's Sheila Walsh, Ruth still emphasized the need to pray for a tender heart to stay sensitive and compassionate in the midst of not always favorable circumstances.

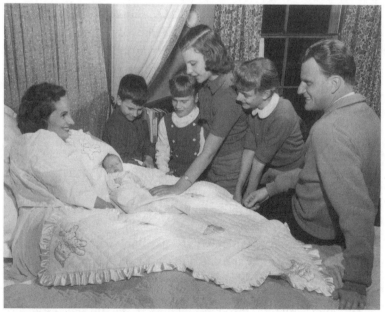

The entire family welcomes the new baby in 1958. From left to right: Ruth, Ned, Franklin, Bunny, Gigi, Anne, Billy.

Ruth was not spared times of depression either. In commenting on a prolonged time of depression she experienced during her pregnancy with her youngest child, Ned, she emphasized the positive side of it: "I'm glad I had that, because it helps to understand how people feel." And then she added, "Thank God that David wasn't always on a perpetual high. What would we do without the Psalms?"[27]

Already in her youth, Ruth learned from her parents' example that God did not promise us an easy life but that he is always at our side. She had no reason to be afraid. Difficulties were part of life for any witness of Jesus. That is why Ruth never complained about her husband's long absences or about her health, which was poor in her old age. When asked how she was feeling, she always said, "Fine," even if she sometimes endured severe pain. The only thing she complained about from time to time was her immobility, because she was mostly bedridden during the last years of her life. When Billy's brother-in-law, Leighton Ford, dug a little deeper and asked her how she was really doing, she replied, "I am as content as a mouse on a glue pad."[28] But on the other hand, she enjoyed the privilege to have lots of time to pray and to memorize Scripture.

As a child, Ruth desired to die as a martyr for Jesus. When I consider the many things Ruth had to bear, I can't help feeling that somehow God took Ruth's desire seriously.

In China, Ruth had experienced that problems and persecution were a normal part of Christian life. Ruth said:

It is we Christians in the West who are living abnormally. Personally, I am grateful for the "abnormality." But if it doesn't last, we must not question, complain, or be bitter. Instead, let us accept each day as the Lord sends it, living obediently and faithfully, not fearing what may come, knowing that the glory ahead will obliterate the grim past, and praying we may be able to say to our Lord, "We are honored to have served . . . under difficult circumstances."[29]

Although Ruth went through a lot herself, she still kept a soft spot in her heart for other people's troubles. She knew how quickly hearts could harden and always prayed that it would never happen to her. People who met her saw how she, as well as her husband, were totally authentic. She was not split into a Sunday and workday Christian. Her faith was her entire way of life. That's why she didn't need to wear a mask. What you saw was what she really was.

Nowhere are we able to express our deepest feelings better than in our prayers. That's why there is no better recipe for a good marriage than to pray together frequently, because in this way you sense your spouse's heart. That is what unites you as nothing else can.

Ruth was as open and direct with other people as she was when speaking to her heavenly Father. To offer a glimpse of Ruth's heart and what she felt about others, I would like to close this chapter on authenticity with a prayer of Ruth's. It's a prayer she said at the end of a speech to several thousand American women from diverse backgrounds in Anaheim in 1969:

> Our Father, thank You for being here. You know there is someone here who is carrying a load too heavy for her. There is someone for whom life has become unbearable, someone who is trying to escape reality through drugs and too much alcohol. When the fog clears, there is reality still staring her in the face. Only, Lord, each time she is a little less able to cope with it. And there is someone here who has to live with problems that can't be solved because there is no solution, some haunted by a tragedy they can never forget, some enslaved by sin they can neither escape nor control, bored by purposelessness and worn out by drudgery. There are some who are tired and discouraged and ready to quit. Lord, help each one to remember that all the fitness You require is to feel our need of You. So, as the blind came in Your day, the sick, the impure, the bitter, the weary, the confused, so may we also come just as we are. Forgive us, please; make us clean and whole. Take us into Your family, and as we leave here we will know that we will never again be alone nor unloved, for You will go with us. You will never leave us nor forsake us, and nothing can ever separate us from Your love. Make us Your eager pupils. May we hear Your words and do them. As we do, we know You will make us sweeter and easier to get along with, especially at home. In Jesus' name, Amen.[30]

3

Humility—Dependent Living

I've had enough trials and tribulations and persecutions and troubles and criticisms and sicknesses to always keep me down before the Lord. Anytime I think I'm anything, the Lord has His way of pushing me right down and saying: Billy Graham, you are dependent on me.[1]

Billy Graham

For more than half a century Billy Graham has been dedicated to the message of salvation. He has never stopped proclaiming the gospel and never stopped admitting his own faults and weaknesses while doing so. To remain humble, teachable, and gracious among success and in the face of sometimes bitter opposition and criticism is the mark of true virtue in any person. . . . Billy Graham's overwhelmingly single most prominent moral quality, his supreme virtue, has been his humility.[2]

David Aikman, former *Time* senior correspondent

I used to worry about Billy. When he started out, there was all that adulation. I was worried he might be tilted off balance by it. But then I met Ruth. Then I relaxed, knowing he had that strength on which to lean.[3]

Paul Harvey, radio broadcaster

It was 1986 in Amsterdam, a few days before the start of the International Conference for Itinerant Evangelists, which was sponsored by the Billy Graham Evangelistic Association. This time I was in Amsterdam as editor of the magazine *Christliches Zeugnis*. I was sitting in a Chinese restaurant and had just placed my order when Billy and Ruth Graham came through the door with Cliff Barrows and T. W. Wilson and were seated at the table next to mine. After they sat down, Billy spoke a prayer of thanksgiving and shared his feelings about the upcoming conference. Because he was sitting closest to me, I could hear most of what he said. I don't remember all the details, but I do remember Billy sharing how he felt unworthy and insecure about being able to teach anything valuable to these

Billy was as dependent on Ruth as she was on him. Ruth was a pillar of strength for her husband, to whom she closely clung throughout her life.

evangelists, some of them from countries where Christians were harshly persecuted. He shared that he had even met some who had scars on their bodies as a result of their brave testimonies for Christ. Billy felt they should be teaching him, not the other way around.

In this brief encounter, I got to know a man who honestly held others in higher esteem than himself. This was not the man I had seen so far, self-assured, full of conviction and power to persuade. I saw a man who was aware of his utter dependence on God,

The cover page of the Amsterdam '83 conference newspaper, with a photo of the author (below right) carrying the Swiss flag.

a man who realized his inadequacy in the face of the challenge before him. His wife's response was typical for her. I don't remember her exact words, but I remember that she laid her right hand on her husband's shoulder. She obviously told Bill, as she called her husband, to relax. He only had to give what he could give; God would take care of the rest.

For years I had hoped and even prayed that at some time God would allow me a glimpse behind the Grahams' public appearances, to get to know the real Billy and Ruth. In retrospect, I regret not having approached them in the restaurant, because I would have experienced another typical side of the Grahams: their friendliness and graciousness toward strangers, even when interrupted in the middle of a meal. And I certainly was a stranger to them. The only personal contact I had had so far with Billy Graham had been after a press conference in Amsterdam in 1983, when I had a brief conversation with him to thank him for being a role model for my life and ministry. I was so nervous that I started speaking in my mother tongue of German without realizing it. In his typically cordial way, Billy asked me to pardon his lack of German language. Perhaps it's understandable that I hesitated to approach him again after my blunder three years earlier. I was therefore more than grateful for the gift of this second encounter, which allowed me a peek behind the public facade of Ruth and Billy Graham.

If there was one trait that was characteristic of the Grahams, it was their humble dependence on the Lord. They had a very sober assessment of who they were and how much they depended daily on God's grace. Billy's brother-in-law, Leighton Ford, himself a great Christian leader, gave a good explanation of what humility is and what it is not in his book *Transforming Leadership*:

> In Jesus we see authority and humility wonderfully coupled together. In him we see that humility is not denying that one possesses a gift; it is recognizing the source of that gift. It would not be humility for a great speaker like Billy Graham to say in false modesty, "I can't speak." That would be an untruth! Humility, rather, is recognizing that our gift comes through us and not from us. Humility is . . . confidence in God, whereas pride is . . . confidence in self.[4]

Or in the words of the famous British preacher and revivalist Charles H. Spurgeon, "Humility is to make the right estimate of one's own self."[5]

Billy and Ruth Graham embodied the biblical truth that God lifts up the humble. Ruth's motto was "Drop to your knees and grow there." When the couple had appointments with kings and presidents, Ruth preferred talking to the service staff. She had a special place in her heart for outcasts and the disadvantaged. Many times she opened her home to them. For her, no one had fallen from grace.

The blood of Jesus was shed for everyone, and it was sufficient for all who confessed their need for forgiveness.

Ruth herself was aware that she needed God's grace just as much as anyone else. For her, there was no such thing as a Christian star, her husband included. There were just forgiven sinners. Jesus was more than a figure in her belief system; he was her dear friend and place of daily refuge. The Bible was more than just a guideline for her; it provided her daily strength and was her line of communication with the Lord, upon whom she fully depended for both the big and small things in everyday life. As a reflection of her conviction, she decided to have the words of Martin Luther's famous hymn carved on a beam above the fireplace in their living room: "*Eine Feste Burg Ist Unser Gott*" ("A Mighty Fortress Is Our God").

Her neighbor Betty Frist, who knew her very well, describes Ruth as a very down-to-earth lady, full of life and energy. She was not the typical pious sort but someone who tackled problems hands-on. She was a resolute, feisty woman without fear. But she also describes her as a woman who totally depended on the help and wisdom of the Lord, knowing that only the Lord Jesus could set things straight. When faced with a problem, Ruth often responded with, "This is the Lord's problem." This was also true when she was unduly criticized. Hadn't the Lord said that he would deal with it himself? Frist said, "Ruth meets all of their critics in one place—on her knees—and deals with them there."[6] Ruth certainly

Ruth Graham walked through life with open eyes and was willing to tackle the challenges around her head-on.

78

took Martin Luther's words seriously: "To believe in God is to go down on your knees."

Frist also observed the same quality in Billy: "To Billy, praying is as necessary as breathing." When she was still living at home, the Grahams' daughter Anne noticed, "Sometimes when Daddy comes to the breakfast table, he's too tired to eat. One morning he told me he'd been up all night praying." Praying was a very natural thing for him because he wanted to stay connected to Jesus, "in whom are hidden all the treasures of wisdom and knowledge" (Col. 2:3).

Billy recognized his utter inadequacy. But he decided to look at God's adequacy instead. He focused on God's wisdom and power rather than on his own deficiencies. For him, prayer was an act of humble dependence.

At Amsterdam '83, I interviewed the well-known Argentine evangelist Luis Palau. Palau worked for Billy Graham for many years as a Spanish translator and associate evangelist. The BGEA later provided the seed money that allowed him to start his own evangelistic ministry.

Luis Palau, called "the Billy Graham of Latin America," in an interview with the author at Amsterdam '83. The Argentina-born evangelist described Billy Graham as his great role model, especially as humility is concerned. In 1970, Graham contributed the seed money for Palau to start his own ministry as an evangelist.

Many describe him as "the Billy Graham of Latin America," although he currently resides in the United States. Palau reveres Graham for his humility and commitment to preach the gospel and describes him as his role model. Upon meeting him, one quickly realizes how much a disciple of Graham he is. In the book *Billy Graham: A Tribute from Friends*, Palau shares an experience with Graham in a hotel room in Essen, Germany, that made a lasting impression on Palau. At the time, both of them were praying with and for a German evangelist whom no one wanted to invite as a speaker. Palau describes how Graham reacted:

> Mr. Graham gave him a few ideas, the German asked a few questions, and we all got on our knees to pray. Mr. Graham began pouring out his heart for this evangelist, asking God to bless him. When his voice became muffled, I thought, "What's he doing?" I opened my eyes to see Billy lying flat in front of the German. Not on all fours, but straight-out flat, face down, on the floor! After the man said good-bye, Mr. Graham said to me, "You know, Luis, the Bible says, 'Humble yourselves under the mighty hand of God' (1 Pet. 5:6). I believe the best thing for an evangelist is to humble himself every day, even physically. I pray a lot flat on my face. In due time, He will raise us up!"[7]

Ray Gustavson, schoolmate of Graham at the Florida Bible Institute and later a member of the evangelistic team, recalls an experience when Graham even prayed like that in the middle of a field:

> When it was Billy's turn, I opened my eyes for it did not seem that he was praying from a kneeling position. And he wasn't! He, in his good suit, was lying prostrate on the ground, with his face downward.[8]

Where had Graham learned the importance of active humility? He writes about it in *The Greatest Lesson I've Ever Learned*, edited by Bill Bright.

In January 1950, a few months after the famous breakthrough mission in Los Angeles, Billy Graham led a mission in Boston at the invitation of Harold John Ockenga, the pastor of the prestigious

Park Street Church. As president of the recently formed National Association of Evangelicals, Ockenga was one of the most respected evangelical leaders of the United States at that time. The mission turned out to be a great success, and this in liberal New England. But God also used it in a special way in Graham's life to teach him an important lesson early in his ministry. Graham describes what happened:

> Surely, I thought, Dr. Ockenga must be taking great personal satisfaction and justifiable pride in what is happening and the important part he's played in bringing it about. One day in the midst of the campaign, I stopped by to see him at the church. His secretary told me he was in his office and suggested I go on in. As I entered, however, I thought she must be mistaken, for Dr. Ockenga was not to be seen. Then a muffled sob caught my attention—and I discovered him prostrate on the floor, his head literally under the rug. He was praying as earnestly and fervently as anyone I have ever seen, humbly acknowledging his unworthiness and his total dependence on the Holy Spirit. He was beseeching God to pour out His blessings on the people of New England through the meetings. There was no hint of pride or self-satisfaction here.[9]

Graham concluded that if this famous, respected leader, with all his education and prestige, felt the need to humble himself before God, lying prostrate on the floor and praying with tears and a contrite heart, how much more would he himself need to do so. He resolved to continue to humble himself actively before God and men from that point onward. Graham emphasized the fact that God does not say in his Word that we should *ask* for humility but rather that we should actively humble ourselves, and then God will grant us grace. But how terrible it must be, Graham concluded, to experience God taking a firm stand against us when we are proud!

One could legitimately argue that kneeling and praying prostrate on the floor are just outward forms of spirituality. Rightly so. Humility is not primarily about our posture when praying and seeking the Lord; it's about what happens in our hearts. It's about actively putting God first and denying the self. And yet I am convinced that many Christians have forgotten the art of kneeling before God and his Word, to their detriment. Are we aware that the loving Father is also the almighty Creator and holy Judge? Are we conscious of the fact that the Bible is God's holy Word to us humans? Do we realize to whom we are praying? It's important to realize who we are and who God is. Humble prayer is the visible expression of our conviction that nothing good can come from us unless we are transformed and empowered by the Holy Spirit. Humility takes Jesus at his word when he said, "I am the vine; you are the branches. If you remain in me and I in you, you will bear much fruit; apart from me you can do nothing" (John 15:5).

As Ockenga was not only a pastor but also a theologian, and as such, one of Graham's great role models, it is interesting to understand what was behind his unusual habit of humbling himself. What was its biblical foundation? What motivated this distinguished scholar to display such unusual, lowly behavior?

In *Power through Pentecost*, Ockenga describes the theology that inspired and motivated him to his humble action of self-denial:

> Self is the Great Hindrance to the Spiritual Life. . . . Self blocks the Spirit from filling the believer with the life of God and of Christ. If self has its way even only

Billy Graham always tried to learn from more experienced Christians. Here he is with Harold Ockenga, who taught him to actively humble himself before the Lord.

partially, it hinders the work of the Holy Spirit. It turns the eye from Christ, it corrupts the spiritual life, it leads man to trust himself and to seek his own. Therefore, self must be denied. . . . In the percentage that we deny self and follow Christ, this is the cross in human experience. Our critical decision rests in whether we will forsake all for Christ, whether we will yield self, self's intellect, self's pleasure, self's affections, self's desires, so that the Holy Spirit may fill us with the life of God.[10]

And in another place, Ockenga starts with Romans 12:1:

"Beseech you therefore, brethren, by the mercies of God, that you present your bodies as a living sacrifice, holy, acceptable unto God, which is your reasonable service." Service is a principle involved in the cross and often stated by Jesus. Herein the cross represents self-denial, sacrifice and service, all of which are involved in being a Christian. "He that loves his life shall lose it; and he that hates his life in this world shall keep it unto life eternal" (John 12:25), and "If any man will come after me, let him deny himself, and take up his cross, and follow me" (Matt. 16:24).[11]

Then he draws the following conclusion: "Unless such self-denial and service are exhibited in the field of missions, evangelism, social service, humanitarianism, the Christian testimony will be invalidated."[12]

Humble dependence on God's daily grace is also the best protection against temptations of all kinds. Talk show host David Frost once asked Billy Graham if he could remember any instances when the devil was working on him. His reply was straightforward:

Yes, definitely. In fact, David, I think people would be rather surprised. I sense it every day, because I'm tempted every day and temptation comes from the Devil. . . . The Devil is constantly after a person like me. . . . I have to be very careful in the life I lead, keeping up my defenses by prayer and Bible study, because the Bible says we're not up against flesh and blood—we're up against principalities and powers and forces of wickedness—we're up against a great spiritual force, and when anybody tries to stand up for the Gospel or stand out for good, he's going to be opposed by these evil forces in the world.[13]

Frost dug deeper and wanted to know in which areas Graham experienced the most temptations. Graham replied:

There are three main temptations that man has—there's the lust of the flesh, there's the lust of the eye, and there's the pride of life; in other words, ego. All three of these are temptations that Satan brings to us every day, tempting us in a thousand different ways and coming at us from different angles.[14]

Frost then asked Graham directly if he had ever been led into temptation by women, which Graham affirmed, adding that he had never touched a woman inappropriately. He had, however, not always had pure thoughts. There were times when he had been sorely tempted. Graham explained that he had to be particularly careful when he was far from home, all alone in some hotel. The biggest temptation, however, was to become proud and feel smug about oneself. Pride had caused Satan's downfall. Pride and idolatry go hand in hand. If you are proud, you focus only on yourself instead of on God.

Graham decided early in his career to work very hard on his character. Over and over again, he asked the Lord to change him so that he could become more Christ-like, because he realized that a blessed ministry had to go hand in hand with

Cliff Barrows and Billy Graham kneeling in profound prayer, with the open Bible before them. The photo was taken just before the famous Los Angeles '49 mission.

a totally committed life, which the Lord could shape according to his plan. The Lord certainly did that with Graham's life.

One of the men who were very close to Graham from the early days when he was studying at Wheaton was Walter Smith. For many years, he was the director of Graham's missions and later the international

Former president Gerald R. Ford described Billy Graham as a "modern-day apostle" and "one of the most selfless men I have ever known," with Ruth being "a vital part of his life's work."[15]

director of the Billy Graham Evangelistic Association. In *Harper's* magazine, February 1969, Smith spoke about his friend Billy Graham:

> The thrilling thing is that he's still as humble as he was at Wheaton. I can't explain his humility. I've never known him to be jealous of any other human being. Such a sincere individual. He believes with every fiber of his being, and when he speaks he speaks with authority—of God.[16]

Russ Busby, who as a photographer accompanied Graham on the most diverse occasions, from crusades to meetings with kings and presidents, concluded that the main reason God used Graham is that he leads people not to himself but to God. Busby quoted a student who after attending the Pittsburgh school of evangelism said, "I went to Philadelphia to meet a great man (Billy Graham) and I came home with no other desire than to serve the Gospel of a great Savior."[17]

Few people know us better than our children. All of the Graham children attribute great humility to both parents. Their daughter Ruth writes in *A Legacy of Faith*:

If I had to name the one overriding character trait that I see in my father, it would be humility. Daddy, I am sure, would object. But I have watched my father's humility operate consistently and on many levels throughout my lifetime. I am constantly touched by the modest way he expresses himself. He is unassuming, even when caught by surprise, which shows his humility to be authentic.[18]

But it was his wife, Ruth, who knew him best. When asked about her husband's main qualities, she would normally point to his strong and unshakable faith and that he really loved people. The fact that Christians should be humble was a matter of fact to her and not worth mentioning.

Ruth never put her husband on a pedestal. She could be very frank, setting the facts straight. Ruth helped her husband keep his feet on the ground, despite the admiration heaped upon him from all sides. She gave him a hard time if he thought too highly of himself or took himself too seriously. Their oldest daughter, Gigi, tells a funny story on this subject. When her father complained to his daughters about how poorly he felt and described all his illnesses at great length, their mother responded, "Stop complaining, Bill, and die as a Christian!"

His co-workers also kept him humble. His close associate Grady Wilson often said, "If the Lord will keep him anointed, I'll keep him humble." Wilson, a gifted evangelist himself, was full of fun and jokes. He needled Graham mercilessly. But the good thing was that Graham could take it in a positive way, joining in the laughter and the fun.

Graham hated arrogance. He was convinced that people who were seeking the truth and looking for role models should experience Christians as modest people who were aware of their weaknesses and therefore completely dependent on God's grace. He feared that he could receive praise that only God deserved. In his speech to twelve hundred missionaries and pastors in Osaka, Japan, in 1956, this fear of taking honor away from God clearly comes to light:

I want to tell you something that I haven't told others on this trip around the world. I feel tonight as if my ministry is going to be very

86

brief. My name has appeared in too many newspapers. It has been placed on too many posters. There has been too much praise given to a man and the Bible says God will not share His glory with any man. . . . If there are any newspapers in heaven, the name of Billy Graham will not be on the front page. Headlines will be about some unknown missionary back in the jungles who has been faithful.[19]

God was able to exalt Billy Graham precisely because Graham's constant goal was to honor God and give him the glory and not to appear bigger than he was. Journalists also noticed his modesty. After the 1949 campaign in Los Angeles, where many well-known people surrendered their lives to Christ, Graham made the following statement to the media: "I feel so undeserving of all the Holy Spirit has done, because the work has been God's and not man's. I want no credit or glory. I want the Lord Jesus to have it all."

In sixty years of articles on Billy Graham in *Time* and *Newsweek* magazines, the humility and modesty of Graham are mentioned again and again. The following excerpts serve to illustrate this fact and at the same time reveal the circumstances of outward success in which he maintained that humble attitude:

In 1949, the tent mission in Los Angeles, which was prolonged by several weeks, proved to be a breakthrough for Billy Graham's far-reaching ministry, as it was widely covered in the media. During this mission, he learned not to trust his own words but the Word of God.

The Rev. Billy Graham had clinched his title as America's greatest living evangelist. The blond, handsome, 31-year-old Southern Baptist minister who has been compared to another Billy named Sunday, had been sweeping the country from coast to coast with old-fashioned revivals. . . . Mr. Graham took Boston by storm this January. . . . And yet Billy Graham takes little credit for his achievements.[20]

In 1949, he was almost unknown to the American public. Today, almost five years later, he has preached to some 8,000,000 persons in gigantic rallies from coast to U.S. coast. . . . His radio and television audience adds up to some 10,000,000 regulars. . . . His book *Peace with God* . . . had sold 125,000 by this week. And his newspaper column, *My Answer*, now appears in 73 papers reaching another 15,000,000 people. But the Southern Baptist minister confesses that "I've never been so awed and frightened as I am facing London."[21]

After the highly successful 1954 mission in England, *Time* magazine wrote:

Ministers who get about the country already report a heavy increase in church attendance and collections. And the clergy of England, at first skeptical about Evangelist Graham, are now warmly grateful. . . . The biggest change in attitude occurred among the press. . . . The newspapers that had scoffed at the "hot gospeller" from the U.S. now wrote editorials of warm praise. Even the *Daily Mirror*'s sharp-tongued columnist, "Cassandra" (William Connor), devoted more than a page to his second thoughts on the man he had called a "Hollywood version of John the Baptist." "I think," he wrote, "that he is a good man. I think that he is also a simple man. And goodness and simplicity are a couple of tough customers. . . . I never thought that friendliness had such a sharp cutting edge. I never thought that simplicity could cudgel us so damned hard. We live and learn."[22]

The same magazine reported:

Billy Graham is the best-known, most talked-about Christian leader in the world today, barring the Pope. He has preached on the steps of the Capitol in Washington and in the shadow of the Iron Curtain, on Korean battlefields and in Hitler's former stadium in Berlin. In England, where religion has long been in decline, 2,000,000 people came in penitent droves. . . . Since 1949, Billy Graham has preached personally to 12 million people and brought 200,000 of them to various stages of Christian commitment. "I may be just a small item on the back page of heaven's newspaper," says Graham modestly. But on earth he has already got enough newspaper publicity to make both Hollywood and the circus envious. . . . Tycoons listen to him respectfully, and grey-headed clerics sit at his feet. . . . The great ones seek him out. Churchill invited him to Downing Street, and Eisenhower keeps one of Billy's red leather Bibles at his bedside. . . . But upper-crust Christians tend to regard the sweaty urgency of evangelistic Christianity as frequently hypocritical and always in bad taste. Billy Graham is different. . . . And yet such eminently low-pressure, dignity-bound clerics as the Archbishop of Canterbury have given Graham their blessing. A farewell dinner given for him in London included 70 peers and peeresses, and even the austerely intellectual *Manchester Guardian* admitted, "He has a holy simplicity." How does he do it? Billy would be able to answer that one right off, and with deep sincerity: by the grace of God. "If God should take His hands off my life," says Billy, "my lips would turn to clay. I'm no great intellectual, and there are thousands of men who are better preachers than I am. You can't explain me if you leave out the supernatural."[23]

The same *Time* magazine article says of Graham that he "sincerely considers himself nothing more but a tool of God" and that "he fights and prays for humility" because "pride is the devil's best weapon."[24]

In *Newsweek*, which reported on the great 1957 mission in New York, Graham calls selfishness "the root of all sin." The same article calls him a "man of humility," a man who "is frank to admit that he has had misgivings."[25] According to *Newsweek*, Graham's sole purpose was to proclaim God's Word as simply and as clearly as possible so that people would understand it and give their lives to Jesus Christ as their Redeemer and Lord.

Graham did not depend on his undeniably excellent gift of speaking but on the power of God's Word and the Holy Spirit, who uses God's Word. He didn't want people to hang on to his ideas but rather to align their lives with God's eternal Word. It was not about what Graham said but what the Bible said. Graham wanted to proclaim God's eternal truths without a lot of Graham background noise. He saw himself as a channel of the biblical Word, nothing more. And to him, this biblical Word was just as relevant in the present day as it was when it was written by the inspiration of the Holy Spirit. His belief was that through this Word God speaks into our lives when we humbly submit ourselves to it.

During the 1954 mission in London, Billy Graham preached in front of the Lord Nelson monument to a huge crowd assembled at Trafalgar Square.

The August 14, 2006, issue of *Newsweek* states that Graham was still learning Psalm 23 by heart, even at his advanced age. The article quotes him as saying:

> The older I get, the more important the eternal becomes to me personally. . . . I can't say that I like the fact that I can't do everything I once did, but more than ever, as I read my Bible and pray and spend time with my wife, I see each day as a gift from God, and we can't take that gift for granted. . . . We pray together and read the Bible together every night. It's a wonderful period of life for both of us.[26]

The article calls humility the "unifying theme of Graham's new thinking." Humility truly characterized Graham's thinking, but the word *new* is not appropriate. The article closes with a description that sums up Graham well: "Billy Graham—a man who has, at journey's end, found refuge in hope and humility."[27]

Graham's humility won many hearts, even those who were originally antagonistic to his message. A columnist for the *New York Daily Worker* once wrote that

Billy Graham, shown with Geoffrey F. Fisher, archbishop of Canterbury. Their mutual appreciation began during Graham's first mission in London in 1954. Archbishop Fisher was especially impressed by Graham's genuine humility.

Graham "speaks with an arrogant humility which is terrifying."

Graham also won many heads of churches to his cause through his gracious and modest behavior. Prior to his Greater London Mission in 1954, which was prolonged and turned out to be a big success, most of the church leaders were quite outspoken about their fears of being spiritually colonized by the Americans. At the end of the twelve-week effort, the archbishop of Canterbury, Geoffrey F. Fisher, emphasized the humility and sincerity of Graham:

> Though there were Americanisms, the methods were totally unlike those of some earlier evangelists who have visited us from the United States. . . . That is due in the first place to the great humility and sincerity of Dr. Graham himself, coupled with a great personal attractiveness. He would take or assume nothing for himself, but was clearly a humble man seeking only to use to the utmost of his ability such vision of truth and such gift of expressing it as God had given him.[28]

Indeed, the Greater London Mission in 1954 triumphed over all skepticism and surpassed the highest expectations. It always touches me anew when I look at the picture of Billy and Ruth Graham arriving in Waterloo Station, making their way through the crowds with only the Bible as a weapon, moving toward the many waiting journalists who thought they were easy prey. "God has called us for this, and so we can rely that he carries us through till the end." This was their belief because they knew their God, and this conviction marked their ministry throughout the years.

Billy's humility and modesty are perhaps more obvious than Ruth's because he was constantly in the public eye and therefore was observed more. Ruth, however, was just as humble as her husband. Nevertheless, she also needed to be continually reminded of how quickly the ego can take over.

A friend once wrote to Ruth, kidding her about the informal way she behaved around VIPs. Ruth responded with a letter saying:

> It doesn't pay to feel important. The only time I ever walked across a stage feeling important, I found out later that my slip was showing. The Lord has a way of cutting us down to size, too. But I hope not to give him another opportunity.[29]

Ruth did everything to avoid giving the impression that she was a superwoman who succeeded in everything. That made her so approachable. The people around her liked to confide in her and share their problems with her. She received many letters from people seeking her advice and spent many hours replying to them. When doing so, she never hid her own weaknesses. She particularly felt that she had failed when it came to her children's upbringing:

> The very first thing in raising children is to be the woman that God wants me to be, and this is where I have fallen so far short. . . . I think how often I have failed my kids on this. I expected more of them spiritually than I was willing to give myself. . . . I'm afraid—and this is a confession—I'm not a good disciplinarian, to the children's detriment. . . .

I usually just give in on a point if the children press it. Or, if I get really upset, I'm likely to be too strict with them when I shouldn't have been. I think a good disciplinarian is much more objective and consistent than that.[30]

As the Grahams' oldest daughter, Gigi experienced quite a strict education, whereas Ned, as the youngest child, tended to be spoiled, as is often the case in families with many children.

Ruth never hid the fact that she sometimes had strong differences of opinion with Billy in the early years of their marriage, but they never argued in

Ruth Graham was a down-to-earth woman who also made sure her world-famous husband's feet stayed on the ground. Describing his great-grandmother, Seth Barker said, "She behaved as normally as any other less-known person and was totally genuine in all she did."

front of the children. Gigi once remarked that she would have preferred for her parents to have argued in front of them. Experiencing that would have helped her to handle disagreements in her own marriage better. When Ruth was asked on camera if she had ever considered divorcing her husband, she replied with a twinkle in her eyes, "Divorcing never, but killing several times."

Once, shortly after her wedding, she was so frustrated with Billy for not taking her with him to downtown Chicago so she could do some window shopping while he and his associates were having a man's day that she prayed to God, "Lord, when you forgive me that I married this man, I promise you to never do it again." She had obviously not lost her sense of humor despite her aggravated state. Yet she could also rave about Billy. One entry in her diary after they had started dating reads:

[Bill] has been an inspiration. Sleeping almost none, [giving] all the time, so dead in earnest, all else falls in line with the longing to make Christ known in all His saving power. Filled with the Spirit, humble, thoughtful, unpretentious, courteous. And the verse stands out vividly: "Neither count I my life dear unto myself." . . . No reserve. Just giving. Desiring only to be well-pleasing to Him.[31]

Decades later, when she was over seventy, Ruth added:

I just thank God for the privilege that He has allowed me to be married to the man that I think is the finest man I know. So it has been a privilege to share him with the rest of the world.[32]

She emphasized that it had not always been easy to be the wife of a famous man, and she had often wished that he had been home more often. But the Lord had never promised that the Christian life would be easy. One way or another, she had always preferred, as she often stated, "to have a little bit of Bill than a lot of any other man."

ᐧᐧᐧ

Ruth and Billy did not consider themselves wise. Instead, they sought God's wisdom. They made it a habit of beginning each day by reading a chapter of Proverbs as well as five psalms. Thanks to this habit, they read the entire book of Proverbs and Psalms every month. In Proverbs, they looked for directions concerning daily life and relationships with their fellow human beings. With their daily reading of Psalms, they sought to strengthen their relationship with God. By studying God's attributes, they wished to focus their thoughts on God and take on a worshipful attitude. While Proverbs provided practical guidance for everyday life and work, the book of Psalms was a guideline for prayer and worship.

For a period of time, I also tried to read Proverbs according to this schedule. In doing so, I realized that the Grahams' lived-out humility and God-fearing attitude had a lot to do with their daily meditation on Scripture. Can anyone read the following Bible verses every month without being affected?

> The fear of the LORD is the beginning of knowledge,
>   but fools despise wisdom and instruction. (Prov. 1:7)

> My son, if you accept my words
>   and store up my commands within you,
> turning your ear to wisdom
>   and applying your heart to understanding—
> indeed, if you call out for insight
>   and cry aloud for understanding,
> and if you look for it as for silver
>   and search for it as for hidden treasure,
> then you will understand the fear of the LORD
>   and find the knowledge of God. (Prov. 2:1–5)

> Trust in the LORD with all your heart
>   and lean not on your own understanding;
> in all your ways submit to him,
>   and he will make your paths straight.
> Do not be wise in your own eyes;
>   fear the LORD and shun evil. (Prov. 3:5–7)

> Above all else, guard your heart,
>   for everything you do flows from it. (Prov. 4:23)

> Wisdom's instruction is to fear the LORD,
>   and humility comes before honor. (Prov. 15:33)

> Before a downfall the heart is haughty,
>   but humility comes before honor. (Prov. 18:12)

> Humility is the fear of the LORD;
>   its wages are riches and honor and life. (Prov. 22:4)

The content of Proverbs still applies today as a guideline for everyday life. Modern-day Christians, even the most earnest ones, often do not have this reverence for God. This is why we often lack obedience and spiritual depth. The first Christians were characterized by holiness and fear of God, and the Holy Spirit granted them growth: "Then the church throughout Judea, Galilee and Samaria enjoyed a time of peace and was strengthened. Living in the fear of the Lord and encouraged by the Holy Spirit, it increased in numbers" (Acts 9:31).

Fear of God does not mean being afraid of him but rather being afraid of not honoring him properly. To fear God means to have a loving reverence for our great God in all things and at all times. He is close to us as a loving Father, yet at the same time, he is also our holy Creator and Master. Both aspects of God are necessary for a healthy and balanced view of him.

The fear of God helps us to distinguish between good and bad. When we fear God, we hate what is evil. According to Ruth, the fear of God also keeps us from the fear of man, because it's more important for us to please God than man. As the Bible says, the fear of God is the beginning of wisdom and knowledge. Ruth believed that Christians in the West have lost to a great extent the fear of God. As a result, instead of capturing the world with the transforming power of the gospel, the world is capturing them. They in turn lose the freedom and the joy that result from a life that shows appropriate reverence to God and follows his healthy guidelines. As a result, they develop destructive habits and attitudes and begin to fear all kinds of things. Ruth put the fear of God in relation to obedience to God's commandments:

> Fear of the Lord puts all other fears in proper perspective. From Genesis to Revelation, fear of God and obedience to God are two key commands. If we fall short in either of these, our children, as well as we, will suffer.[33]

In a time when fear of the future is growing globally, capturing so many people and leaving them paralyzed, the only real way out is to acknowledge God Almighty and to trust in his love. The only remedy for fear is to fear the Lord, who has everything under control and who makes all things work for the good of those who love him (Rom. 8:28).

Psalms was Ruth's favorite book of the Bible because it conveys both sides of God's nature, his holy side and his merciful, loving side. Psalms often begin with a sinner's brokenness and end with thanksgiving and praise to a God who loves us with unending love, and whose specialty is solving problems. Many of Ruth's poems are structured like the psalms, which start with an outline of a problem or a dilemma and end with thankfulness and the experience of God's peace after our eyes are drawn away from the difficulties and pain to his eternal love for us. Ruth herself describes it like this in one of her poems:

> And I lay, where for long in despair I had lain,
> entered, unshod, the holy,
> there where God dwells with His pain—
> alone with the pain of the price He had paid
> in giving His Son for a world gone astray—
> the world He had made.
> My heart lay in silence,
> worshipped in silence; and questioned no more.[34]

Humility means recognizing who we are and who God is. A humble person is someone who is dependent on God. Perhaps one should say that it is someone who is aware of his dependency on God in all things. Although we all rely on God for his blessings, we are not always aware of our utter dependency on him. Facades of some older Swiss buildings are inscribed with the saying *"An Gottes Segen ist alles gelegen"* ("Everything depends on God's blessing").

A proud person thinks that his abilities, experience, and education are what bring him success. In contrast, Billy completely depended on the Holy Spirit. As a result, he was filled with the profound certainty that God would manage to imprint the gospel on people's hearts despite his own inadequacies as an evangelist. His dependence on God also allowed him to remain calm even when criticized. Graham once noted in his diary that his greatest victory was that his Lord had given him the strength not to defend himself but instead to pray for those who criticized him unjustly. He usually felt a deep peace as a result.

Ruth radiated tranquility and peace even more than Billy. This was based on her faith and her knowledge that God's fatherly love carried her. She knew who she was in Jesus Christ. Day after day, she trusted in the Holy Spirit's support. She was an example of a life fully dependent on God. Her youngest son, Ned, testifies to this in a lovely way:

> With Mother, I have seen true righteousness in a human being on a level that I've never seen before. There was absolutely no insecurity in the woman. There was total peace and confidence of who she was in God through Christ. There was a complete dependence and openness to the work of the Holy Spirit in her life. She hungered and thirsted after righteousness constantly. I've never seen anything like it.[35]

An important sign of humility is a willingness to learn. The Grahams were keen to learn from whatever sources they could find. Ruth was a good listener, and Billy tried to learn something new from every encounter he had, even if the people he met were not committed Christians. Their daughter Ruth describes this character trait of her father:

> I have always known my father to operate out of an intense desire to improve himself—whether by staying current with news (he subscribed to an array of magazines and newspapers), reading books on various subjects, or absorbing wisdom from others. He is extremely curious and is constantly asking questions. Ever aware of his need for growth, he maintains the posture of a learner—which is a posture of humility.[36]

Billy's most important mentor besides his wife, Ruth, was his father-in-law, Nelson Bell, who was active in a number of ministries in the Presbyterian church after his retirement as a medical missionary abroad. For many years, Bell also wrote a regular column, "The Layman and His Faith," in the magazine *Christianity Today*, which he founded together with his son-in-law. Billy rarely contributed to the magazine himself because he felt that he couldn't measure up to all the great theologians who wrote for the magazine.

His purpose was to provide the evangelical movement with a biblical foundation and to show that believing and thinking weren't mutually exclusive. On the contrary, he felt that both sides could be inspired in the following way: He who believes, thinks further; he who thinks, believes more deeply. To Billy Graham, the Bible as God's revealed Word was always the starting and pivotal point of all reflective thinking.

Billy had already received an upbringing that had been completely Scripture-oriented, with a Calvinistic touch. His parents attended the small Associate Reformed Presbyterian Church in Charlotte. Every child had to learn the Shorter Catechism by heart, which summarizes Calvin's theology in 107 concise questions. Billy's mother had a Bible calendar in the breakfast room.

Billy Graham with his father-in-law, Nelson Bell, who was an important mentor to him. Together they launched *Christianity Today* as a magazine that "addresses the great social issues of our days" from a biblical point of view and thus gave the evangelicals a voice.

Each day, she tore off the page with the corresponding Bible verse for her children to memorize.

In Montreat, Ruth and her five children regularly attended the local Presbyterian church. Well-meaning Baptist friends of Billy's wanted to convert Ruth to the Baptist faith, but anyone familiar with Ruth's character was aware that this was an impossible undertaking, because the label of the churches was irrelevant to her. There wasn't a Baptist church in Montreat anyway. According to Ruth, God was not interested in denominational formalities. He was everywhere where people allowed room for him and where his Word was proclaimed. Ruth's opinion was that, if anything, it was Billy who should switch churches. He was the one who had not remained true to his parents' denomination when he was ordained a Baptist pastor in Florida. That's why she sometimes referred to him jokingly as a backslider. But it wasn't that bad. When Billy was at home on a Sunday, he and the family attended the local Presbyterian church. And Ruth also felt very close to the Baptists.

Billy Graham's theology never wandered far from his parents' Calvinistic faith. His close relationship with his father-in-law, Nelson Bell, was of great influence in this area. Many of Graham's theological role models subscribed to the ideas of the Geneva reformer John Calvin, particularly regarding the key emphasis Calvin placed on Bible study and biblical teaching for personal and societal transformation. Two key points of Calvin's theology were humility and total commitment to the Word of God. This theology influenced both Ruth and Billy more than either of them were ever aware. They inherited the fundamental importance of thorough Bible study as well as God's sovereignty from the Calvinistic Presbyterians and passion for evangelism and mission work from the Baptists—truly not a bad combination!

Calvin points out that as God's ambassadors we should proclaim God's Word and not our own very limited wisdom:

God cannot bear with seeing his glory appropriated by the creature in even the smallest degree, so intolerable to him is the sacrilegious arrogance of those who, by praising themselves, obscure his glory as far as they can.[37]

According to J. I. Packer, no theologian or preacher depended so exclusively on Scripture than Calvin. Ruth and Billy were good disciples of John Calvin in their humble Bible-centeredness.

Many theologians, beginning with Augustine, have mentioned humility as the cardinal virtue of Christian discipleship. Andrew Murray makes it clear in his inimitable words:

> Until we seek humility in Christ as our chief joy and welcome it at any price, there is very little hope of a religion that will conquer the world. . . . The truth is this: pride must die in you, or nothing of heaven can live in you. Under the banner of truth, give yourself up to the meek and humble spirit of the holy Jesus. Humility must sow the seed, or there can be no reaping in heaven. Do not look at pride as only an unbecoming temper, or at humility as only a decent virtue. The one is death, and the other is life; the one is all hell, the other is heaven.[38]

God was able to use Billy and Ruth as his worldwide ambassadors so wonderfully because they continuously made an effort to live a humble life devoted to him. They were convinced that pride is the hardest enemy to detect because it attacks us from behind. And when we think we are least vulnerable because God is using us in a mighty way, we are in fact most vulnerable. True humility is the best protection against the enemy's attacks because God gives his grace to the humble. Only by walking in God's grace can we stay on top of what is coming. Only in a position of humble dependence can we ride the mighty wave of the Holy Spirit that the Bible predicts for the end times in midst of increasing turmoil. And to keep the balance, we need to be empty-handed and free of all kind of false bonds and idols.

Ruth spoke of the brokenness one needs to be able to do God's will. She said to herself, "Kneel and be broken, rise and be healed!"[39]

Only if we seek God's will and glory alone can we bring his presence and message to people in need. If anyone was aware of this, it was Billy Graham. Let us take his words to heart that he shared in his very first book, *Calling Youth to Christ*, while ministering as an evangelist for Youth for Christ:

> The root of all sin is pride. Perhaps the greatest sin that has crept into the lives of Christians is the sin of pride. No young person can expect victory and inward rest until the capital I has been conquered. God commands us to humble ourselves. We are never told to pray for humility! That is our job! If we are to live above the clouds, the sin of pride will have to be confessed and forsaken. It is deadlier than the poison of a rattlesnake. It stunts, stifles, weakens and destroys Christian victory.
>
> When I was a student at Wheaton College a great revival swept our campus. Dr. Harold Warren was the human instrument, but it was the Holy Spirit who did the job. From ten o'clock in the morning until eleven at night on two successive days, classes and meals were forgotten as students confessed their sins and God took over. The sin that was confessed most often publicly and privately was the sin of pride. Students, staff and faculty alike realized that this awful sin was ruining their individual victory with God. If that is your sin, confess it today and be rid of it.[40]

Billy's mother, Morrow Graham, put the secret as to why the Lord laid his hands on her son in a nutshell when she connected her son's success with his attitude of standing back and giving all honor and glory to the work of the Holy Spirit: "I may sound like a very prejudiced mother who can see no fault in her child, but I believe God has honored Billy all these years because he has so consistently maintained that kind of an attitude and right spirit."[41]

I would like to close this chapter on the importance of a humble dependence on God with the appraisal of a theologian and evangelist who was associated with Billy Graham since his time as an evangelist for Youth for Christ in the mid-1940s. Stephen F. Olford, president of

Encounter Ministries, aptly and succinctly summarizes what made Graham stand out and what can serve as an example for us all:

> I believe one of the main reasons why Billy Graham has been so used of God throughout the years of his evangelistic ministry is because of this virtue of humility—both as a discipline and as a disposition. No one in our time has been subjected to more praise, on the one hand, or criticism, on the other, and yet has maintained that sweet spirit of meekness and teachability. God has set him forth as an example for us to follow. So let us imitate him, even as he has followed Christ in the virtues of holiness, happiness, and humility.

4

Intimacy—Living in God's Presence

With private issues, Mother went to God. She worked out her struggles on her knees; God was her sofa place. As a result, Mother's relationship with God was and is very intimate. God truly is her confidant, friend, husband, and father—He is her everything.[1]

Ruth "Bunny" Graham, daughter

I feel a great need of getting alone with God. . . . I want to spend much time in reading the Word and praying. I must sit at the feet of the Lord and have Him fill me again. Christ Himself felt the need of getting off by Himself for spiritual refreshment. I feel a constant battle with the Devil when I am preaching the Gospel.[2]

Billy Graham

Ruth has come as near as anyone I know to fulfilling the command of Christ to "pray without ceasing." She calls prayer her "continuing conversation" with God. Her impact on Billy, the children, friends, relatives, and the thousands of others whose lives she's been able to bless is due in great measure to the fact that her whole life is criss-crossed by prayer. From childhood, she has had daily audiences with the King of Kings and Lord of Lords, who uses earthly thrones as his footstools.[3]

Betty Frist, neighbor

During her study of theology at Wheaton, Ruth Graham was considered not only one of the prettiest students—according to Billy she was always being asked out on dates—but also one of the most committed ones. She had made it a habit to get up early and spend two hours devoted to God before attending lectures. Her deep faith, however, didn't make her unbearable in the sense of being a "holier than thou" type. On the contrary, Ruth was a fun-loving person who was always up to mischief. Her father once called her "an interesting mixture of deep spirituality and mischievous fun."

If the word *unconventional* ever applied to someone, it did to Ruth. She didn't let herself be squeezed into any mold and by no means into any religious one. She couldn't stand religious showing off. Upon entering the Grahams' home, I couldn't help noticing the following saying on the wall: "God loves you and I'm trying."

Specifically because Ruth had such an honest relationship with God, she could be an ordinary human being and didn't have to pretend anything. For her, there was no separation between Sunday and weekday Christianity. A plaque hanging over the sink in the Grahams' kitchen reads, "Divine service will be conducted here . . . three times daily." For Ruth, there was no division between everyday chores and "spiritual" activities such as prayer and evangelism. Everything has to be done as a service to God, whether it's big or small from

This word of Ruth Graham welcomes the people visiting the Graham home. It displays both Christian conviction as well as her humor.

a human perspective. Ruth said, "If it's God's will for me here and now to do the washing up, then I want to do this gladly, by this honoring the Lord."

Because of her husband's frequent absences, Ruth was often alone and didn't have anyone with whom she could discuss her problems. She was a very sensitive person. Both of her sisters described her as the most sensitive of them all. In her youth in China, she even carried out a "very solemn burial" for a dog.

The best way Ruth found to express her feelings was in poetry. Many of her poems

Happy reunion of the Grahams aboard the *Queen Elizabeth* in New York. Ruth and the children returned by ship from Switzerland, where they spent the summer of 1960, and Billy arrived by plane from Germany after concluding a speaking tour.

were later published, although she had originally not intended to make them public because they were personal prayers in written form. If you want to understand Ruth Graham's heart, you have to read her poems. Ruth often wrote them to help her deal with personal issues and so as not "to develop an ulcer," as she wrote in the preface to *Ruth Bell Graham's Collected Poems*. In her poems, you can feel some of the deep conflicts of her innermost being. At the same time, they express her desire for an intimate relationship with God.

Ruth's reference point throughout her life was—as she expressed it—"the living Word and the written Word." The time she spent alone wasn't easy for Ruth. As an evangelist, her husband experienced exciting times with God. Everyone was talking about Billy, and Ruth had to take care of the household and the children, which wasn't always particularly thrilling. She had no other choice but to have her own experiences with God. Ruth's reaction when her husband had the opportunity to proclaim the gospel to a large crowd for the first time and she had to stay home with the kids is revealing in this context. In March 1950, *Life* magazine ran a major report about Graham's mission in Columbia, South Carolina, under the headline "Billy in Dixie," with a full-cover photo of her husband, accompanied by the following text:

> Not since the great days of Billy Sunday 27 years ago had South Caro-linians seen anything like it. Billy Graham, a 31-year-old evangelist who rose to prominence barely six months ago in Los Angeles, was staging a spellbinding revival campaign in Columbia, SC. . . . When the afternoon came, more than 40,000 spectators, including Governor J. Strom Thurmond and former Secretary of State James F. Byrnes, overflowed the stadium.[4]

Was Ruth overjoyed or frustrated about not being able to attend because of her motherly duties? Ruth provides the answer herself in a diary entry: "God is not limited to Columbia. The same God so marvelously working there is in the house with me. I shall have a little revival of my own."[5]

Ruth was well aware of the dangers of self-pity and therefore took a proactive role as a partner in missions at her husband's side. On the one hand, she did so by taking care of the children. On the other hand, she actively participated in her husband's missions by encouraging him on a daily basis during their phone conversations and by praying fervently for his evangelistic ministry. Her daughter Anne describes it as follows: "I would go down to my mother's room late at night. I would see the light on underneath the door and I'd go in, and she would be on her knees in prayer."[6]

Anne sees this as the reason why she, as a daughter, never had the impression that her mother was missing anything:

> As I look back on my childhood, I cannot remember any impression whatsoever that my mother was ever lonely. She may have been lonely,

but I never saw it. I believe that our Heavenly Father, our Savior, saved my mother from loneliness, because of her daily walk with the Lord Jesus; He was the love of her life. It was her love for the Lord Jesus, with Whom she walks every day, that made me want to love Him and walk with Him like that.[7]

Anne's older sister, Gigi, was impressed by the fact that their mother never let the children notice the great burdens she had to bear. Ruth made it a habit of bringing all her worries and cares to God. She didn't want her life to be determined by circumstances but by the Bible's promises. Her goal was to live on the level of God's kingdom and place the eternal above the temporal, the invisible above the visible. Ruth once remarked that God often practically pushed her to himself in challenging times. But Ruth also actively kept up her relationship with God, even in her everyday routine. Gigi describes it like this:

> All these years her immediate reaction has been to throw herself on the Lord and the Scriptures. As a child I can remember her leaving her Bible open in a prominent place, so she could just get a verse every now and then. We found her often by her bed, on her knees. She had her Bible anywhere she was in the house, sometimes even on the ironing board. There would be a verse that she would be gleaning and meditating upon.[8]

The many long periods without an adult to talk to, which were due to Billy's frequent absences, drove Ruth into God's arms. The children were no substitute for her husband. All three daughters left home and married before they were twenty years old. Their brother Franklin was very rebellious in his youth and therefore not an ideal conversation partner. So Ruth was glad to have her youngest, Ned, with her for some years. When he also left home to attend a boarding school in England, she was home alone, with many pets but no human counterpart. She describes the feelings she had when she became aware that none of the children were home and that she would be completely alone:

I dreaded returning to that now empty house. But as I entered the front door and looked down the length of the hall and up the steps leading to the children's now vacant rooms, suddenly it wasn't empty. I was greeted by a living Presence, and I realized anew how true His last words were: "Lo, I am with you always" (Matt. 28:20).[9]

Ruth was thankful that she had been prepared for the long stretches of loneliness during her school years in North Korea, far away from her parents: "It was to the Bible that I turned for comfort during the times of homesickness in North Korea."

Since that time, Ruth had cultivated a close relationship with her heavenly Father. She had experienced how her God was sufficient in all situations. Time and time again, she also felt how his Word, the Bible, spoke to her very directly. She saw the Bible as a love letter from her Creator and divine Friend that had been written to her personally. People who met Ruth were always greatly impressed by her natural relationship with God. In her book *Special People*, Julie Nixon Eisenhower describes a personal encounter with Ruth Graham: "Ruth's approach to her religion is very personal. She is close to God, close to the Bible. . . . Praying seemed as natural as our conversation had been."[10]

Ruth had read one of her favorite verses to Julie from her worn Bible, Psalm 37:4, which says that we should delight ourselves in the Lord, and even enjoy him. Ruth had encouraged Julie to seriously study the Bible, explaining that once she began doing so, she would increasingly enjoy doing it.

President Nixon's daughter was greatly impressed by her meeting with Ruth: "She undeniably enjoyed great inner peace. She had not answered all my questions, but somehow that seemed less important now. I was eager to know more about the Bible, and about Ruth herself."[11] Soon afterward, *Newsweek* magazine reported that Julie Nixon Eisenhower was regularly attending a Bible study led by a staff member of Campus Crusade for Christ.

Someone who had the opportunity to witness Ruth's relationship with God firsthand was a college student who led the worship music prior to Ruth's adult Sunday school class at Montreat College. She wrote after Ruth's passing:

> Once I realized Mrs. Graham would arrive early to pray each week, I began to come earlier just for the opportunity to pray with her and to have any moments I might get to talk to her. Mrs. Graham was always very gracious and personable. She would always inquire as to what was going on in my life and say, "Well, let's pray about that." I knew I had the opportunity that few would ever have—to sit by the feet of one of the greatest women of faith. It became very clear to me that Dr. Graham was able to be who he was because of Mrs. Graham. I was amazed at her knowledge of the Scriptures, but what impressed me more than her knowledge was her absolute Love for the Scriptures. It was very clear that Jesus was her very best friend. When speaking of Jesus, there was almost a twinkle in her eye and such love and passion in her voice that you could believe He was standing right there with her.[12]

Sometimes the expression is used too hastily, but it truly applies to Ruth Graham: she was in love with Jesus. This was evident to me also when I watched the few existing filmed interviews with Ruth. Whenever she spoke about God's love and faithfulness in her life, something lit up in her eyes, similar to what you see when people have just fallen in love—and fortunately also in people who have been in love for a long time. Wouldn't it be great to be able to say about all Christians that their eyes begin to sparkle when they speak about their divine Friend?

A faculty member who helped lead the adult Sunday school class at Montreat College also had the chance to get to know Ruth and her faith in a personal way. He was also deeply impressed by Ruth:

> It was wonderful to see her love for God and His Word. . . . She had a genuine love for the students and for all who she was associated with. I recall her sharing her "Bible belt" with us. It was the strap she used

110

to hold her Bible and her journal together! She encouraged us all to read and study the Bible with a journal handy so that we could record what God was saying to us. Both Dr. Graham and Mrs. Graham had a unique way of talking to you as if you were the only one that mattered at that time. I am impressed that such world-renowned people honestly care for that one individual who stands before them at that time. Ruth Graham was the best model of Christ-likeness that the students and I could have had.[13]

Ruth's love of God marked her life: "I cannot remember when I didn't love the Lord. My earliest recollections are of deepest gratitude to God for having loved me so much that He was willing to send His Son to die in my place."[14]

Her childhood in China left a big impression on Ruth. Her father, Nelson Bell, had served there as a missionary doctor. She had learned the importance of prayer and Bible study at an early age from her parents. The Bells lived a joyful, relaxed Christianity. John Pollock describes the Bell family atmosphere in his book on Nelson Bell, *A Foreign Devil in China*, this way:

> Each day in the Bell household began with prayers. . . . Both girls noticed, with the unfailing perception of childhood, that their father positively enjoyed these daily prayers; they came to realize the importance of his own devotional hour and their mother's devotional time after finishing her household duties.[15]

The Bells were great examples of happy people, which was the result of their deep relationship with God. Grandfather Bell made a particularly deep and lasting impression on his grandchildren. Once when Gigi showed us the house where her grandparents had lived after their return to the US, she remarked:

> My grandfather was always a role model for me of a Spirit-filled, happy Christian who lived out his faith. The house of my grandparents was always filled with laughter. The positive attitude to life was contagious. My grandfather was fun, and he always had time for his

grandchildren. He started every day on his knees praying also for us. When my grandmother became ill, he cared for her. He described it as a great privilege to push her around in her wheelchair. He was a real gentleman. He never disappointed me as a Christian man, never.

Ruth had a close relationship with her father. She inherited from him her wide range of interests but also an intimate relationship with God. She also had the habit of rising early, seeking God and reading his Word. God spoke to her through the Bible; she spoke to God in prayer. She always made an effort to read the Bible or have a short chat with God even during the most routine, everyday chores. That's how she tried to remain in permanent fellowship with God.

Sometimes Ruth expressed this attitude as "practicing the presence of God," referring to the three-hundred-year-old classic by Brother Lawrence, *The Practice of the Presence of God*. What does this mean? Brother Lawrence explains it like this:

> The soul's eyes must be kept on God, particularly when something is being done in the outside world. . . . Although the habit is difficult to form, it is a source of divine pleasure once it is learned. . . . In the beginning of this practice, it would not be wrong to offer short phrases that are inspired by love, such as "Lord, I am all Yours," "God of love, I love You with all my heart," or "Lord, use me according to Your will." . . . The first blessing that the soul receives from the practice of the presence of God is that its faith is livelier and more active everywhere in our lives. This is particularly true in difficult times, since it obtains the grace we need to deal with temptation and to conduct ourselves in the world. . . . By practicing God's presence and continuously looking to Him, the soul familiarizes itself with Him to the extent that it passes almost its whole life in continual acts of love, praise, confidence, thanksgiving, offering, and petition.[16]

Ruth considered prayer a continuous conversation with God. What helped her was the fact that she had made it a habit to memorize Bible verses very early in her life. She could thus recall Bible verses when she was cooking, ironing, and so on. Her grandson Tullian Tchividjian, head pastor of the well-known Coral Ridge Presbyterian Church in Fort Lauderdale, Florida, testifies to her life of intimacy with God:

> My grandparents have been walking with God for more than 70 years, and they know him better than anyone else I know. Their simple, single-hearted devotion to their Lord saturates virtually everything they say and do. My grandmother is in her late eighties with severe physical limitations, but she still pursues fellowship with God with every last bit of energy she possesses. Every time I spend a few days with them, I leave with a renewed passion to know God the way they do.[17]

It had once again proven true that grandparents can have an enormous influence on their grandchildren, not only through their prayers but also by the living testimony of their relationship with God. One can rightly speak of ancestral blessing here, which is passed on from one generation to the next.

According to Gigi, all of Ruth and Billy Graham's children and grandchildren have adopted the faith of their grandparents, even though they have also been through ups and downs, like all people. It is especially painful that the extended Graham family was not spared its share of divorces. Yet none of the children or grandchildren ever gave up their parents' and grandparents' faith. On the contrary, the crises appear to have brought them closer to God.

Some of Ruth's poems clearly convey how much she suffered with her children and grandchildren when they went through tough times. In addition, Ruth was

Tullian Tchividjian, one of Gigi Graham's sons, is following in his grandfather's footsteps as a passionate preacher of the gospel.

physically impaired after a severe fall in 1974 after trying to test a zip line attached to a tree for her grandchildren. Yet this did not prevent her from seeking God and enjoying his presence in every possible way.

Even when she was bedridden and could hardly see anymore, Ruth had a stand attached to her bed that held sheets of paper containing Bible verses. Her personal assistant printed them in large letters. Ruth particularly loved to memorize psalms. The August 14, 2006, issue of *Newsweek* reported how Ruth used the summer months to learn Psalm 90 by heart:

> Teach us to number our days,
> > that we may gain a heart of wisdom. . . .
> Satisfy us in the morning with your unfailing love,
> > that we may sing for joy and be glad all our days. . . .
> May your deeds be shown to your servants,
> > your splendor to their children.
> May the favor of the Lord our God rest on us;
> > establish the work of our hands for us—
> > yes, establish the work of our hands. (Ps. 90:12, 14, 16–17)

Billy also learned many Bible verses by heart. Yet in the same *Newsweek* article mentioned above, he states regretfully, "I have friends that have memorized great portions of the Bible. They can quote [so much], and that would mean a lot to me now."[18]

Like Ruth, Billy made it a habit to read Bible verses during the day. For him too, an open Bible was the expression of his desire to always remain connected to God. When asked how he kept up the discipline of reading the Bible, he replied:

> Wherever I am in the world, whether it be here or at home or in a hotel or at someone's house, I place my open Bible where I will see it frequently. Whenever I notice it I stop and read a verse or two or a chapter or two or even for an hour or two. This is not for sermon

preparation or study. This is just for my spiritual nourishment—my food.

When asked if there were also times when he didn't read the Bible for a while, he answered, "Oh, I don't think I've ever done that. I told you, it's my spiritual food. I don't miss meals."[19]

Basyle "Boz" Tchividjian, my first contact with the Graham family, had the following experience, which made a lasting impression on him:

> One incident I will never forget and that has always been an encouragement to me occurred during the 1988 Republican National Convention in New Orleans. One evening my friend and I were looking for a car to borrow so we could drive around the city. As a twenty-year-old college sophomore, sadly God was not a priority in my life, and I was simply interested in getting out into the city to have some fun. My grandfather's assistant had rented a car when we arrived, and thus I decided to go to Daddy Bill's hotel room to see if he would allow us to borrow the rental car. We arrived at his hotel at about 9 p.m. Keep in mind, this is during the middle of a huge convention where Billy Graham could have been at any number of political social gatherings. He probably could have had his pick of which one to attend. Thus, I was a little surprised when he opened his hotel room door wearing his pajamas. As we entered the room, I noticed his Bible open on his bed. At that moment, God convinced my heart in a significant way. Here was Billy Graham, "America's preacher," in New Orleans during a political convention attended by many influential and famous people and he chose to spend his evenings sitting in his hotel room reading Scripture and spending time with his heavenly Father. Needless to say, I left his room that evening forever impacted and without the car keys!

Basyle added that he always saw at least one Bible lying open somewhere at his grandparents' home. And every evening they knelt together before going to bed to thank God and to pray for current issues as well as the politicians in office.

Ruth and Billy had their set time with God. For Ruth, it was early in the morning, before attending to the children. Billy often lay awake at night and used this time for prayer. But they both also tried to stay "online" with God during the day. Larry Ross, who was Graham's media and public relations manager for more than twenty years, reports how at the first interview he organized for Graham, he told Graham's personal assistant, T. W. Wilson, that he had reserved a room at the NBC studio where they could pray together. Wilson had laughed and replied:

> You know, Larry, Mr. Graham started praying when he got up this morning, he prayed while he was eating his breakfast, he prayed on the way over here in the car they sent for us, and he'll probably be praying all through the interview. Let's just say that Mr. Graham likes to stay "prayed up" all the time.[20]

I can still remember Graham's reply when he was asked at Amsterdam '83, the first International Conference for Itinerant Evangelists, how often he prayed, because it really flabbergasted me: "To be honest, I try to take the biblical admonition seriously to pray without ceasing. Even now I pray in my heart to God to lead me when answering your question."

After my return from Amsterdam, I made it a point to remain connected to God in all situations as well. But I quickly found out that it's not that easy. But the Bible would not encourage unceasing prayer if it wasn't a great help for a victorious Christian life and a fruitful ministry.

> Rejoice always, pray continually, give thanks in all circumstances; for this is God's will for you in Christ Jesus. Do not quench the Spirit. (1 Thess. 5:16–19)

Ruth and Billy's goal to remain constantly connected to God is certainly one of the secrets of their blessed lives and ministries. You cannot understand the phenomenon of Billy Graham without pointing to this couple's intimate relationship with God. Pleasing their divine Friend was more important to them than pleasing people. They didn't want to disappoint God. They talked to him about all their issues as well as shared their victories and defeats with him. He was the constant in their turbulent lives, which lay widely exposed to the public. Living in close fellowship with God and seeing their identity and value as his beloved children allowed them to celebrate great victories as well as endure harsh criticism.

Their personal staff certainly helped keep Billy from becoming conceited despite all the admiration he received. And with her unpretentious, down-to-earth manner, Ruth most certainly helped Billy remain the same, simple follower of Christ and announcer of the gospel all his life. But more than anything else, Billy's close, personal walk with God kept him on his humble, stable course. When my wife and I visited him at his home shortly before his ninetieth birthday and asked him what Jesus meant to him, his answer was typical. After reflecting briefly, he said only one word: "Everything!"

Ruth knew right from the start that she would always be the second most important person in his life. But that didn't bother her, because Jesus was the most important person to her too—even more important than her husband. What she especially loved about her husband was that, like her father, he was a man of God, a man of strong faith because he knew his God so well.

The Grahams were people like you and me, with ups and downs, successes and failures and disappointments. They did not always live up to their own ideals and stumbled from time to time just like anybody else. They would be the first to admit this. But one quality made them stand out: their deep love of God. Jesus Christ was much more than their Redeemer, Lord, Friend, and Counselor. He was their very life, or as Billy put it above, their everything. Their lives can be properly understood and valued only when viewed in this light.

No one can lead others closer to God than one is himself. In fact, the primary task of a Christian leader is to lead people to God's heart. If he doesn't do that, he ties people to himself or to concepts, strategies, and methods. The primary goal of leadership is the development of Spirit-filled and Spirit-led people who in turn lead others to make God's agenda their agenda. In this way, they help them to achieve their God-given potential in their lives. We must entertain a love relationship with Christ ourselves if we want to lead others to an intimate walk with him.

Before Jesus appointed Peter to be the leader of the church in Jerusalem, he carried out a sort of job interview with him. We might have wanted to know if Peter could be trusted not to betray Jesus again in the future. We might have asked him if he had become prudent enough to balance his undeniable passion. We may have also asked him to summarize the key points of the Sermon on the Mount. Undoubtedly, these would all have been good things to ask. But Jesus asked Peter something completely different. He posed a question that you can only ask very close friends:

> When they had finished eating, Jesus said to Simon Peter, "Simon son of John, do you love me more than these?" "Yes, Lord," he said, "you know that I love you." Jesus said, "Feed my lambs." (John 21:15)

Jesus asked him the most intimate question you can ever ask: "Do you love me?" Jesus asked this question because he was appointing the person who, as the leader of the church, would be the role model for many others. One attribute for future leaders was obviously more important to Jesus than all the rest: their deep bond with him. If a leader is passionately connected with Jesus, he can lead the people entrusted to him into the same kind of close relationship. We can trust someone who, despite all his weaknesses and imperfections, loves Jesus above all. He will lead those entrusted to him not to himself but to the one and only Shepherd who deserves the name: Jesus Christ.

118

In Ruth and Billy Graham, God found people who loved him above everything else. That's why he could entrust them with many of his sheep and call them to a worldwide ministry as his ambassadors, even if they weren't "perfect" Christians.

What about us? Do we love Jesus Christ above all else? Or have we lost the first love of our life, as had the Christians in Ephesus (see Rev. 2:1ff.)? Or are we like the Laodicean Christians (see Rev. 3:14ff.), who had become lukewarm followers? We often do not notice such things for some time because we still function as Christians on the outside. Have we given our lives to God unreservedly? Does he sit on the throne of our lives?

Bill Bright, the late founder and longtime president of Campus Crusade for Christ International, was not only my boss but also my spiritual mentor and role model. He and his wife, Vonette, were examples for me and my wife as Christians completely devoted to God. They decided to evaluate everything based on whether it honored Jesus and helped to fulfill the Great Commission:

The last photo of the author (middle) with his spiritual mentor and friend Bill Bright (right), founder of Campus Crusade for Christ, who was already affected by his illness. Vonette Bright is seen at left.

Then Jesus came to them and said, "All authority in heaven and on earth has been given to me. Therefore go and make disciples of all nations, baptizing them in the name of the Father and of the Son and of the Holy Spirit, and teaching them to obey everything I have commanded you. And surely I am with you always, to the very end of the age." (Matt. 28:18–20)

Bill and Vonette Bright wanted to obey the Great Commission because they loved the one who gave this mandate and they didn't want to disappoint him. When I used to ask Bill what we should pray for, the answer always went something like this: "Pray that I lead a holy life and that I never lose my first love!"

These two characteristics probably go together: not losing our first love for God and leading a holy life. Love is the greatest motivation for wanting to please the beloved in every way. True love makes obedience to God easy; without love, obedience becomes a heartless, legalistic ritual, and that's the last thing God wants of us. Obedience, on the other hand, is an important expression of our love and bears fruit not least in the form of joy. Jesus described the relationship between love, obedience, and joy in the following way:

As the Father has loved me, so have I loved you. Now remain in my love. If you keep my commands, you will remain in my love, just as I have kept my Father's commands and remain in his love. I have told you this so that my joy may be in you and that your joy may be complete. (John 15:9–11)

In his talks about the end times, Jesus connected a disregard of the biblical standards with a loss of love in society: "And many false prophets will appear and deceive many people. Because of the increase of wickedness, the love of most will grow cold" (Matt. 24:11–12).

Graham's main message was "God loves you!" and again "God loves you!" and yet again "God loves you!" The best reply to this is to turn to God and submit our lives to Christ's leadership, the one who loves us so much and wants only the best for us. There is nothing as fulfilling as being united with our Maker and Father, who gave us everything in giving his Son. Love is the language God uses to draw us to himself. To prove his love to us, he sent his Son as a sacrifice for all our sins and let him die a horrible death for us. He wanted to show us that we are not only his creatures but also his friends. "Greater love has no one than this: to lay down one's life for one's friends" (John 15:13). Love is also the language when we are seeking the appropriate response to God's love.

When God gives his children spiritual gifts and authority, he does so to reveal his love and care. When God provides signs and wonders, he doesn't do so to demonstrate his power but rather to show us his love and to draw us to his heart. Spiritual gifts should always point to God as the giver of the gifts. According to Galatians 5:22, love is the firstfruit of the Holy Spirit's presence in our lives. God's love is poured into our hearts by the Holy Spirit (see Rom. 5:5).

Love is therefore the most important sign that God lives in us. The longer and the more we live with God, the more this love increases. The amount of genuine love we have for God and our neighbor is the thermometer of our spiritual lives. As long as we abide in God's love, we "reign" over circumstances, and difficulties lose their power over us.

Jesus describes love for our spiritual brothers and sisters as the most important sign that we are his disciples: "By this everyone will know that you are my disciples, if you love one another" (John 13:35). Love for God and love for our fellow human beings stem from the same source. When we learn to drink of this spring every day, it has a healing influence on all the other areas of our lives and ministries.

Ruth and Billy Graham's relationship with the triune God was not a partnership of convenience but a loving relationship. They knew that God wasn't interested in their skills or service as much as in themselves.

Ruth and Billy Graham's intimate relationship with God contributed greatly to their unfeigned modesty and humility as well as to the fact that they remained faithful to their Lord and Friend throughout their lives, through all the highs and lows. For them, prayer was an expression of humble dependence as well as their childlike belief in God's omnipotence. But it was primarily an expression of their intimate relationship with their divine Friend, whom they wished to please in all things.

To conclude this chapter, let's listen to Billy as he speaks about the role of prayer in our lives:

Before they built their mountain home, Ruth and Billy Graham often retreated to a small cabin high in the hills above the village of Montreat for times of relaxation and reflection.

A Christian grows when he prays. . . . The person who waits to pray until he feels like it will never pray. The devil will see to that. The Bible says you are to pray without ceasing. That means that you can be in a spirit of prayer while driving the car, walking down the street, working in the office, or wherever you may be. Every Christian should have a quiet time alone with God every day. Your spiritual life will never be much without it. Prayers should be filled with praise to God, with thanksgiving for all the wonderful things He has done. Self-examination should be in your prayers, as you confess shortcomings. God is interested in hearing your personal requests, no matter how small. You should seek guidance in prayer. An important thing to remember is that you should pray that God's will be done and not your will. People make mistakes. God doesn't. . . . Learn the secret of prayer. Christ's prayer life was one of the most amazing and impressive features of His earthly ministry. He prayed with His disciples. He prayed in secret. Sometimes He spent all night in prayer. If He, the sinless Son of God, could not live His earthly life without constant fellowship with God, can you?[21]

5

Focus—Disciplined Living

Billy Graham has been a great inspiration to me for over half a century. No one has had a greater impact on world evangelism and on more people, nor has maintained such a total focus on the Gospel of our Lord Jesus Christ than has Billy.[1]

Bill Bright, founder of Campus Crusade for Christ

My mother is very feisty and whether he [Billy] asked for her opinion or not, believe you me, she gave it. . . . Today he would not only consult her opinion, he would respect it and honor it and listen to her. She has enormous wisdom. . . . She didn't let him get sidetracked for a moment, and she has kept him focused.[2]

Anne Graham Lotz, daughter

If there is any single factor in Graham's staying power and the steady extension of his global ministry, it is in his determination to keep sharp the cutting edge of the Gospel.[3]

David Poling, pastor

123

For many years, T. W. Wilson was Billy Graham's closest associate and always took the room next door when they were at a hotel. If Graham was working, then Wilson was on duty. He was Graham's personal assistant, adviser, and, practically speaking, also his bodyguard. Graham confessed that he leaned on him in practical ways perhaps more than on any other person. No one had a better insight into Graham's life and way of working when he was going about God's business. And it was Wilson who described Graham as "the most completely disciplined person I have ever known."[4]

Billy's daily routine was clearly structured. This was especially the case when he was preparing the evening messages during missions. During this time, starting from three in the afternoon, he didn't want anyone around him, not even Ruth.

Ruth was also extraordinarily disciplined when she was having her personal time with God or was preparing her own ministries, such as leading a devotional or teaching adult Sunday school.

Someone who knew Ruth very well was Cliff Barrows. He served as choir director at Graham's missions for over sixty years and occasionally as master of ceremonies at conferences. In addition, he produced the weekly radio broadcast *Hour of Decision* in the Grahams' home, which made Billy Graham known nationwide. He later also led World Wide Pictures, the television department of the BGEA.

The Barrowses were not only close co-workers of the Grahams but also personal friends. I sensed the closeness of Cliff Barrows to the Grahams when he introduced his very dear and beloved friend Billy Graham at the 2012 Christmas celebration at the Billy Graham Training Center at the Cove near Asheville. In this light, what Barrows says about Ruth has great weight: "She was a tremendously fun woman. She was also a woman of great discipline. She disciplined herself in the knowledge of the Word. She got that love from her father and mother and her training in China."

Ruth's strength of character, determination, and fearlessness can be understood only within the context of the environment in which she grew up. Her time in China and North Korea formed the foundation for and was the prerequisite to Ruth's ability to master the diverse challenges at her world-famous husband's side and to become the pillar of support her husband needed. Therefore, it's helpful to take a closer look at Ruth's childhood in China.

Ruth's parents, Dr. Nelson and Virginia Bell, moved to China in 1916 after marrying. Ruth's father worked there as a missionary doctor until the outbreak of World War II. After the abdication of the Manchu emperor in 1912, Chinese warlords took over the government completely in 1916. In 1919, the Treaty of Versailles favored the Japanese, to the detriment of the Chinese. The additional factor of revolution-inspired communists in Russia created an explosive situation within China. Bandits from all sides took advantage of the ensuing power vacuum; groups of citizens fought on all fronts.

Ruth was born into this environment in 1920 as the second of four children. With her siblings, she experienced all the horrors of a land in upheaval. Ruth and her older sister, Rosa, once said that they couldn't remember a single day when they didn't hear gunfire. They had learned from their parents to stay calm and to trust God because in the midst of the raging battles, he was always in control. Ruth felt that during this time in China she lost all fear, once and for all. From then on, fearlessness was one of her trademarks.

During their youth in China, the Bell children also learned about the value of a disciplined search for God. They depended on God to protect them and to carry them through each day, as all foreigners in China were hated for their supposed "exploitation of the country."

Ruth experienced a harsh youth and was confronted with the world's misery and the consequences of godlessness at an early age. She also experienced long periods of loneliness in Pyongyang, the capital of modern-day North Korea, where her parents had sent her for further education. There she was prepared for "a lifetime of good-byes," as she once put it. But both in Korea and in China she learned the value of an orderly and disciplined lifestyle. In China, she saw daily what

125

happens when clear rules and a guiding hand are lacking. However, she also saw how God caused a radical change and renewal in people's lives, bringing them both comprehensive healing and purpose in life. Her parents were not only doctors but also evangelists; their lives radiated the love and concern of a Father God who cares about each individual. The Bells wanted healing not just for the body but for the entire human being. Ruth thus experienced firsthand how, through God's power, broken people became shining witnesses for Christ and were restored and found purpose in their lives. She was particularly impressed by the complete transformation of a Chinese woman who had previously kidnapped children and sold them as prostitutes. After conversion, that woman sang praises to God as she cared for the sick.

Despite the difficult environment, Ruth had a happy childhood, filled with love and laughter. The Bells laughed a lot; this positive atmosphere had a great deal to do with the parents' strong faith. Ruth couldn't recall a morning when her father didn't kneel to pray for his family and patients and read the Bible. Reading the Bible together was as much a part of family life as mealtimes and games. Ruth's mother, Virginia, knew how to juggle many tasks and still stay relaxed. In addition to managing the household and bringing up four lively children, she worked as a nurse at the women's hospital. Yet she never gave the impression that she was stressed because she adhered to the motto of the great China missionary Hudson Taylor:

> The sweetest part, if one may speak of one part being sweeter than another, is the rest which full identification with Christ brings. I am no longer anxious about anything, as I realize this; for He, I know, is able to carry out His will and His will is mine. It makes no matter where He places me, or how. That is rather for Him to consider than for me; for in the easiest positions He must give me His grace, and in the most difficult His grace is sufficient.[5]

Thanks to her parents, Ruth was able to enjoy a loving, sheltered childhood filled with strong faith, despite raging power battles and terrible wartime events.

In later years, it took quite a lot for Ruth to lose her composure. She had a strength and resoluteness that astonished everyone who knew her closely. Her faith was unshakable and her peace in all circumstances legendary, despite the fact that she was a very sensitive person. She was convinced that if God asks us to do something, he also provides the necessary strength to carry out the assignment. Nevertheless, we must stay true to our personal calling with all our strength; God doesn't do it for us.

Ruth always found it important to set priorities. To do this, she learned to say no to anything that did not help fulfill the divine mission. Ruth lived a promise-oriented life rather than a problem-oriented one. If God wasn't worried about something, she didn't have to worry about it either. She admitted, however, that she often became weak and let herself be unnecessarily burdened by worry. When that happened, God would speak to her clearly, not audibly but always unmistakably, telling her she should leave things up to him. Miracles were his department. She should concentrate on the possible and leave the impossible—for example, her sons' conversion—to him.

In hard times, she needed to learn that God is sovereign, so there was no reason for her to take herself too seriously. Ruth had her own way of getting people's feet back on the ground if they were in danger of getting too self-centered. Her husband experienced that time and again. Longtime associate Gerald Beavan describes her influence on Billy like this:

> Ruth has been the rudder for much of his life to keep him focused. She has been a very faithful prayer supporter. She is very plainspoken, and if Billy wanted to do something ridiculous she would say, "Oh, come on, Bill," and he wouldn't do it.[6]

No one helped Billy stay true to his evangelistic task more than his wife. She helped him to decline offers from film companies and even from several US presidents for posts as an ambassador or cabinet member. Ruth felt that there were enough politicians, and it was her husband's task to be God's ambassador and to transmit the gospel in unabridged and understandable form to all people, independent of their cultural backgrounds and political persuasions. "Stay out of politics!" was an admonition Billy repeatedly heard from Ruth. She reminded him to limit his advice to spiritual and moral issues. Billy later hinted that he would have been wise to heed Ruth's advice more closely. At the opening speech of Lausanne '74, the International Congress on World Evangelization in Lausanne, Switzerland, Billy stated:

> A third error is to identify the gospel with any particular political program or culture. This has been my own danger. When I go to preach the gospel, I go as an ambassador for the kingdom of God—not America. To tie the gospel to any political system, secular program, or society is dangerous and will only serve to divert the gospel.

Graham learned his lesson from the Watergate scandal. President Nixon did not live up to the trust Graham had placed in him. In retrospect, Graham felt it was a great mistake to have even indirectly endorsed Richard Nixon during the election campaign by inviting him to say a word of greeting at one of his crusades.

The Grahams had known the Nixons for many years before the latter became president of the United States. They particularly held Nixon's mother in high esteem, as she was a very devout woman. Because of their long-standing friendship with the Nixons, Billy Graham's attitude is understandable. It was nevertheless wrong and damaged his reputation as a pastor for many Americans. To his credit, he showed more discerning judgment in later years; yet he continued to be criticized for being too naive, or at least for his idealistic views. Many felt he had let himself be used as an ideological puppet by the Soviets by accepting their invitation to hold a speech at a disarmament conference during the Cold War. He was often harshly criticized for his ministry behind the Iron Curtain. But his only goal was to share the gospel of Jesus Christ; even KGB members needed to hear the Good News.

Helene Bos, a well-known Dutch prayer movement leader, told me of an encounter she had with Graham that had a lasting effect on her. In the autumn of 1982, she participated at an international meeting of prayer intercessors in North Carolina. One evening, they were joined by Ruth and Billy Graham. Billy poured out his heart to the seventy people present. The harsh criticism he had received even from fellow Christians about his recent tour of the USSR had been very painful for him, all the more since several KGB members had opened their hearts to Jesus at the meetings in Moscow. Billy said, "Who tells them the gospel if we shut our mouths because of fear of being misused? Do the communists not need to hear the gospel too?" As he said that, he could no longer hold back his tears over the fact that people who did not know the Lord were lost. Bos concluded, "I have seen his tears. I have seen his compassion for people who were lost without Jesus. I do not care what people say about Billy Graham's naivete when preaching behind the Iron Curtain."

This picture makes it clear why Billy received offers to star in films.

David Epstein, head pastor of Calvary Baptist Church and staff member at the last mission of Billy Graham in New York in 2005, defends Graham in a similar way:

There have been people who have taken issue with him on secondary matters, like why he would stand with a particular person on a podium or make a statement in Russia that was thought to be politically naive. I would say: "Give the guy a break!" Billy Graham was called by God to be an evangelist, to preach the Gospel. Let's honor a servant of the Lord who's preached the Gospel. He's not done it angrily or polemically, he's done it by lifting up Christ. He has never dishonored Christ by any fiscal or moral or mean-spirited scandals. So let's give him credit, let's give him some space; he's been faithful. When people persist in being critical, I say, "OK, here's the last thing I am going to state: all the women in my life—my mother, my wife, my sisters—came to Christ through Billy Graham."[7]

Billy Graham is by nature an extremely friendly gentleman who certainly wouldn't want to offend anyone. That's why he always found conflicts very difficult, in contrast to Ruth. Their daughter Gigi once asked him why, at an event held by *Time* magazine for all who had ever appeared on the cover, he had been so nice to Bill Clinton, who

Graham's close friendship with President Richard Nixon, shown here while vice president in a 1960 photo with Billy, would cause problems for Graham later on.

was sitting next to him, despite the recent revelation of Clinton's affair with Monica Lewinsky. He explained his behavior by saying that it was his duty to share God's love and forgiveness and that it was the Holy Spirit's task to convince and convict people of their sins.

Graham's foremost goal was always to focus on God's love and grace extended to sinners. In doing so, he leaned on the Bible as God's revealed Word. Ruth was a great help to him in this respect. After his first sermon at the 1949 Los Angeles Mission, where it seemed that he relied more on Jonathan Edwards's famous sermon "Sinners in the Hands of an Angry God" than on the Bible, Ruth did not hold back her opinion: "You've got to stick with the Bible. That is your source of power."[8] And it was certainly not the last time that Ruth reminded him that his role was primarily to transmit God's Word, not his own thoughts or someone else's. He was unquestionably convinced of this, but he had to hear it again and again to remain true to his conviction. During the mission in Los Angeles, he learned how to research God's Word when preparing a message. Because the campaign was extended by several weeks, he ran out of prepared sermons and was forced to dig deeply into God's Word by himself. He discovered that God provided him with a new message every day.

Because he had received the messages directly and personally from God's heart, they were well received by his audience. The more he let God's Word speak, the more people made a decision for Jesus Christ. He decided to quote from the Bible as much as possible. The more he did, the clearer it became to him that an ambassador of God must transmit God's thoughts, not his own, and this in an undiluted way.

At the same time, Graham wanted to set himself apart from many of the past evangelists who, in his opinion, appealed too strongly to people's feelings, which had resulted in listeners not knowing what they were so excited about when the event was over. He was afraid that such emotionally charged conversions would not stand the test of time. Nevertheless, in countries that had no tradition of major missions, he continued to be criticized for his too-passionate, over-emotional style of speaking. Those countries did, however, gratefully acknowledge that he was at least trying not to take advantage of the emotional character of a mass event and did not try to play with his listeners' feelings. An article titled "A Convincing Billy Graham" in the June 20, 1955, issue of the Swiss magazine *Schweizer Illustrierte Zeitung* described his preaching style at the Zurich Hardturm Soccer Stadium: "Contrary to the occasional criticism of Graham's presentation style, the evangelist spoke clearly and simply, and appealed more to the listeners' intellect than to their feelings." The Swiss *St. Galler Tagblatt* reported, "Although these words weren't new, they

Many people wished that Billy Graham, when ministering behind the Iron Curtain, would explicitly take sides against communism. But he deliberately abstained from doing so, seeing himself as an ambassador of Christ, not of a political system. This picture was taken at a crusade in October 1977.

were presented in such a way that they sank into the hearts and consciences of all who heard them with the power of a profound, living conviction."[9]

Billy Graham was often criticized for his heavy use of modern marketing methods. The German magazine *Der Stern* mentioned in its June 27, 1954, edition that never before in Europe had they seen such a big American-style advertising campaign but that this did not completely explain Graham's success:

> Who would have believed that in the age of the hydrogen bomb, religious topics could fill the press for weeks? But modern methods of marketing and curiosity alone certainly do not account for Billy's tremendous success. Everyone who has heard him understands that

132

the secret of his success lies in his personality.[10]

It was always essential for Graham that the content of the biblical message be the focus of his campaigns. It made no difference if he was speaking to forty thousand people or to one individual. He writes in his autobiography:

> I never go to see important people—or anyone else—without having the deep realization that I am—first and foremost—an ambassador of the King of kings and Lord of lords. From the moment I enter the room, I am thinking about how I

In 1955, Billy Graham preached in the fully packed Zurich Hardturm Soccer Stadium. The evangelistic message was simultaneously transmitted to the nearby Förrlibuck Field. Many had to be satisfied with a radio transmission.

> can get the conversation around to the Gospel. We may discuss a dozen peripheral things first, but I am always thinking of ways I can share Christ and His message of hope with them. I make every effort to be sensitive to their position and their viewpoint, but I rarely leave without attempting to explain the meaning of the Gospel unless God clearly indicates to me that it is not the right time for this person. No one has ever rebuffed me or refused to listen to me.[11]

It was equally important to Ruth not to get stuck in other people's suggestions, no matter how well meant, but to point to the only one who can truly help us all: Jesus Christ. She knew how to meet people at their own level, right where they were at the time.

As an excellent listener with a fine feeling for people's true needs, she was able to convey a clear sense of personal interest and caring to those she was counseling. Yet she did not simply stop at this; she always guided her conversation toward biblical truth. She did it in such a way that it could be received more as an encouragement than a command. In this way, she carried out a particularly effective ministry to those who had damaged self-esteem or lives marked by failure and breakdowns. Because she herself openly confessed her weaknesses and errors, people she talked to were also open and honest. She was able to show countless people God's undeserved grace and awaken in them a readiness to let God work in their hearts.

I have met people who have heard far too many messages conveying demands they could not meet. Such people would have hardly responded to a traditional evangelistic sermon, but Ruth was able to win them over to a life lived by Christ's grace.

Ruth's gift was not only to show compassion but also to set others back on their feet by showing them the Redeemer's wonderful love. She always pointed to Jesus and what he had done for us human beings with his death on the cross. Her main focus was the new life we can receive when trusting in Jesus. For Ruth, there was no place for self-pity. She experienced this challenge herself in the times of solitude when Billy was gone for weeks and later in the midst of physical suffering after her accident. Nor did she allow the people she counseled to feel sorry for themselves. She was very frank about this point: self-pity hinders us from experiencing God's help and healing. It was important for Ruth to package the gospel in a listener-friendly but at the same time uncompromising way. Christ's death on the cross should not be glossed over. When asked by an actress in London how Christ's crucifixion should be explained to children, Ruth replied, "Exactly as the Bible does. God died for my sins. Whatever you do, don't underestimate or try to soften the horror or the glory of it!"[12] When her children were still at home, she often told them stories of Christian martyrs to show them what it means to take up Christ's cross. But she also did it to make it clear to them the power that lies in faith in Christ.

In his book *Nearing Home*, published in 2011, Billy reflected on the secret of his wife's inner strength, quoting one of Ruth's favorite Bible verses:

> "Neither death nor life, neither angels nor demons, neither the present nor the future . . . nor anything else in all creation, will be able to separate us from the love of God that is in Christ Jesus our Lord" (Rom. 8:38–39).
>
> In the weeks before her death, my wife, Ruth, repeated these verses over and over to us. Ruth was always thinking of others. This was her secret for getting through so much of life with joy. She never focused on her problems, she turned her attention to Christ, and He always led her to someone who needed a word of encouragement or a listening ear.[13]

Ruth remained an encourager and an evangelist all her life. Twila Knaack, who worked for the BGEA for some time, once observed at an evangelistic outreach in Las Vegas how an oddly dressed hippie suddenly entered the office and started asking lots of questions. While the other staff members were having their coffee break and were chatting with each other, Ruth Graham sat in a quiet corner with the visitor. She answered his questions in a kindhearted manner using her well-worn Bible, which was full of underlined verses and notes, and told him of Christ's love. When the man understood what Christ had done for him at Golgotha, both knelt in prayer and the man confessed his sins and gave his life to Christ.

While Ruth passed on the gospel in a more personal setting, Billy usually did it from a podium. As he put it, "That is my sole mission—to hold a beacon for the soul-sick, hopeless, to repent and find their way back to the comfort of Christ."[14]

Prior to the New York Mission, which received nationwide attention and was extraordinarily blessed, he expressed his role even more clearly in an interview in *Newsweek*: "My only specialty is soul-winning. I'm not a great philosopher, not a theologian, not an intellectual—God has given me the gift of winning souls. In New York my object is the winning of souls."[15]

I have compared Graham's earlier sermons with his later ones and discovered that as he grew older he emphasized God's love more strongly as well as the cost of discipleship. Yet the core message never changed: Christ's work of salvation on the cross and the need for a personal changing of ways. He kept this focus throughout his life.

In his autobiography, Graham describes in detail what brought him to the conviction never to miss preaching Christ's redemptive work on the cross:

On June 23 (1954), we moved on to Germany. Accompanying us was German-born industrialist John Bolten, who had recommitted his life to Christ during our 1950 meetings in Boston. Exactly a year before our German meetings, something had happened to focus the message I was preaching; and John was part of that change. In 1953 he had been with us during a series of Crusade meetings in Dallas's Cotton Bowl. One night my preaching did not seem to have spiritual depth or power, although a number of people did come forward at the invitation. After the meeting, John and I took a walk together, and he confronted me. "Billy," he said, "you didn't speak about the Cross. How can anyone be converted without having at least one single view of the Cross where the Lord died for us? You must preach about the Cross, Billy. You must preach about the blood that was shed for us there. There is no other place in the Bible where there is greater power than when we talk or preach about the Cross." At first I resisted his rebuke. The Cross and its meaning were, more often than not, a part of my sermons. But that night I could not sleep, and before morning came I knew he was right. I made a commitment never to preach again without being sure that the Gospel was as complete and clear as possible, centering on Christ's sacrificial death for our sins on the Cross and His resurrection from the dead for our salvation.[16]

For over fifty years, Graham stuck to this resolve, to his last official mission in New York in 2005.

The Swiss theologian Karl Barth once said that he loved it when Billy Graham held up the Bible and said to the crowd, "The Bible says." However, the two men held different convictions in other areas. In 1955, Barth visited one of Graham's crusades in Basel, Switzerland, where Graham, as was often the case, preached about Jesus's words to Nicodemus, "You must be born again." Barth found many words of praise, but he felt the words "you must" were too strong. According to Barth, God was the main actor when it came to saving mankind. Barth's opinion was that conversion had already happened at Golgotha. Nonetheless, in his later years, he made some positive statements about Graham's invitation to inquirers to come forward as a sign of their decision to follow Jesus Christ.

Mr. Graham, don't ever let anybody criticize you for the fact that it [the decision] doesn't last, because for one fleeting moment in that person's life he stood before God. That will always remain with him to his dying day; he will never forget that one moment when he stood before God.[17]

Billy Graham and Karl Barth respected each other even though they did not always share the same theological views.

137

Despite their theological differences, Barth agreed with Graham that there was no task more important for the Christian church than to proclaim the gospel of Jesus's death on the cross for the salvation of men. Barth said:

> The Church will die and petrify if it does not proclaim the Good News. Christians have been told to "Go out and preach the Gospel!" The injunction is not "Go and celebrate services!" "Go and edify yourselves with the sermon!" "Go and celebrate the Sacraments!" "Go and present yourselves in a liturgy." . . . The one thing must prevail: "Proclaim the Gospel to every creature!" . . . Where the Church is living, it must ask itself whether it is serving this commission or whether it is a purpose in itself?[18]

Billy Graham could only add his hearty amen to such a clear statement. Graham and his co-workers wouldn't let anyone or anything divert them from their goal to proclaim the gospel and call people to a decision. They were aware that God's enemy would do everything he could to prevent their ministry of calling people to repentance and salvation in Christ.

In meetings with pastors, Graham repeatedly emphasized the need to preach the gospel in a way that everyone understands:

> When you go into the pulpit next Sunday, preach with clarity and simplicity. Preach to the people in language they can understand. The fact that you shoot over the heads of your congregation doesn't prove you have superior ammunition. It just proves you can't shoot.[19]

At the Lausanne Congress on World Evangelization in 1974, Graham called on participants assembled from all over the world to always remain conscious of their main task:

> Certainly we have some doctrinal differences, some cultural and political differences. But we are one in the Spirit. We shout with one voice, "Jesus alone saves!" We have one task—to proclaim the message of salvation in Jesus Christ. In rich countries and in poor, among the educated and uneducated, in freedom or oppression, we

138

are determined to proclaim Jesus Christ in the power of the Holy Spirit so that men may put their trust in him as Savior, follow him obediently, and serve him in the fellowship of the Church, of which he alone is King and Head.[20]

Graham closed with an appeal: "My fellow evangelists and missionaries, if men are lost, as Jesus clearly taught they are, then we have no greater priority than to lift up a saving Christ to them."[21]

Robert O. Ferm writes in *Cooperative Evangelism* that Graham was criticized time and again because of the people he worked with in his missions. The result of Ferm's investigations speaks for Graham's uncompromising proclamation of the Bible message: "It has been agreed by both his supporters and opponents that Billy Graham has never trimmed or diluted the message of the Bible."[22]

The foundation for Graham's goal-oriented, disciplined character was laid in his childhood.

Billy Graham was born in 1918 in Charlotte, North Carolina, the son of a dairy farmer and the oldest of four children. From an early age, he had to help milk the seventy-five cows. Milking time was determined by the cows. With his brother, Melvin, he had to get up before daybreak. When he returned from school in the afternoon, he often had to do another round of milking. Their mother, Morrow Graham, said:

> I looked forward to our evenings together as a family. Everyone gathered in the family room. It was the most important thing in our life, this time of Bible reading and prayer. I know that Billy Frank recalls those instructional periods as among the most important in his life, helping him to become saturated with the Bible. . . . Our children have thanked us and told us these times together taught them what they wouldn't have learned on their own.[23]

It was equally important for Billy's father to set priorities and to stick to them in a disciplined way. God and his Word came first, then everything else. While Morrow prepared the sandwiches, Father Graham helped the children learn a Bible verse by heart for that day. Going to church on Sundays was a necessity. For Billy, church wasn't exactly a highlight of the week. He preferred to play baseball or drive around in old cars to impress young ladies. But he did take note that church-going obviously didn't hurt, as his parents were happy people. After Billy turned to Christ as a teenager during one of Mordecai Ham's fiery evangelistic campaigns in his hometown of Charlotte, this disciplined spirituality became so important to him that he continued it into adulthood.

During his time at the Bible College in Florida, he regularly retired to a secret place to set up his own prayer altar, which nobody knew about except him. Often he would spend two, three, or four hours there alone with the Lord.

He brought problem after problem before the Lord and asked him to help him respond in a way that would please the Lord. He confessed losing his temper and being rude to other people. And he would often hear the Lord respond, "You must speak to that person." He admitted that growth was slow in some areas, but over time he saw progress.

That is why in his books and speeches, especially those directed to young people, Graham always emphasized the value of discipline in all areas of life:

> Living in this world of gadgets and amusements, with its tremendous emphasis on sex, plenty of leisure time, a lot of money, plus insecurity and sophistication, today's teenagers face real problems. . . . A key lesson we need to learn in high school is to discipline ourselves. . . . Lose the battle with sex—and you lose the battle of life! . . . Unless you are reading and studying your Bible systematically, your efforts for Christ are being robbed of much of their effectiveness. . . . I would get as much Bible training as I possibly could, no matter for what field I was headed. . . . Abraham Lincoln once said: "I will prepare myself and some day my chance will come."[24]

Graham goes into more detail about the need for a disciplined, goal-oriented lifestyle in the book *The Holy Spirit*:

> If we Christians realized that God Himself in the person of the Holy Spirit really dwells within our bodies, we would be far more careful about what we eat, drink, look at, or read. No wonder Paul said, "But I buffet my body and make it my slave, lest possibly after I have preached to others, I myself should be disqualified" (1 Cor. 9:27). Paul disciplined his body for fear of God's disapproval. This should drive us to our knees in confession.[25]

Graham was very conscious of the fact that this applied to him personally as well. At the same time, he warned about misunderstanding discipline and thus painting a false picture of God: "God does not discipline us to subdue us, but to condition us for a life of usefulness and blessedness."[26]

In the same focused way in which he kept a personal relationship with God and worked on eradicating character weaknesses, Graham also worked to improve his speaking abilities during his time in Florida: "I knew I wanted to be a preacher, a revivalist preacher. And I practiced sermons hour after hour, preaching right from the Bible. Any old stump along the river was a good pulpit, even if I didn't have anyone to listen to me."[27]

Many people with great talents never achieve much because they are undisciplined. On the other hand, we all know people who have average talents but do extraordinary things as a result of discipline and constant practice. More important than having specific abilities is having clearly defined goals we aim for with our entire strength and will. In an increasingly complex age, which is simultaneously superficial and chaotic, there is a great danger of letting ourselves be distracted. Jesus pointed out the dangers to his disciples long ago: "The seed that fell among thorns stands for those who hear, but as they go on their way they are choked by life's worries, riches and pleasures, and they do not mature" (Luke 8:14). If we don't learn to discern, we will be led by the prevailing spirit of the times. Graham brought it to the point:

Many people are being lulled to sleep—spiritual sleep—by entertainment today—TV, movies, and so on. Many are oblivious to God's grace and lack Christian discipline. We need more discipline in our lives; we need to think. Everything is pre-digested for us. It takes real self-discipline to turn off the TV and pick up the Bible.[28]

Billy Graham always made sure to have enough time to study the Bible and read good books.

In the midst of all our well-meaning Christian activities, we can forget our most important Christian task, which is to cultivate a relationship with God. Today, more than half a century after it was spoken, Graham's exhortation to church leaders in Germany in 1954 is more valid than ever:

We are all busy like machines. If the average Evangelical would attend all of the official meetings he is expected to go to, then he wouldn't be able to carry out his ministry of the Gospel. He would no longer be capable of praying, he wouldn't have any time left for the quiet time with God. Invitations to this or that or yet another event clutter our desks. If we accepted even just half of them, we would be at committee meetings most of the day—until God himself was "committed and organized" to death. I pray to God for a desire to have fewer board meetings and less organization and more prayer meetings and more from God. That's the greatest need we have today.[29]

Without a clear goal or focus, it is difficult not to be absorbed by second-rank matters. Only when we have a clear goal before us can we resist the enemy's distractions and stay on the path of reaching the goal of our lives.

One of the most focused people I know is the current president of Campus Crusade for Christ International, Steve Douglass. Many years ago while facing a big challenge, he decided to leave out one meal a day to find more time to seek the Lord. With only a short break, he has continued this habit for over twenty years, because he realized the blessing of a focused, disciplined life. He experienced that having discipline in one area helped him to have more discipline in other areas too. Douglass never seems to be in a hurry. He always has time for his staff because he deliberately decided to take time for the really important and not be sidetracked by the secondary.

Another very focused person was the Scottish revivalist Duncan Campbell. My wife and I were closely acquainted with his daughter Sheena for many years, and she shared many personal stories of her father with us.

In 1949, at the same time when Billy Graham had his breakthrough mission in Los Angeles, a revival broke out in the Hebrides Islands in Scotland that would last for several years. Village after village was touched by the presence of God. Hundreds came to know Christ as their Savior and Lord. Two old sisters, both over eighty years old, one blind, the other frail, stood on the promises of God's Word all their lives, praying for revival until God showed them that he wanted to use a Scottish Presbyterian pastor by the name of Duncan Campbell to be the human instrument to bring revival to the Hebrides. After a personal crisis, Campbell had rededicated his life to Christ, reentering the Faith Mission he was part of earlier. He was invited to preach on the island of Lewis. Wherever Campbell preached the gospel of salvation, scores of people were convicted of their sins and gave their lives to Christ. Campbell and the other preachers were literally overwhelmed by people who wanted to get right with God. Recently, I asked Campbell's son Archie what most characterized his father. His answer: "He was a man who was totally focused, twenty-four hours a day focused." Campbell describes the reason for his focused passion: "Can we be casual in the work of God—casual when the house is on fire, and people in danger of being burnt?"[30]

Both the two sisters and Campbell did not give up until they saw their prayers answered. The same was true for Billy Graham, whose evangelistic campaigns in Scotland were accompanied by mighty showers of God's blessing. Fellow evangelist Luis Palau attributes the blessing of Graham's campaigns in Scotland to the determination of the Scottish believers and the focus of the Scottish leaders, stressing that the clergy had a common goal and were united as they never had been before. Graham supported this fact in a meeting with several hundred Scottish ministers preceding his six-week Glasgow Mission in 1955: "All the elements of revival are here. Glasgow is the most prayed-for city in the history of the Christian Church. It will not be a miracle if we have a revival. It will be a miracle if we don't."[31]

A Christian's life and ministry is not a one-hundred-yard dash but a marathon, and with every marathon there are crises. That's when it's important to keep our eyes on our goal. Sometimes it helps to set intermediate goals. We shouldn't be disappointed if we don't advance as quickly as we wish, as long as we move forward. Billy and Ruth Graham also failed time and time again and had to learn how to depend on God's mercy and forgiveness. The difference between a winner and a loser is that the winner always gets up again after he has fallen.

We must learn how to live on daily forgiveness. Just as we regularly exhale the used air when breathing and inhale pure air, we must also, as Christ's disciples, continually confess our sins and lay down our burdens at God's feet, to then claim Christ's forgiveness and the Holy Spirit's empowerment. The apostle Paul uses the Greek Olympic Games as an example to show the value of being goal-oriented and disciplined:

Do you not know that in a race all the runners run, but only one gets the prize? Run in such a way as to get the prize. Everyone who competes in the games goes into strict training. They do it to get a crown that will not last, but we do it to get a crown that will last forever. Therefore I do not run like someone running aimlessly; I do not fight like a boxer beating the air. No, I strike a blow to my body and make it my slave so that after I have preached to others, I myself will not be disqualified for the prize. (1 Cor. 9:24–27)

Discipline has to do with setting priorities and the value we attribute to something. The reason for a lack of discipline often lies in the fact that we don't place enough value on something. I would never have been able to finish this book if I hadn't been convinced that the lessons I learned from studying the Grahams could also be helpful to others.

The apostle Paul didn't shy away from using military and war as illustrations when he was trying to teach his disciple Timothy the value of goal-oriented discipline: "Join with me in suffering, like a good soldier of Christ Jesus. No one serving as a soldier gets entangled in civilian affairs, but rather tries to please his commanding officer" (2 Tim. 2:3–4).

Billy Graham repeatedly found himself at war against the destructive powers of the day. In the early years of his ministry after World War II, when the Russians had an atomic bomb and Mao Tse-tung had risen to power in China, he, like most of his contemporaries in the Western world, saw communism as a great danger that needed to be opposed with all might. He felt that the most important way to do this was to call people to God through the gospel and to help the American people experience moral and spiritual renewal that would finally affect all areas of society. He believed that it was God who governed war and peace.

We Christians shouldn't be strangers to discipline when we consider that the word *discipline* has the same root as the word *disciple*. A good student follows his teacher's instructions carefully. The Holy Spirit is our teacher, or, as the disciple John says in John 14–16, our *parakletos*: someone who has been called (*kletos*) to stand by our side (*para*) and to show us the way. We can keep our focus only if we've learned to listen to the gentle voice of the Holy Spirit. It is dangerous to enter the battle without God's orders. We need to be not only filled and empowered by the Holy Spirit but also guided by him. Only then are we capable of instructing others in God's purposes. The apostle Paul expressed it this way in his letter to the Galatians: "Since we live by the Spirit, let us keep in step with the Spirit" (5:25). And in his letter to the Romans, Paul even equates our being a child of God with being led by his Spirit: "For those who are led by the Spirit of God are children of God" (8:14).

Billy Graham was always very aware that God himself must "start the race" and that it is dangerous to run ahead of God. In this way, he was able to resist outside pressure from people who thought he should do one thing or another. For example, he was willing to carry out a mission in New York City only after receiving a clear

In this photo from 1983, Billy Graham chats with Alexander Solzhenitsyn, author of *The Gulag Archipelago* and winner of the Nobel Prize in literature. Solzhenitsyn liked Graham's focus on the gospel of Christ but missed a clear statement against the persecution of religion in communist USSR.

yes from God. He did not wish to march into battle without his divine companion. Graham's close co-workers testify that he kept on asking the question, "What is God saying we should do?" A secret of his successful leadership was that he never wanted to embark on anything of his own accord but always waited for God's "Go!" His associates could trust that he undertook only things he had thoroughly tested before God:

> Such sensitivity to the Spirit has typified Billy's decision-making process over the decades. Throughout his ministry, Billy followed. He was a highly effective leader with clarity of purpose because he was determined that nothing would short-circuit his responding to the nudges of the Holy Spirit. In facing ambiguous circumstances and hearing competing voices, the complexities pressed him to long hours of reflection, prayer, and seeking the applicable biblical wisdom.[32]

Biographer William Martin states the same fact more succinctly: "Billy Graham . . . has carried with him since his mid-teens an obsessive determination to discern and perform the will of God."[33]

Ruth also stayed true to her calling at Billy's side and as the mother of five children and grandmother of twenty-two grandchildren. In a speech, she encouraged a group of American women to provide the help their husbands needed:

> God, you know, created each of us to be a helpmeet for her husband; in other words, a help suited to meet his needs, wishes, desires—tailor made, if you wish, with a few alterations now and then. My advice to any young girls who are not yet married is: Marry a man to whom you don't mind adjusting! God tailors a wife to fit her husband, not the other way around.

Ruth recommended that the women present not hold impossible expectations of their husbands: "Some women expect their husbands to be to them what only Jesus Christ himself can be. Remember, you married a man, not God."

She encouraged the women to try to slip into their husbands' shoes. Husbands want nothing more than a wife who is loving and respectful. Ruth made this truth clear in her humorous way with an everyday experience: "Some time ago I saw a filling station in Las Vegas with a sign that said, 'Free Aspirin and Sympathy.' Now, are we going to let a filling station beat us at our game?" Ruth repeatedly emphasized that it was not a wife's duty to make her husband good but to make him happy. "You see, only God can make him good. We are to take care of the possible and trust God for the impossible."

You could get the impression that Ruth saw wives only in a submissive role and that she felt it was only the women who had to compromise. But that would be completely misjudging her. She advised her three daughters that there were times when it was appropriate to outwit their husbands rather than submit to them. Based on this advice, it is clear that Ruth did not equate the biblical concept of submission with subservience. According to Gigi Graham, her mother did a lot of outwitting. Ruth always expressed her opinion clearly, often more frankly than Billy wished. But her head told her that in the end somebody had to decide. It was Billy who did so for ministry matters; she was the boss at home. She also took care of all practical matters, as Billy was often away and was less of a handyman than Ruth. Ruth made sure that the family had a pleasant, comfortable home.

Ruth loved fireplaces more than anything. But Billy felt that two were enough. When he was on one of his journeys, she instructed the workmen to add as many fireplaces to the house as possible. When Billy returned, there were five of them. In Ruth's defense, the fireplaces really look good in the Graham home. My wife and I immediately felt at ease, and the house has a lovely, homey atmosphere. The house was to a great extent designed by Ruth, and the builders carried out Ruth's instructions to the letter. When it was finished, they all felt the end product was a success, despite initial doubts.

148

Ruth had reached her goal, and the family had a cozy home on the mountain to which they could retreat.

After Ruth passed away in June 2007, the Wheaton College alumni magazine summed up Ruth's contribution at her husband's side:

> She knew what she wanted and on any project she had definite opinions on how things would be carried out. . . . Ruth was the epitome of a woman whose own calling was to be a life partner in her husband's work. As he made decisions that affected many people, she was a visible extension of his personhood—her grace and charm a reflection of the constituency that she, too, represented.[34]

Ruth saw herself as a full-fledged partner at her husband's side in his ministry. She did not feel relegated to the background. Her roles as wife, mother, and assistant to her husband were a great privilege for her. She could fully identify with her husband's mission.

Ruth Graham and her three daughters on the Great Wall in China. From left to right: Ruth (Bunny), Anne, Ruth, and Gigi.

Together, they tried to fulfill his God-given mandate. When she was asked what the secret of her marriage was, she replied, "The heart of our marriage has been our mutual love for and commitment to Christ."[35]

Even before she married Billy, Ruth had decided to fully support him in his tasks. A letter she wrote to her parents is enlightening:

> To be with Bill in this type work won't be easy. There will be little financial backing, lots of obstacles and criticism, and no earthly glory whatsoever. But somehow I need Bill. I don't know what I'd do if, for some reason, he should suddenly go out of my life. And Bill needs someone to understand him, someone who would be willing to take the quiet place of praying for him. . . . I knew I wouldn't have peace till I yielded my will to the Lord and decided to marry Bill. I must admit I have had real peace since doing so.

This letter reveals Ruth's readiness to set aside her own ambitions and be a source of support Billy could count on. In later years, she emphasized that their different character traits greatly enriched both of their lives:

Ruth and Billy enjoying one of the rare spare times together at the seaside.

> Too often, early love is a mirage built on daydreams. Love deepens with understanding, and varying viewpoints expand and challenge one another. So many

Ruth was always smartly dressed, even at home. She felt that her Creator deserved that honor. Gigi is shown standing between her parents.

things improve with age. A recent advertisement read: "Things of true quality need not fear the years—it only improves them." So it is with marriage.[36]

When they married, someone told Ruth, "If two agree on anything, one is unnecessary." A prerequisite for fruitful differences of opinion, however, is that both marriage partners have a common life goal that provides a bond.

Many years later, in an interview with someone whose life and marriage were in trouble and who sought advice, Ruth related:

The important thing is to know when to argue. You should never argue when tired or preoccupied or sleepy. That doesn't leave us much time. . . . (laughs) Try to look as nice as you can. Tone of voice is very important. Rules of courtesy are very important. See, I come from a long line of strong-minded, hardheaded individuals. Some people are much more flexible, milder, I would say, so there were times . . . but we celebrate our fiftieth this August.[37]

Ruth was often a great help in preventing Billy from being distracted by second-rank matters. She wanted to do her utmost to prevent him from ever straying from his God-given mandate and to help him keep his message focused on the biblical center, and she succeeded in doing so. J. Lee Grady stated in *Charisma & Christian Life* magazine:

What is amazing to me is that Graham's message hasn't changed during the 60 years he's been in ministry. Even after he began sending his crusades on television and writing daily columns for newspapers, he didn't modify the conditions of repentance. Though he became friends with American Presidents, he didn't compromise his morals, sell out to special interests, or cash in on his celebrity. And when an increasingly secular culture began selling the idea that all religions are the same, Graham held his Bible in the air—maintaining that salvation comes only through Jesus.[38]

All of their lives, Ruth and Billy transmitted unabridged biblical truths with great sensitivity. At a time when many Christian leaders tell people what they want to hear and therefore lose their prophetic power, it is necessary to proclaim God's Word fully and not to adapt the message to ruling opinions and culture. Otherwise, it loses its cutting edge and healing effect. Today, tolerance is the prevailing motto—truths, not the Truth. Any kind of absolute is frowned upon. Jesus's claim to be the way, the truth, and the life and his statement that no one can come to God except through him (see John 14:6) simply do not fit into our age of relativism and individualism. It will be a great challenge for us Christians to continue to stand firm on the biblical truth of salvation solely through Jesus (see Acts 4:12). This is the only way people can recognize the truth and be saved.

The Grahams emphasized that our fellow human beings depend on us to clearly point them to the only One who can help: Jesus Christ, the Son of God and Redeemer. "Again, if the trumpet does not sound a clear call, who will get ready for battle?" (1 Cor. 14:8). Warning voices will also be necessary in the future because God especially speaks to us in the midst of problems and difficulties. Ruth once used an analogy: "Trouble is just the old sheepdog nudging us back to the shepherd."[39]

It's not easy to avoid creating a causal connection between a crisis and the possible sins of the people affected by the crisis and yet still point out that God uses crises and catastrophes to call us to repent. Jesus referred to a familiar event to illustrate this truth: "Or those eighteen who died when the tower in Siloam fell on them—do you think they were more guilty than all the others living in Jerusalem? I tell you, no! But unless you repent, you too will all perish" (Luke 13:4–5).

How should a Christian reply to the horrifying terrorist attacks of September 11, 2001, when many were asking how a God of love could allow such a terrible thing to happen? Billy Graham was asked to give a message at the National Day of Prayer and Remembrance on September 14 in the National Cathedral of Washington DC. Here are some excerpts from his speech:

> We come together today to affirm our conviction that God cares for us, whatever our ethnic, religious or political background may be. The Bible says that He is "the God of all comfort, who comforts us in all our troubles" (2 Cor. 1:3–4 NIV). No matter how hard we try, words simply cannot express the horror, the shock and the revulsion we all feel over what took place in this nation on September 11. It will go down in our history as a day to remember.
>
> We especially come together to confess our need of God. We have always needed God from the very beginning of this nation, but now we need Him especially.
>
> The Bible's words are our hope: "God is our refuge and strength, an ever present help in trouble. Therefore we will not fear, though the earth give way and the mountains fall into the heart of the sea" (Ps. 46:1–2 NIV). . . .
>
> Yes, there is hope. There's hope for the present because I believe the stage has already been set for a new spirit in our nation. One of the things we desperately need is a spiritual renewal in this country. We need a spiritual revival in America. And God has told us in His Word, time after time, that we need to repent of our sins and we're to turn to Him and He will bless us in a new way. There is also hope for the future because of God's promises. As a Christian, I have hope, not just for this life, but for heaven and the life to come. And many of those people who died this past week are in heaven right now, and they wouldn't want to come back. It's so glorious and so wonderful. And that's the hope for all of us who put our faith in God. I pray that you will have this hope in your heart."[40]

Graham concluded his message with the following words:

> Here in this majestic National Cathedral we see all around us symbols of the Cross. For the Christian, the Cross tells us that God understands our sin and our suffering, for He took them upon Himself in the person of Jesus Christ. From the Cross, God declares, I love you. I know the heartaches and the sorrows and the pains that you feel. But

I love you. The story does not end with the Cross, for Easter points us beyond the tragedy of the Cross to the empty tomb. It tells us that there is hope for eternal life, for Christ has conquered evil and death and hell. Yes, there is hope. . . . My prayer today is that we will feel the loving arms of God wrapped around us and will know in our hearts that He will never forsake us as we trust in Him.[41]

The daughter of Billy Graham, Anne Graham Lotz, was asked at the same time to give her views on 9/11 on *The Early Show* on CBS, which was broadcast nationwide. Anne is the author of several books and is an excellent Bible expositor. According to her father, Anne is the best Bible teacher in the family. She has the exceptional capacity of skillfully connecting a current topic to the core of Christian faith, without being harsh. Her response to 9/11 is a fine example of remaining true to biblical truth while maintaining sincere empathy.

Anne began by expressing her deep sympathy for the families involved. She asked the God of peace and compassion to come into the lives of those families in a special way to take care of their needs. When the CBS interviewer asked, "If God is good, how could God let this happen?" Anne replied:

God is also angry when He sees something like this. And I would say also that for several years now, Americans, in a sense, have shaken their fists at God and said, "God, we want You out of the schools, we want You out of our government, we

Anne Graham Lotz, daughter of Ruth and Billy Graham, is a gifted Bible teacher and prophetic voice in the United States and beyond. One of Anne's favorite statements is, "God does not call you to be successful—only faithful."

want You out of our business, we want You out of our marketplace."
And God, who is a gentleman, has quietly backed out of our national
and political life, our public life, removing His hand of blessing and
protection. And we need to turn to God, first of all, and say, "God,
we're sorry that we have treated You this way, and we invite You now
to come into our national life. We put our trust in You. We have our
'In God We Trust' on our coins. We need to practice it."[42]

Anne was then asked for some closing words to the nation in view
of the event, which, according to the interviewer, had changed the
world forever. Anne tried to put herself in those people's situation.
At the same time, she stayed true to her evangelistic calling and kept
her focus on inviting people to a closer relationship with God:

> I pray that God will use this event to change us forever in a positive
> way and to strengthen our faith in Him. I thought of all those people
> who have died in this tragedy, and it doesn't matter right now what
> political affiliation they had or what denomination they belonged to
> or what religion or what the color of their skin was or if they were
> old or young or their stock portfolio. What matters is their relation-
> ship with God. I would like to see Americans focus on the primary
> things—things that are more important than entertainment and plea-
> sure and making more money.[43]

Jeffrey Donaldson, a member of the British Parliament from Bel-
fast, Northern Ireland, received a copy of the transcript. Like many
others, he believed Anne Graham Lotz's words applied not only to
the United States but also to the United Kingdom and even beyond.
After confirmation from other leaders, Anne was asked to give the
main address at the National Parliamentary Prayer Breakfast at
Westminster Hall in London, the first person from outside of Great
Britain to do so.

Anne certainly has inherited from her father the gift of being
a prophetic voice to the world. Ten years after 9/11, in September
2011, *Christianity Today* asked her about the changes since 9/11.

First, she shared about her personal changes as she experienced a personal revival and a renewed vibrancy in her relationship with God leading to an increased fervency in prayer, a clearer insight into God's Word, and a sharpened focus in ministry. Then she pointed out that God's wake-up call is stronger than ever, and it concerns us all:

> But the alarm did not fade away. Instead, I have heard it reverberating throughout the past 10 years: from Hurricane Katrina to the record-breaking floods, forest fires, tornadoes, droughts, and snow storms; to

There was a period when Billy Graham was on the cover of more renowned magazines than any other public figure.

> the collapse of our major financial institutions; to the economic recession. . . . The alarm keeps resounding because so many people have not heeded, or even heard, the warning.

And what is the warning? Simply this: It is five minutes to midnight on the clock of human history. Judgment is at the door. Jesus is coming! It's time to wake up and get right with God! Are you listening?[44]

6

Integrity—Responsible Living

Billy Graham has for all these years been so self-disciplined and has so disciplined those around him that he has never been seriously touched by anything that would suggest contradiction to the message he proclaims.[1]

Fr. Richard Neuhaus, founder of the Institute on Religion and Public Life

Let us not be concerned about the praise—or even the undeserved criticism—of men, but let us be supremely concerned about the will and the approval of God.[2]

Billy Graham

Graham's no milquetoast. He has strong convictions and views about many things. But at the same time, he demonstrates his genuine desire to serve under the authority of those who will keep him from stumbling financially.[3]

Bill Pollard, member of the BGEA board

Shortly after World War II, Billy Graham traveled to Europe for the first time for Youth for Christ, first to Great Britain and then on to the European continent. He traveled with co-evangelist Charles "Chuck" Templeton and received a very special welcome in Paris. At that time, France's capital was a popular vacation spot for members of the Allied Forces, and countless prostitutes on the streets were on the lookout for customers. Young men in civilian clothes like Billy and Chuck were rare and therefore a particularly sought-after prey.

Chuck recounts how he and Billy were approached at least fifty times in broad daylight by such women as they walked from the Arc de Triomphe down the Champs-Elysees to their hotel. The women were often very aggressive—they stood in Billy's or Chuck's way or grabbed their arms. Chuck tells how one very brash woman freely presented her charms by opening her coat, revealing that she was wearing nothing at all underneath. Billy moved on, grim-faced, and said, "Chuck, we've got to get out of here."[4] They hurried on and literally shoved the many women aside. Arriving at the hotel, they were speechless over the conditions in Paris.

In the evening, they went to a typical French restaurant. While they were still looking at the menu, two young women sat down at their table and ordered drinks. They spoke no English, so it was a very difficult conversation. After Chuck and Billy paid, the women didn't want to let them leave and latched themselves firmly arm in arm with the men. The one with Billy was particularly adamant and simply would not let go of him. Billy glanced at Chuck with a desperate look on his face. What should he do? They had learned to act like gentlemen. Chuck pulled a face. "Guess we'll have to walk them home."[5] Luckily for him, his companion appeared to live across the street from the restaurant. Once they were inside, Chuck quickly realized that he had been led into a trap because he heard a man's voice. He fled into the bathroom and hid his wallet there. He came out after a short while and saw the young woman return to the restaurant where they had met. After retrieving his wallet, he went back to the hotel.

When he got there, Billy was not to be found. After waiting for two hours, Chuck started to get worried. He considered calling the police, but what would he tell them? He had no idea where Billy could be. Finally, Billy came rushing in shortly after midnight, sweating profusely. He frantically shared what had happened. Billy had wanted to at least escort the young lady to her front door. But she hailed a taxi, and they kept driving and driving until they reached the outskirts of Paris. Billy wanted to pay and pulled out his wallet. The taxi driver took not just the money but the entire wallet. Billy explained what happened next:

> The girl had me by the arm and she led me toward this place where she lived. It was a dump. We got inside and she closed the door. I was trying to think of something I could say or do to let her know I was leaving. She went over to the bed, and without a word, unbuttoned her dress, tossed it aside and fell back on the bed. And Chuck, she was stark naked! I turned, opened the door and got out of there. In the street, I started to run. I don't know how far I ran; it could have been a mile or two. When finally I stopped, I looked around. I had no idea where I was. I was going to hail a cab, and then realized I didn't have any money. I asked some people the way to the downtown area but they just looked at me or rattled on in French. So I started to walk. I walked and walked and walked until I saw the Eiffel Tower in the distance. Then I knew where I was.[6]

Many years later, Charles Templeton kidded Billy Graham about this experience: "Hello, Bill. How's the Midnight Runner?"[7]

This little-known story from the early days of Graham's evangelistic ministry is a good illustration of his attempts to withstand temptation and to lead a life of moral integrity. Like Joseph in Egypt, his commitment to moral purity was sorely tested in Paris. Just as when Potiphar's wife tried to seduce Joseph, no one would have known if Billy had given in to this sexual temptation. But Billy, like Joseph, lived his life before the eyes of God. Integrity can only grow on this kind of foundation.

The Paris experience certainly impacted Graham deeply and caused him to be extremely careful in his dealings with women throughout his life. As he was in the habit of reading a chapter of Solomon's Proverbs every morning, he was always reminded of his special welcome on the European continent and his naivete when dealing with a certain type of woman at that time:

> For the lips of the adulterous woman drip honey,
>   and her speech is smoother than oil;
> but in the end she is bitter as gall,
>   sharp as a double-edged sword.
> Her feet go down to death;
>   her steps lead straight to the grave.
> She gives no thought to the way of life;
>   her paths wander aimlessly, but she does not know it.
> Now then, my sons, listen to me;
>   do not turn aside from what I say.
> Keep to a path far from her,
>   do not go near the door of her house,
> lest you lose your honor to others
>   and your dignity to one who is cruel. (Prov. 5:3–9)

Every temptation we overcome with God's help gives us strength to withstand the next temptation. It is a great help, however, if we can count on the support of a trusted friend.

Graham's and Templeton's experiences in Paris are not unusual for people who travel a lot. In some countries, certain females can be so pushy that you have to avoid them completely. I once visited a place that was so unfriendly and dreary that I was very thankful for the sociable people I thought were other guests in my hotel, until I noticed they just wanted me as a customer.

One does not have to go to Paris to make moral compromises. The question is, Am I prepared to lead a life that lies openly before God? Am I ready to ask God immediately and sincerely for forgiveness when I fail in some way and let myself be filled with the Holy Spirit again? Do I want to live a life that honors God, not a life without sin but a transparent life before God, not trying to hide anything? Do I ask my brothers and sisters in Christ for help? Am I prepared to be accountable to them?

Integrity means to live responsibly in all areas of one's life, both private and public. Life and ministry must be in harmony with each other to form a unified whole. Words and deeds must agree. Promises must be kept. Integrity also means to put all our cards on the table and not be governed by selfish motives.

Billy Graham's foremost concern was to lead a life of integrity in all areas—a life beyond reproach, one that honored God and didn't tarnish God's name. When he was asked what he wished to be remembered for, he said, "Integrity! That's what I've worked for all my life."[8] Integrity is truly a quality you have to work on all your life with all your strength. As Henry Blackaby and his son Richard write in their book *Spiritual Leadership*, "Integrity is not automatic. It is a character trait that leaders consciously cultivate in their lives."[9]

In a personal encounter, Henry Blackaby, author of the bestseller *Experiencing God*, remarked that in his opinion Graham's great effectiveness came from the fact that he always took care to lead a life that lived up to God's standards. He never stumbled, like so many other evangelists, because early on he set down some specific security measures and clear rules for himself and his core team. Blackaby says:

> He also developed a team of friends to monitor whether he was keeping this standard. While some might consider this safeguard excessive, it kept him from scandal for over half a century of high-profile ministry.[10]

It was important for Graham and his team to counteract the bad reputation most evangelists had. Every mass evangelist was automatically compared with the fictional character Elmer Gantry.

In 1927, Sinclair Lewis, who later received the Nobel Prize for literature, wrote the satirical novel *Elmer Gantry*. The novel describes a young narcissistic man who seeks fame, fortune, and power and pursues his goal by becoming an evangelist. He feigns faith and enjoys the success he experiences with his trusting followers. Yet his actions are completely contradictory to his preaching. Elmer Gantry doesn't love God; he loves the money, alcohol, and women's admiration, which are part of his life as an evangelist. He is a first-rate charlatan.

The novel was widely acclaimed and hotly debated. Many felt Sinclair Lewis had exaggerated but wasn't that far off the mark. There were unfortunately quite a number of Christian evangelists who resembled Elmer Gantry in many ways. From then on, Elmer Gantry was a synonym for Christian hypocrisy and charlatanry. The novel was dramatized in 1928 and premiered on Broadway in New York. It was later made into a film, with Burt Lancaster starring as Elmer Gantry, a role for which he received an Oscar. The topic of the Christian charlatan is still so up-to-date that an opera of the same name premiered in November 2007 in Nashville.

In the early years of his growing popularity, Billy Graham could not avoid being compared to Elmer Gantry again and again. Almost always, the comparison was to Graham's advantage. Even his greatest critics testified that he sincerely believed in what he preached. Nor were there ever any scandals about money or women. The only things critics repeatedly reproached him for were—in their opinion—the way he proclaimed the gospel and that his message was too simple. There was a reason why no concrete reproaches for any Elmer Gantry–style behavior could be made: the Modesto Manifesto, a code of conduct to which Graham and his team ascribed. Before we look at the code in detail, I would like to describe Graham's personal experience with an evangelist that would fundamentally change his life.

Even as a young man, Graham had a dislike for theatrical preachers whose personal integrity was questionable at best. This was the

162

reason why, at the age of sixteen, he didn't want to attend Mordecai Ham's mission in his hometown of Charlotte, despite his parents' repeated encouragement. Billy's father was a member of a group of Christian businessmen that had been formed after a previous revival meeting conducted by Billy Sunday in Charlotte. These same businessmen had invited Mordecai Ham to come. During a meeting in the Graham home, the leader of the group prayed that through this revival meeting God would awaken someone to the faith who would carry the gospel to the far corners of the earth.

Ham's mission, which went on for several weeks, was hotly debated all over Charlotte. One thing impressed the young Graham: Mordecai Ham was bold and relentlessly called things by their name. Graham admired fighters. He loved the comics about Tarzan, who had fled to the jungle because he had had enough of the hypocritical life as the son of an English lord. If one believed the critics, Ham appeared to have something of a Tarzan-like air about him, swinging from tree to tree, as it were, regardless of any obstacles along the way. Graham became curious and decided to see for himself by attending the tent meetings. He recounts how he experienced Ham:

His words, and his way with words, grabbed my mind, gripped my heart. What startled me was that the same preacher who warned us so dramatically about the horrible fate of the lost in the everlasting lake of fire and brimstone also had a tremendous sense of humor and could tell stories almost as good as my father's. I became deeply convicted about my sinfulness and rebellion. And confused. How could this evangelist be talking to me, of all people? I had been baptized as a baby, had learned the Shorter Catechism word perfect, and had been confirmed in the Associate Reformed Presbyterian Church with the full approval of the pastor and elders. . . . So why would the evangelist always be pointing his bony finger at me? . . . I was so sure he had singled me out one night that I actually ducked behind the wide-brimmed hat of the lady sitting in front of me. Yet, as uncomfortable as I was getting to be, I simply could not stay away.[11]

Graham became increasingly aware that, despite his good Christian upbringing, he did not have a personal relationship with Jesus Christ. He continues his story:

> And then it happened, some time around my sixteenth birthday. On that night, Dr. Ham finished preaching and gave the invitation to accept Christ. After all his tirades against sin, he gave us a gentle reminder: "But God commendeth his love toward us, in that, while we were yet sinners, Christ died for us" (Rom. 5:8, KJV). His song leader, Mr. Ramsey, led us all in "Just As I Am"—four verses. Then we started another song: "Almost Persuaded, Now to Believe." On the last verse of that second song, I responded. I walked down to the front, feeling as if I had lead weights attached to my feet, and stood in the space before the platform. That same night, perhaps three or four hundred other people were there at the front making spiritual commitments. . . . As I stood in front of the platform, a tailor named J. D. Prevatt, who was a friend of our family with a deep love for souls, stepped up beside me, weeping. Putting his arms around me, he urged me to make my decision. At the time, in his heavy European accent, he explained God's plan for my salvation in a simple way. . . . He prayed for me and guided me to pray. . . . No bells went off inside me. No signs flashed across the tabernacle ceiling. . . . I simply felt at peace. Quiet, not delirious. Happy and peaceful. My father came to the front and put his arm around my shoulders, telling me how thankful he was. Later, back home, when we went to the kitchen, my mother put her arm around me and said, "Billy Frank, I'm so glad you took the stand you did tonight." That was all. I went upstairs to my room. . . . Then I went over to my bed and for the first time in my life got down on my knees without being told to do so. I really wanted to talk to God. "Lord, I don't know what happened to me tonight," I prayed. "You know. And I thank You for the privilege I've had tonight."[12]

Despite his positive experiences with this fiery, old-time preacher, Graham was acutely aware of the dangers of serving as an evangelistic preacher. How easy it was for an evangelist to prompt even justified criticism!

He wanted to take all possible measures to prevent himself and his team from being blamed for actions and attributes associated with the fictional character Elmer Gantry. Graham was very afraid that they could taint God's name through their mistakes or acts of carelessness. Particularly in the period just after World War II, all sorts of preachers with questionable motives emerged in the public arena. Sociologist William Martin writes of this time:

> For evangelists it was like being a stockbroker in a runaway bull market. As in other fields, however, the boom attracted some whose motives were less than sanctified, who fell prey to the temptations described in Scripture as "the lust of the flesh, and the lust of the eyes, and the pride of life" (1 John 2:16), but better known by the street names: sex, money, and power. Despite good intentions and behavior, Graham and his associates occasionally found themselves the objects of suspicion and condescension from ministers and laypeople alike. They learned that Elmer Gantry . . . was a deeply entrenched cultural stereotype.[13]

In 1948, at a mission in Modesto, California, Billy Graham felt it necessary to gather his core team together for a frank discussion. He asked Grady Wilson, Cliff Barrows, and Bev Shea to withdraw for an hour and to write down why the so-called mass evangelism and the traveling evangelists had such a bad public reputation and what could be done about it. How could they set themselves apart in a positive way from the fictional character of Elmer Gantry? What were evangelists often justly blamed for, and what practical measures could they as a team take so as not to make the same mistakes?

When they exchanged their notes afterward, they had amazingly all written down the same points. They all agreed that in the future they would do their utmost not to fall into those same traps and thereby dishonor God. Together they decided to make an agreement before God and each other that would help them live with integrity in four critical areas and not give cause for criticism. This agreement later became known as the Modesto Manifesto. Graham said, "We made a series of resolutions or commitments among ourselves that would guide us in our future evangelistic work."[14]

Graham described this private agreement as "a shared commitment to do all we could to uphold the Bible's standard of absolute integrity and purity for evangelists. . . . In reality, it did not mark a radical departure for us; we had always held these principles. It did, however, settle in our hearts and minds, once and for all, the determination that integrity would be the hallmark of both our lives and our ministry."[15]

The agreement made by the Graham core team in November 1948 in Modesto contained four points that would enable them to minister for decades beyond reproach.

The core team members who formulated the guidelines for the ministry in 1948, which later became known as the Modesto Manifesto, are pictured here together with pianist Tedd Smith. From left to right: Tedd Smith, Cliff Barrows, Billy Graham, George Beverly Shea, Grady Wilson. The photograph was taken in 1975 at the Mississippi Mission.

1. We will never criticize, condemn, or speak negatively about other pastors, churches, or Christian workers.
2. We will be accountable, particularly in handling finances, with integrity according to the highest business standards.
3. We will tell the truth and be thoroughly honest, especially in reporting statistics.
4. We will be exemplary in morals—clear, clean, and careful to avoid the very appearance of any impropriety.

Graham and his team were convinced that it was not a Christian's task to criticize brothers and sisters of faith. They had experienced too often how particular evangelists had spoken ill of other pastors. This had led to divisions between them and the pastors, and the body of Christ at large, which had hindered a fruitful and blessed cooperation between the evangelists and the local churches. It also had made follow-up with new believers difficult. Graham said:

> We were convinced, however, that this was not only counterproductive but also wrong from the Bible's standpoint. We were determined to cooperate with all who would cooperate with us in the public proclamation of the Gospel, and to avoid an antichurch or anticlergy attitude.[16]

Cliff Barrows later stressed that specifically this decision not to judge other Christians had been necessary and essential. The decision certainly contributed greatly to the positive opinion most people had about Graham and the Billy Graham Evangelistic Association.

Jesus Christ underlines in the Sermon on the Mount that we are judged as harshly as we judge others:

> Do not judge, or you too will be judged. For in the same way you judge others, you will be judged, and with the measure you use, it will be measured to you. Why do you look at the speck of sawdust in your brother's eye and pay no attention to the plank in your own

eye? How can you say to your brother, 'Let me take the speck out of your eye,' when all the time there is a plank in your own eye? You hypocrite, first take the plank out of your own eye, and then you will see clearly to remove the speck from your brother's eye. (Matt. 7:1–5)

This is a basic spiritual principle. If we judge mercilessly, we also will be judged without mercy; if we show lovingkindness and grace to others, we will receive the same. Don't we all depend on the mercy of God and our fellow men?

Billy and Ruth Graham were loving and gracious to others throughout their lives and transmitted that type of behavior to their team members. They believed that judgment was God's business, not theirs. They not only refused to criticize others but also refused to defend themselves when they were criticized. They wished to stick to their divine mission at all costs and not let themselves get sidetracked.

Graham once remarked that he would never have been able to do any evangelistic work if he had defended himself against all the criticism he received. He expected God to defend him. Graham's diary entries reveal that this attitude did not come about without great inner battles. But it is obvious that the refusal to defend themselves when criticized significantly contributed to Graham's effective ministry. In this way, he avoided wasting time and energy, which he instead was able to use for his world-spanning ministry.

One time, however, Graham felt moved to reply publicly to an article that had appeared in *Time* magazine.[17]

Billy Graham, President John F. Kennedy, and Senator Frank Carlson bow their heads in prayer at the annual Presidential Prayer Breakfast in 1961.

It was during the presidential candidacy of John F. Kennedy, who was Catholic. Judging from a previous article in the same magazine, one might have concluded that Graham felt Protestants had every reason to oppose Kennedy's candidacy because he was Catholic. In a letter to the editor, which he wrote during the 1960 mission in Basel, Switzerland, Graham set the record straight that his statements had a different meaning in the original context. The letter ended with the following words: "I might also add that I deplore all forms of religious bigotry!"[18] For once, Graham felt it necessary to take a stand because it was primarily not about his own reputation and honor but concerned American Christians as a whole.

Graham's and his team's decision not to criticize or defend themselves when being criticized is exemplary. Yet at the same time, Graham always took constructive criticism seriously, mainly when it was about the long-term results of his ministry. Together with Ruth and their closest associates, he placed such criticism before God and asked him for advice on what they could learn from it. When there was something to be learned, they accepted such free advice thankfully and took the necessary steps to increase the effectiveness of the ministry. They tried to evaluate everything from the perspective of God's Word but left judging others to God, because in their opinion he alone is qualified and authorized to do so.

Time and again, preachers and organizations fell into disgrace because they hadn't been careful with their finances, or because they gave the impression that they carried out the ministry to get rich at their admirers' expense. When Graham began his ministry as an evangelist for Youth for Christ, it was customary during an evangelistic rally to ask at least once for a so-called love offering, the entirety of which was then given to the evangelist. Many traveling preachers used all their motivational skills to make the love offering as large as possible. This deplorable custom aroused suspicion and mistrust so that increasingly even people who had been supportive at the start began questioning the evangelists' sincerity.

With their professional and transparent accounting, Graham and his team made it a point not to let even a hint of suspicion arise that they were benefiting personally from the people attending the missions. That's why they decided to refrain from taking up love offerings and instead drew a fixed salary. It was agreed that Graham would have a salary equivalent to that of a pastor of a larger church.

It later became apparent how important this decision was. Finances were a regular topic of public debate at the larger evangelistic events. Thanks to the media, people always knew exactly what Graham's salary was. In 1950, two years after Graham and his team formulated the Modesto Manifesto, the Billy Graham Evangelistic Association (BGEA) was founded, mainly to manage the donations and be accountable for ministry finances. Local committees were responsible for the finances for the missions. They set up a budget, raised the necessary funds, and provided an accurate accounting for all financial transactions. People who later examined the BGEA's bookkeeping records attested that "the integrity and soundness of its finances have been unquestioned."[19]

To this day, the BGEA provides its annual report to anyone who asks for it. As far as disclosure of accounts is concerned, the BGEA goes farther than many other nonprofit organizations. Dan Busby, vice president of the Council for Financial Accountability, praises the BGEA: "They continue . . . to be a leader in accountability. Their track record across the decades speaks for itself."[20]

The *Tribune Business News* writes:

> After Graham's more than 50 years in ministry, Christians and non-Christians know the North Carolina preacher's reputation for financial integrity. . . . Unlike some evangelists, Graham has satisfied critics by going beyond standards required by the Internal Revenue Service, keeping an active and independent board of directors, not taking money from local mission appearances and publishing an annual audit of ministry finances.[21]

Thanks to the decision in Modesto, Graham and the BGEA passed the accountability test.

Over the years, innumerable people followed the invitation of Billy Graham to leave their seats and walk to the front as a sign of their commitment to follow Christ, as here in a mission in Chicago in 1962.

Many preachers' tendency to exaggerate the number of people attending their events gave them a bad reputation and discredited evangelistic preaching in general. The evangelists were tempted to seek greater recognition and financial support by reporting the largest possible numbers. In Modesto, the core team decided that no one should be able to accuse them of inflating the numbers. Therefore, they decided to always use official numbers confirmed by an independent source. If several figures were on the table, they would use the lowest figure, unless there was an obvious mistake. It often happened that journalists then made it clear that the BGEA's official numbers by no means reflected the full impact of Billy Graham's ministry.

The low-key stance toward attendance statistics contributed significantly to the extraordinarily good media reports Graham received as an evangelist, mainly in the United States and also increasingly in Europe. Because he was honest about numbers, he was also considered to be honest in other areas. The opposite also holds true. If someone doesn't tell the truth in one area, you can't believe that person in other matters.

Building trust takes time, but it can be lost overnight. That's why the core team around Graham felt it was important not to risk that long-earned trust. The result would have been doubt about his message and perhaps even about God himself, whose representatives they considered themselves to be. It was important to be particularly careful about numbers, be it funds or the results of one's work. Graham and his team considered it vital never to give cause for criticism in this regard.

☙

During his time at a Bible college in Florida, Graham had a shattering experience. The school's director, whom Graham viewed as a spiritual role model, "was discovered to be at least in the planning stages of adultery."[22] Some students had observed this and made the story public. As a result, several teachers and a quarter of the students left the school. At first, Graham could hardly believe what had happened. With time, he became conscious that God wanted to use this incident to teach him not to build upon even the most seemingly upright people but only on God and his promises. It became very clear to him that even the most devout people are susceptible to all kinds of sins. Graham said, "It was a big learning experience for me in many ways, and it taught me to be very careful myself."[23]

The incident in Florida was vividly present in Graham's thoughts when the core team in Modesto decided to set up guidelines to help them lead morally irreproachable lives. Shortly beforehand, they had heard of several other evangelists who had been accused of immoral conduct. That's why they wanted to be especially careful in this matter. So they agreed never to be in a room alone with someone of the opposite sex, except for their own family. That way, they would not be tempted or even give room for false interpretations. They were convinced that even the slightest rumor resulting from such carelessness could significantly damage the ministry. Graham said, "From that day on, I did not travel, meet, or eat alone with a woman other than my wife. We determined that the apostle Paul's mandate to the young pastor Timothy would be ours as well: 'Flee . . . youthful lusts' (2 Tim. 2:22)." Decades later, when Hillary Clinton asked him for a personal conversation, Graham agreed under the condition that they meet in the middle of a restaurant where everyone could see them. Two incidents prove that such strict security measures are justified.

A newspaper once tried to stir up controversy by reporting that Graham had been seen in the company of a pretty blonde in the streets of New York. Billy was actually out shopping with his daughter Bunny. It was at least a compliment to his daughter. Another time, a well-known singer, who had recently divorced her equally well-known husband, publically expressed her special affection for Graham, which gave the impression that she had a particularly close relationship with the evangelist. The woman was probably only well-intentioned and wanted to contribute to Graham's campaigns with her excellent singing. However, it was a big story for the media. When confronted with the woman's statement, Graham replied that he knew nothing about the lady's joining the team but that she was welcome to attend the mission as a member of the audience.

Graham and his team did their utmost to prevent compromising situations from even occurring. T. W. Wilson, Graham's associate, always checked the hotel rooms before Graham entered for women lying in wait. This caution was justified, as there are always those seeking to discredit Christians in the public eye. A spiritual leader

from a country that forbids Christian missions once told me that for a long time he was not able to leave the house without his wife because he was in danger of women flinging themselves at him and embracing him. As others

Billy Graham with Ruth and their son Ned in front of their home in Montreat. In their personal life as well as in Billy's public ministry, they upheld marriage and family values.

173

had already experienced, the resulting photo would then be passed on to government officials, who were just waiting for a reason to discredit Christian leaders.

Graham and his team were not only praised but also criticized for their strict moral code. Voices were raised that rebuked them for "demonizing women." Such people were convinced that one could not live out such an attitude without being unloving. How did a close friend of Ruth and Billy Graham experience this? Millie Dienert reports:

> I have always appreciated, from a moral point of view, how clean the men have been in their attitude toward the secretaries. The doors are always left open. There is a high regard for the lack of any kind of privacy where a boss and his secretary are involved. At times, I thought they were going a little too far, that it wasn't necessary, but I'm glad they did it, especially today. They have kept everything above reproach. When you are working on a long-term basis with the same person, constantly in hotels, where the wife is not there and the secretary is, that is a highly explosive situation. You have to take precautions. I have always respected the way they have handled that. It has been beautifully done.[24]

In his last television interview, Wilson provided a wonderful testimonial about his friend:

> Billy has always been an encouragement not only to me but to all team mates. That's why I think people throughout the team have stayed with him so long. We believe in him. We know that he is a man of integrity. I've often thought to myself and I've said it to a few people: Don't think Billy could fool me, even if he tried. I'd see him in the hotels. I'd see him wherever he goes, because he doesn't go anywhere by himself. And this is in itself a very good thing because if somebody misappropriates the truth and accuses him of something, there is always somebody with him. . . . If he is not for real, I don't know anybody who is.[25]

Bev Shea, who usually accompanied Graham's sermons with a hymn and celebrated his one hundredth birthday in extraordinarily good health in 2009, emphasized that throughout the years of their ministry together, he had never been disappointed by Graham. Cliff Barrows also affirmed that he had never regretted his lifelong decision to stand beside Graham. Because the core team members trusted

This photo shows three friends who worshiped their Lord together for more than sixty years. What a testimony! From left to right: Cliff Barrows, Billy Graham, Bev Shea.

one another implicitly, they could also share openly if something wasn't working properly or if they noticed something negative in one of the other team members. This openness was an important factor in recognizing mistakes early on and being able to make the necessary corrections.

Billy's greatest help in living a morally blameless life and not straying off the path was his wife.

Ruth and Billy often held different opinions. From his upbringing, Billy was not accustomed to outspoken women expressing their opinions as openly as Ruth and their three daughters did. But he couldn't change Ruth. And Ruth not only didn't want to change but also was convinced that her Bill needed a strong partner, someone who would hold a mirror up to him in all honesty. After a few verbal clashes, Ruth began to pray for wisdom and the ability to recognize the right opportunities when to tell Billy her opinion. Billy suddenly paid more attention to her views, and Ruth felt understood and taken seriously by her husband.

If there were occasional heated arguments between the two, they were never carried out in front of the children. When asked about the secret of a good marriage, they replied that marriage should be a "union of two good forgivers." Despite all "happy incompatibility," as she once described their different characters, Ruth felt that the time at home with her husband was the most satisfying. Being on the road with Billy, on the other hand, was like being alongside a general in a war, and vacations with him were like being with a race car driver who took the least number of pit stops, and, if he took any at all, they had to be as brief as possible. Ruth said, "I cannot keep up with the man." She therefore had to find her own pace and rhythm for life and work.

When he was older, Billy spent more time at home than during the years of his worldwide ministry. They had much more time together and greatly enjoyed this time. Visitors always noticed how Billy's eyes lit up when Ruth entered the room or when he spoke of her. Both said that in advanced age a new romance had been kindled between them. Billy often knelt beside Ruth's wheelchair and tenderly kissed her forehead. After Ruth's passing in June 2007, Billy missed her very much. He has a large photograph of her in his bedroom.

One of the reasons why Ruth and Billy's relationship lasted all those years and even improved is Billy's decision in Modesto to lead a morally impeccable life. Equally important, however, was that they both continually worked on their relationship. Because Ruth was a friend and partner who loved him and sincerely supported him, and because they both consciously cultivated romance especially as they grew older, Billy never needed to seek other women to meet an unfulfilled need. The same holds true for Ruth. As their marriage progressed, she experienced a husband who became increasingly tactful and sensitive to her needs and who made sure she was taken care of.

Integrity is also important in the relationship between parachurch movements and local churches. Many mistakes have been made in this area that were detrimental both to the movements as well as to the churches. In light of this fact, Graham and his team felt it was very important to establish guidelines early on about this subject as well.

According to Graham and his core team, the churches were the key players in an evangelistic mission. They saw themselves as servants of the local Christians. They were convinced that it was thanks to the longtime, faithful service of the local churches that the evangelistic outreaches bore any fruit.

Surveys confirm that most churches didn't regret having participated in a Graham crusade. As a traveling evangelist, Graham received surprisingly little criticism about his relationship to the local churches. When in an interview with *Look* magazine in February 1956 he was criticized that his evangelistic ministry was not sufficiently linked to the local Christian churches, he replied that he was quite surprised at the remark, as he had received hundreds of letters from pastors after missions who thanked him for his efforts and told him what positive fruit they had seen in the churches as a result. He told that he never went to a city without being invited by the local churches first. His ministry was completely integrated in local church life. Graham then remarked:

> We believe that the church, with all its faults, is Christ's organization upon earth. We shall continue to do everything we can to promote and build His church on earth. All of the people who make commitments to Christ in our meetings are sent back to the church for teaching, instruction, fellowship and worship.[26]

Despite his decision in Modesto not to judge other Christians, Graham could not avoid forming his own opinions and testing whether others held up biblical standards or not. How did Graham form a judgment on an issue based on God's Word without being judgmental at the same time?

At the Amsterdam '86 press conference, I asked Graham what he felt the reason was for the European churches' spiritual weakness and what we European Christians could do to change the situation.

Graham obviously wanted to avoid criticizing the European churches too harshly, yet his reply was nevertheless clear:

> I think that in Europe—I don't wish to criticize the Church in Europe—all right, to put it in a different way: in America and Europe it's particularly necessary to promote biblical preaching and teaching more strongly. We have lost the conviction that the Bible is God's authoritative Word.

He then at least implied that Europe, and especially Germany, might have played a role in this: "Somewhere in the later part of the last century and in the early part of this century we began to have a new theology, in the beginning coming perhaps out of Germany, and things began to change."

It was important for Graham and his team that they—unlike many other evangelists—were not perceived as being judgmental but as humble Christians who were supporting and enhancing the local churches with their specific gift of holding missions and training people in personal evangelism. Graham held the local churches in high regard and saw his evangelistic ministry more as a support to the work of the local churches. He was convinced that local Christians made the greatest contribution to any evangelistic mission.

His personal assistant, T. W. Wilson, himself a gifted evangelist, described the crucial role of the local churches for the long-term effects of a mission in the anthology *Evangelism in the Twenty-First Century*:

> If crusade evangelism is to be a factor in winning people to Christ in the next century, local churches must be involved. Not only does Billy Graham require the invitation from local churches before he comes to a city, he also must be sure that the churches will be actively and integrally involved in the crusade. The local church is not a tool for the use of the crusade; the crusade is an evangelistic tool for the local church. Too much of crusade evangelism comes into cities today, records decisions, and leaves without making disciples. I know

of no other institution on earth that is better equipped to make disciples than the local church. Crusade evangelism should serve the church rather than the church serve the crusade.[27]

Wilson continued, "Crusade evangelism is a 'before,' 'during,' and 'after' process."[28] Local churches were crucial in the organization of major missions. The lasting fruit of the event was directly in proportion to the churches' intensity of prayers by local believers that preceded

A young counselor prays with an even younger inquirer during an evangelistic crusade in the 1960s.

it. Everything depended on the preparations and the follow-up efforts.

During the preparations, the importance of personal evangelism needed to be transmitted to the helpers and staff:

Without prayerful one-on-one witnessing, a Billy Graham crusade would have little impact on the area in which the crusade is held. . . . Perhaps the most effective participation of the local church is for every Christian to realize that he or she has been called to be an evangelist. Certainly some believers have the gift of the evangelist. That does not mean, however, that other Christians are not to evangelize! One may have the gift of giving or serving, but all Christians should give and serve. Effective personal evangelism is ultimately the key to effective crusade evangelism. One of the greatest benefits crusade evangelism can give a group of local churches is the clear communication of the command for all Christians to witness and evangelize. Every evangelist, Sunday school teacher, pastor, elder, deacon, and church member should be a personal "soul-winner."[29]

179

Wilson then underlined the key role of counseling those who had become believers so that they could become true followers of Christ:

> The Great Commission (Matt. 28:19–20) mandates that followers of Christ make disciples, rather than simply elicit decisions. Those who are involved in crusade evangelism must also be obedient to the command of our Savior. It is therefore imperative that persons involved in crusade evangelism seek to make disciples. With the Graham organization, we have seen our ministry, sometimes through trial and error, place more and more emphasis on discipleship in the local church. We believe that no less effort should be placed in follow-up and preservation than in planning or in reaping. Too much of crusade evangelism has emphasized immediate decisions, only to ignore the future discipleship of the converts in local churches. . . . If crusade evangelism continues to be a factor for the kingdom in the twenty-first century, it will be the result of disciple-making rather than decision-making.[30]

Because there was a growing consciousness that the before and after of a mission were the most important parts, Wilson drew his positive conclusion:

> The future of crusade evangelism is bright. And the reason for such optimism is that, in many crusade ministries, the crusade is emphasizing the making of disciples through the local church. And the making of disciples is precipitated by prayer and hard work.[31]

Graham and his team were never interested in quick success. They were always concerned with lasting spiritual fruit, which was only possible as the result of an upright life and ministry. They would never have been able to carry out their long-lasting, blessed ministry for over sixty years if they had not ensured integrity in all areas, both in their personal lives and in their work. If we want to earn the confidence of Christians and non-Christians alike and keep it over the years, we must dedicate ourselves to the pursuit of integrity in all areas with all our strength. Clear guidelines such as the Modesto Manifesto can be a great help. We thus do not have to make new decisions each time but can simply fall back on the general agreement when faced with a difficult situation.

Graham's conscious decisions to live responsibly and to be accountable for all areas of his life contributed significantly to the fact that he never fell from grace. Jay Dennis summarizes this in *Leading with Billy Graham*:

> Without accountability, vulnerability is heightened. Those in ministry who have morally fallen have most often lacked a system of accountability. Billy Graham has stayed above reproach because he first determined to place himself under accountability to God. But he has also placed himself under accountability to a board of directors and the man who traveled with him all over the world, T. W. Wilson.[32]

In order to live responsibly, we need to have a group of friends around us who will go with us through thick and thin, who will share our joys and our sorrows, who will know us well enough not to be easily fooled by outward masks or pretence.

Wilson's younger brother Grady, who served on the Graham team as an associate evangelist, was this kind of friend. Grady Wilson was a passionate man, full of eagerness for God's cause, but also always up to pranks. No one could describe things as vividly as he could, yet Grady had both feet firmly on the ground. He preferred a relaxed atmosphere, but at the same time, he didn't want things to get sanctimonious and problems to be idealized. His down-to-earth, realistic manner helped Graham not to get carried away. I would therefore like to close this chapter on integrity with an excerpt from the preface of his book *Count It All Joy*, where Wilson writes the following about his boss and friend Graham:

> Because of our close-knit relationship, whatever hurts Billy hurts the other team members and me. Really, that should be true of any interaction among Christians. When Billy is struck, we bleed, too.

Billy has been attacked for various reasons—some out of jealousy, some sincere. Years ago he was misunderstood because he believed in integrating the races, misunderstood because he had compassion for the poor, and now misunderstood for his emphasis on peace during the heated nuclear buildup. Sometimes he has been attacked for his connections with presidents, royalty, and other world luminaries. But Billy Graham is also the friend of the "average citizen" or "common folks," as most of us label ourselves. He is totally devoid of arrogance and pride.

Public figures have all kinds of legends and myths repeated about them. Billy has had more than his quota, and it's according to who's looking at him. People have tried to lump the BGEA with unsavory stereotypes of evangelism, especially in our early days. They accused us of being flamboyant and flashy, hypocritical Elmer-Gantry types. That ilk of criticism has now virtually disappeared. Almost nonexistent today is criticism of the BGEA's financial dealings. The Association has striven for absolute, bedrock honesty. . . . Billy has asked me repeatedly, "Grady, why has God set us apart for this ministry?" He has aired this wonder to crowds in our crusades on every continent. He has emphasized and reemphasized, "If God removed his hand from me, I couldn't continue. I'd fall flat on my face." And any truly called servant of the Master would concur with that sentiment.

All of us are awfully human. That's the basic premise of the gospel we preach. All of us are sinners. We have faults, "warts and all." Because Billy is painfully aware of his humanity, he stays close to his Lord in spiritual discipline and prayer. . . .

Readers and reviewers will be asking, "How can you be objective doing a book, in part about your relationship with your closest friend?" . . . Believe me, I've tried to find fault from time to time. Most any friends critique each other. I've looked, maybe not with a jaundiced eye, but I've looked. I've known thousands of godly men and women during my ministry. They read like a Christian "hall of fame," but Billy Graham is the best, most-devoted Christian I've ever known!

Many years ago one of our Team members left us. He tried desperately to make Billy look bad, but it simply didn't work. Yes, Billy has foibles. Don't we all? He has flaws, and he's the first to admit them. I've seen Billy perturbed or upset just a few times, and then only after an outright lie or innuendo about the ministry had appeared in the media. And I've never heard a foul word escape from his lips. It has been often noted that "a person who doesn't have any temper isn't worth much." Billy has a temper, but he keeps it in check.

As this book is released I have known Billy Graham almost a half-century. And our ministry for Christ becomes more wonderful every day. It reminds me of that chorus we used to sing in our early evangelistic meetings: "Every day with Jesus is sweeter than the day before; Every day with Jesus, I love Him more and more."[33]

7

Faith—Living by God's Word

Faith was the very heartbeat of life at Little Piney Cove. We began and ended each day as a family on our knees in prayer. . . . But while my father, due to his demanding schedule, lived out faith for us largely from afar—and he loved us very dearly—Mother lived out her faith in front of us day in and day out.[1]

Ruth "Bunny" Graham, daughter

If the Lord has given Billy the gift of evangelism, Ruth has been given the gift of faith. Like a quiet stream, it runs deliberately and very deep. It is the center of her life. It touches the lives of all those who cross her path.[2]

Julie Nixon Eisenhower, daughter of President Richard Nixon

Lord, many things in this Book I do not understand. But Thou hast said, "The just shall live by faith." All I have received from Thee, I have taken by faith. Here and now, by faith, I accept the Bible as Thy word. I take it all. I take it without reservations. Where there are

184

things I cannot understand, I will reserve judgment until I receive more light. If this pleases Thee, give me authority as I proclaim Thy word.[3]

Billy Graham

One of Billy Graham's important traits is his childlike faith. He is convinced that nothing is impossible for God. Even as a young person while working for Youth for Christ, he traveled to Europe shortly after the end of World War II to help initiate a spiritual revival.

Mel Larson describes the pioneering spirit of Youth for Christ at that time:

The fire grows and grows. The fire cannot go out, for the Fireman is God. Human hands cannot quench it, nor human weaknesses dim its glow. Burn on, Youth for Christ, burn on! May millions of embers from your blaze shine through eternity. And, oh, may your flames spread rapidly . . . and burst into a world-sweeping revival![4]

As the first full-time staff member, Graham was right up at the front. Many years later, after having become a world-famous evangelist, he returned to Europe in 1954 to hold evangelistic missions. His only weapon was the Bible.

In many photos, by no means only as a preacher in the stadiums, he is shown holding the Bible. His faith in the God of the Bible was unlimited. One of the main messages of the Bible has always been that God answers prayer spoken in faith. Graham said, "You pray and you tell God that you believe. You trust in Him. You present Him with a problem, and if you have real faith, by heavens, you get an answer. No question about it."[5]

Once he lacked twenty-five thousand dollars to launch a regular radio broadcast. He did not know whether this idea had come from the Lord, but if it had, he was totally sure they would receive the money for it by midnight. Together with his associates, he fell on his knees and prayed for twenty-five thousand dollars. Cliff Barrows said, "He just asked God to help him out." But as they counted the donations in the evening, there was only twenty-four thousand dollars. Graham remarked that they had prayed for twenty-five thousand dollars and God could have given it if he wanted them to start the radio mission. A few minutes later, Grady Wilson checked the hotel mail. In Graham's box were three letters. One contained a five-hundred-dollar check; in each of the other two letters were checks for two hundred and fifty dollars. Their God was good for "small things" like giving twenty-five thousand dollars for a project. But to Graham, he was even powerful enough to change the city of New York:

> It is my personal conviction that sometimes we depend too much on favorable conditions, contrived methods and human know-how—and trust too seldom in him who has said, "With men this is impossible: but with God all things are possible." Our going to New York is certainly not a demonstration of faith in our own methods, for we know that New York would be impervious to a merely human effort. We are daring to go because we know "with God all things are possible."

Ruth's faith was equally strong. She experienced in her childhood how God protected her and her family in the middle of a civil war in China, surrounded by bandits. She spent her middle-school years far from her parents in the city of Pyongyang, in present-day North Korea, which was then occupied by the Japanese, and found her sustenance in God. Both in China and in Korea, she heard from many missionaries about how they experienced God's power in extreme situations. Ruth observed how her parents, thanks to their strong faith, remained calm in the midst of cannon fire because they knew they were being protected by God. Their trust in God stood the tests of everyday life.

In China and Korea, Ruth learned to bring all her problems directly before God and to trust that he would deal with them. One biblical promise she especially leaned on was Proverbs 14:26: "Whoever fears the LORD has a secure fortress, and for their children it will be a refuge."

In an article in *Christianity Today*, she urged readers to fear only God: "We live in a world wracked by fears and anxieties. . . . But God assures his church in Revelation, 'Fear none of those things which are to happen.' We are to fear only the Lord. It is the fear of God that puts all other fears in proper perspective."[6]

Billy Graham and Cliff Barrows producing the weekly radio broadcast *The Hour of Decision*. Beginning in 1950, through his messages on ABC, Billy Graham could regularly be heard all over the United States.

Ruth knew no fear because she experienced early on that she could count on the God of the Bible completely. He had everything under his control and was reliable. Her thinking was based on God's promises, and she also spoke and lived that way. Ruth loved to emphasize the absolute trustworthiness of God and his biblical promises, thus building up the faith of those who came in contact with her. She boldly proclaimed how God faithfully kept his promises in her life. That knowledge was the most precious gift in her life. She encouraged people who had little faith to ground their belief in God's promises and to pray boldly. She explained that there was nothing to lose in doing so except perhaps one's problems: "God loves to be reminded of His promises. He never rebukes us for asking too much."[7]

Yet Ruth also repeatedly pointed out that we should always remain conscious of the fact that God alone knows what is best for us in any specific situation. "Often I have made a request of God with earnest pleadings even backed up with Scripture, only to have him say 'No,' because he had something better in store."[8]

The hardest times were the most blessed for her, because in those times she experienced Jesus Christ most distinctly as the One who is completely trustworthy. When people confided their troubles in her, which was often the case, she would immediately say, "Let's bring it to the Lord."

In a 1993 interview, she stated, "There are things today that I am still concerned and praying about that haven't reached a final solution, but I know because in the past He has never failed, that He is not going to start failing now," only to add, "My prayer is that I won't fail Him."[9]

In another interview she had given a few years earlier to the German magazine *Lydia*, she emphasized the importance of maintaining an attitude of faith and seeking God's face in difficult situations:

I think it's important to look to God who helps us bear our burdens. When situations of stress arise, I try to remain in the strength that prayer provides. If we follow the Apostle Paul's advice to pray "without ceasing," we have to do that during our daily routine. Anyway, I do a lot of spontaneous praying; whenever someone comes to mind, or when I have promised to pray for someone, I immediately stop and pray.[10]

Ruth's faith grew over the years. She knew her God and that he would take care of her, her children, and the many people whom she cared for because he knew what was best for all of them. Ruth believed in the power of prayer because she believed in an almighty God who was able and also willing to make the best of every situation.

I cannot overstate the power of prayer. When I get upset about something, our son Ned is fond of saying, "Mother, God is not a little bit sovereign." We know we live in the devil's world, but God is still omnipotent. He is sovereign.[11]

Ruth wanted a prayer room installed in the attic of the chapel at the Billy Graham Training Center, the Cove, located near Asheville, and she designed it herself. She placed a globe in the middle and put two of her favorite verses on the wall:

Now to him who is able to do immeasurably more than all we ask or imagine, according to his power that is at work within us, to him be glory in the church and in Christ Jesus throughout all generations, for ever and ever! Amen. (Eph. 3:20–21)

Do not be anxious about anything, but in every situation, by prayer and petition, with thanksgiving, present your requests to God. And the peace of God, which transcends all understanding, will guard your hearts and your minds in Christ Jesus. (Phil. 4:6–7)

Ruth's faith was truly unshakable. Her God was in control, wasn't he?

Ruth's faith was severely put to test with her sons, Franklin and Ned. For many years, her two sons distanced themselves from the faith of their parents and fell into bad company. As a loving and caring mother, Ruth grieved over the situation and was continually in danger of forgetting that God cared more about the well-being of her sons that she ever could.

During those difficult years, the faith and persistence of Monica, the mother of the late church father Augustine, was a great motivation to her. Monica persisted in praying for her son, who had gone astray, and expected God to lovingly intervene in his time. Just like Ruth, Monica had fought for and wept about her son. In this difficult time, the bishop of Carthage gave Monica a word of blessing that she clung to from then on and that brought peace to her bewildered heart: "Go thy way and God bless thee, for it is not possible that the son of these tears should perish." Ruth also took these words as God's encouragement for her situation and kept on believing. And just like Monica's son Augustine, Ruth's restless sons finally found their calling in God and as a result have become missionaries of God's love and forgiveness.

Augustine's much-quoted statement of confession proved true in the lives of Franklin and Ned Graham: "Lord, you have made us for yourself, and our hearts are restless till they rest in Thee." Ruth also experienced the truth of another of Augustine's sayings: "Faith is to believe what you do not see; the reward of this faith is to see what you believe."

In general, one never heard Ruth complain, despite the fact that she suffered from increasing pain in her advanced age. She knew that God's love was sustaining her. All heavy burdens had to pass before God first and therefore had a deeper significance:

Perhaps our secret of "grace under pressure" lies in accepting that pressure is from the Lord. At least permitted by Him. . . . For the child of God, are there any secondary causes? Satan must get God's permission before he can touch Job's possessions, much less Job. So when Job lost everything, he worshipped and said: "The Lord gave and the Lord (not Satan) hath taken away; blessed be the name of the Lord." It is this knowledge that enables us to accept the unacceptable. We can take whatever comes as from His hand, submit to it, and learn of Him all He seeks to teach us through those circumstances.[12]

This knowledge of God allowed Ruth to make the best of all the difficulties and challenges she encountered, and through them all, her trust in God grew deeper and deeper.

Ruth was very impressed with Dan and Mel Piatt, staff members who had lost their son, daughter-in-law, and young grandchild in a car accident. The three were buried on the Piatts' twenty-eighth wedding anniversary, but they could not attend because they were in Australia preparing for a mission. When Ruth met Dan several months later, she did not encounter a bitter person but instead a man of faith who believed in God's goodness and faithfulness even in the face of tragedies. Dan recounts:

Ruth, this is the greatest, the most tremendous experience we have ever gone through. Not once has our faith in the goodness and the wisdom of God faltered. The hardest time is at night when we can't sleep. Then the Bible verses that we have memorized over the years come to sustain and strengthen us. All we ask of God is that He teaches us everything that He wants us to learn from this experience.[13]

Ruth herself went through many ordeals, but she never doubted God's faithfulness. While Billy shouted "God loves you" to his audiences, Ruth spoke mainly about God's faithfulness. Her God had never failed her, even in the darkest hours. He had shown his faithfulness in countless situations.

Ruth was not born with this kind of faith. Vonette Bright's book *The Greatest Lesson I've Ever Learned* contains an account of an experience Ruth had that opened up a whole new dimension of believing prayer. Ruth described how she discovered the transforming power that lies in an attitude of thankfulness in all circumstances.

Once again, Ruth was worried about one of her sons, who was turning away from God, and she couldn't sleep.

> When it is dark and the imagination runs wild, there are fears that only a mother can understand. Suddenly the Lord said to me, "Quit studying the problems and start studying the promises." Now God has never spoken to me audibly, but there is no mistaking when He speaks. So I turned on the light, got out my Bible, and the first verse that came to me was Philippians 4:6: "Be careful for nothing; but in every thing by prayer and supplication with thanksgiving let your requests be made known unto God." And verse 7: "And the peace of God, which passeth all understanding, shall keep your heart and minds through Christ Jesus." Suddenly I realized that the missing ingredient in my prayers had been "with thanksgiving." So I put down my Bible and spent time worshiping Him for who He is and what He is. . . . I began to thank God for giving me this one I loved so dearly in the first place. I even thanked Him for the difficult spots which taught me so much. And you know what happened? It was as if someone suddenly turned on the lights in my mind and heart, and the little fears and worries which, like mice and cockroaches, had been nibbling away in the darkness, suddenly scuttled for cover. That was when I learned that worship and worry cannot live in the same heart: they are mutually exclusive.[14]

To remind herself that one should always begin by praising God, she put up a sign in her house: "Praise, pray, and peg away!"

Ruth was by nature a very thoughtful and reasoning person. Contrary to Billy, she always reflected on everything. She was capable of drawing all kinds of spiritual lessons from everyday life. As a sensitive person, she also had a melancholic side. However, it was important to her to look at everything from God's perspective and not to be blocked by the problems. After all, the Bible teaches that God uses all things to work for the good of those who love him (see Rom. 8:28). That gives us every reason to focus on the positive. Her guiding principle was, "Make the most of all that comes and the least of all that goes." Her daughter Ruth experienced it in this way:

> Mother constantly urged us to go through life accentuating the positive and de-emphasizing the negative. . . . Mother lived out what she taught us: She counted the hours that shone, and she worked hard to model an upbeat, positive outlook for my siblings and me.[15]

All of the children confirm that their mother was a great encouragement to them because of her profound attitude of faith. When she entered a room, it was as if an inexplicable peace came in with her. God's peace was a result of her unshakable trust in his goodness and care for us, like a good shepherd's care for his sheep. In his sovereignty, her God reigned over all circumstances. So she also wanted to live above circumstances by aligning her thinking, speaking, and acting with God's eternal truth in the Bible, which is unshakable. She even described it as utter foolishness to be ruled by circumstances when considering God's sovereignty:

> Either He is sovereign or He is not. If He is not sovereign, He is not God. Therefore when we become so preoccupied with and dismayed by circumstances and certain people that we doubt God's ability to handle them in His own way, and in His own time, then we, too, are fools.[16]

$\sim$

The first one to benefit from this kind of faith was Billy himself. He often succumbed to self-doubt and needed encouragement. He once wrote in his diary that Ruth always had a suitable Bible verse on hand to match the situation. She was to him like an ever-flowing source of support and inspiration. In a letter he wrote to her in 1963, shortly before their twentieth wedding anniversary, Billy put his thankfulness to Ruth into words:

> Your love and patience with me in my ups and downs . . . have meant more to me than you will ever know. Your counsel, advice, encouragement and prayer have been my mainstay—and at times I have almost clung to you in my weakness, in hours of obsession, problems and difficulties. . . . One reason that in spite of my own lack of spirituality, discipline and consecration I have found favor of the Lord is because of *you*.[17]

Billy's faith was more of a "faith despite." His children state that the possible problems and difficulties always came to his mind first. Because of that, they teasingly called him "Puddleglum." Puddleglum is a character from the fantasy series the Chronicles of Narnia by C. S. Lewis. As a born pessimist, Puddleglum always has a dark view of things. Just like Puddleglum, Graham tended to see the glass half empty instead of half full. But when Graham was active on the spiritual front, he was a completely different person. He was full of faith, and nothing could deter him from the goal of proclaiming the gospel under all circumstances. When it rained cats and dogs during a mission, he would walk up to the microphone, request everyone to be quiet, and then pray to God to make a dry hole above them, and the rain would stop, as it happened, for example, at a mission in 1997.[18]

Graham was firmly convinced that when God gives us a mandate, he also gives us everything we need to carry it out. He was never afraid for his own security, despite the fact that he frequently received death threats. He reassured those who were concerned about his security that they needn't worry; God would protect him until he had carried out his commission.

Graham's associates and close friends experienced him as a man of faith, as someone who always looked upward or, as his daughter

Gigi once put it, someone "who always looked at things with eternity's values in mind." With this attitude, he encouraged the people around him and strengthened their faith. Grady Wilson put it this way:

> Every associate of his, every close friend would have to admit that Billy is an inspiration to others. Being with him is an uplifting experience. Some people low-rate you. They pull you down. You become downtrodden and depressed in their presence. Billy is exactly the opposite. The radiance of Christ exudes from his person and being with him is a blessing.[19]

Billy Graham playing golf with American comedian and actor Bob Hope. There was a witty saying that Bob had the hope and Billy had the faith.

Wilson then added that, admittedly, just like with other people, there were times when it was better to leave Billy alone. Especially at home, Billy was not always a hero of faith. He was glad he could lean on Ruth's positive disposition and practical life skills. Next to his belief in God, Ruth was the second big constant in his life. She was his anchor and gave him the stability he needed.

Ruth didn't just *possess* a strong faith; her faith characterized her life, or as her granddaughter Berdjette Tchividjian Barker once aptly said, "I don't think her life reflects her faith; I think her life is her faith."[20] The long-standing pastor of her home church, Calvin Thielman, once described her as "religion in shoe leather," emphasizing that her faith was reflected in practical, everyday life.

Ruth's faith showed itself in small but vital acts of love. She felt sent by God to people who needed help. Her faith was a hands-on faith but also a joyous, liberating one, free from all legalistic musts and ought to's. She loved to speak to God directly and pour out her heart to him. Her faith was fresh, joyful, free, and sometimes even impertinent. I am convinced that God loved Ruth's bold communication with him because it was a sign of her affection and deep trust in her divine Friend.

Her poems, which are more like written prayers, show that she spoke to God like a trusted friend. She did not see God as her assistant to fulfill her plans. Instead, her daily goal was to be God's best possible assistant to help him carry out his plan. She often began the day praying, "Lord, what can I do to help you today?"

Ruth trusted God's love and care for her so much that she could also express her displeasure with him when he took his time in answering her prayers, just as the psalmists did in the Old Testament. One of her shortest poems—or prayers—went like this:

> We are told to wait on You.
> But, Lord, there is no time.
> My heart implores upon its knees,
> "Hurry! . . . please."[21]

There were, however, also times when things went too fast for her; then she sounded more like this:

> A little more time, Lord,
> just a little more time.
> There's so much to do,
> so much undone.
> If it's all right with You, Lord,
> please stop the sun.
> There's forever before me
> forever with You;
> but a little more time
> for the so much to do.[22]

Some of the prayers written as poems show how Ruth, after wrestling with God, found peace in her confidence that God did things his way, not according to her ideas:

> As I was praying day and night,
> night and day,
> quietly God was saying
> "Let there be light"—My way.[23]

As a very active person with a tendency to regard every need as a personal duty, Ruth did not find it easy to sit still and leave matters to God. Her God was the specialist for impossible things. She made it a point to "take care of the possible and trust God for the impossible." Commenting on a woman whose trust in God's possibilities was too small, Ruth said, "This poor woman was trying to do God's work for him."

Billy once phoned Ruth from a mission in Tokyo when Ruth was staying with her daughter Gigi in Paris and entertaining guests. Billy was very agitated because Franklin, who at the time was not even twenty years old, had just gotten engaged to a young European woman in Nome, Alaska. Franklin had not yet made a clear decision for Christ. The same was true of his fiancée. Billy was desperate. He was in Tokyo, Ruth was in Paris, and their son was way up in Alaska. Gigi then heard how her mother encouraged her dad: "Well, honey, don't worry, the Lord will work it all out. He is still in control. I love you, too. Good-bye."[24]

None of the guests noticed any sign of disturbance in Ruth following the news of Franklin's unexpected engagement. She was completely focused on her guests and made no mention of any kind of problem she might be facing. Several weeks later, the same guests thanked her for the lovely evening. What had impressed them the most was the peace Ruth had radiated. What a wonderful testimony of a person who rested in God's love and peace and therefore was able to pass these qualities on to others.

In 2007, at the opening of the Billy Graham Library in Charlotte, North Carolina, Billy was honored for his steadfast faith throughout the years. He passed the praise on to his wife: "I miss terribly my wife, Ruth. I want to honor her and tell you how much I love her and tell you what a wonderful woman she has been. More than me, she deserves to be here today."

After Ruth's death, Billy described the role she played in his life and ministry as follows:

> My wife, Ruth, was the most incredible woman I have ever known. Whenever I was asked to name the finest Christian I ever met, I always replied, "My wife, Ruth." She was a spiritual giant, whose unparalleled knowledge of the Bible and commitment to prayer were a challenge and inspiration to everyone who knew her. . . . A night never went by, when we were together, without us holding hands and praying before we went to sleep. Ruth also was a wonderful mother. Her task wasn't easy since I was away from home so much, but she handled our children with both great love and wise discipline. She felt it was her calling, and without her willingness to bear the major responsibility for raising our children, my work simply would not have been possible. She spent hours every week teaching them the Bible and praying with each of them. She also was full of fun, always ready to play a joke on someone. Our children all knew that life was never dull with Ruth around! . . . Whenever she heard of anyone in our community who had a need, she always was there to help with food or flowers or in other ways. Many people went to her for advice and counsel or just to pray with her. . . . She was a gentle, smiling and kind person whose primary goal was to live for Christ and reflect His love. In her last days she talked repeatedly of heaven, and although I will miss her more than I can possibly say, I rejoice that some day soon we will be reunited in the presence of the Lord she loved and served so faithfully.

Like Ruth's, Billy's faith was founded on the reliability of God's Word. What the Bible said was what God said, and when God said something, it was 100 percent trustworthy. Billy believed that the

197

main problem was not primarily a lack of faith among unbelievers but a lack of faith among believers in the validity and authority of the Bible.

During his time as an evangelist for Youth for Christ, Graham often had disputes with his partner evangelist, Chuck Templeton. Templeton became increasingly convinced that the Bible was not totally reliable. After completing an evangelistic campaign in Europe with Youth for Christ in 1946, Templeton decided to enroll at the theologically liberal Princeton Theological Seminary. He prompted Graham to do the same so that he too would have a "proper" theological education. Graham had only received a bachelor's degree from Wheaton College, and that was in anthropology, not theology.

Because Graham had always held Templeton's opinion in high regard and felt himself intellectually inferior to him, he took the suggestion seriously and honestly questioned himself. Should he catch up on his theological studies at a renowned university? In addition, he had been persuaded to take on the part-time presidency of Northwestern in Minneapolis by the previous officeholder shortly before his death. Wouldn't it be fitting for a college president to have a proper theological education from a distinguished university? Graham inquired at several universities regarding what was required to earn a higher academic degree. But their answers were less than encouraging, as he would have to learn the ancient biblical languages. That alone would have taken him forever, according to Graham.

The question of whether the Bible was reliable and authoritative for life and faith began to trouble him more than the question of a proper education. Questions such as "Is the Bible truly inspired by the Holy Spirit?" and "Is it the Word of God, or does it, as many theologians stated, simply contain God's Word?" weighed on him. He wondered whether his friend Templeton was right in saying that you couldn't sacrifice common sense only to uphold the faith. Graham felt torn between the faith of his childhood, which had sustained him in the most diverse situations, and his friend's enlightened opinions.

He describes his feelings in his autobiography:

My respect and affection for Chuck were so great that whatever troubled him troubled me also. I had similar questions arising from my own broadened reading habits. I wanted to keep abreast of theological thinking at midcentury, but brilliant writers such as Karl Barth and Reinhold Niebuhr really made me struggle with concepts that had been ingrained in me since childhood. They were the pioneers in what came to be called neo-orthodoxy. While they rejected old liberalism, the new meanings they put into some of the old theological terms confused me terribly. I never doubted the Gospel itself, or the deity of Christ on which I depended, but other major issues were called into question. The particular intellectual problem I was wrestling with, for the first time since my conversion as a teenager, was the inspiration and authority of the Scriptures. Seeming contradictions and problems with interpretation defied intellectual solutions, or so I thought. Could the Bible be trusted completely?[25]

Graham increasingly asked himself if he as an evangelist even had a message to pass on if the Bible could not be counted on any longer. But what about the apostle Paul's words to his disciple Timothy that God's Word—at that time the Old Testament—was inspired by the Holy Spirit? Paul had received the very best possible education of his time. Hadn't the apostle Peter said that God's prophets didn't transmit their own words but had spoken as moved by the Holy Spirit (see 2 Pet. 1:21)? Even Jesus said that heaven and earth would pass away but his words would not (Matt. 24:35). Didn't Jesus himself often quote the Old Testament as God's completely reliable Word? At least according to the inside testimony, the Bible was inspired by God and could therefore be trusted as authoritative.

While Graham was dealing with such questions, he was invited to speak at the Forest Home Resort Conference Center in San Bernardino, California, along with renowned theologians such as Wheaton College's director Louis Evans and the "revival expert" J. Edwin Orr. The latter had just received his doctorate from the University of Oxford. Graham did not feel sufficiently qualified to speak with such greats: "I felt intimidated by so many bright and gifted leaders, which just added to my generally low spirit at the time. I would just as soon have been at Forest Lawn, the famous Los Angeles cemetery, as at Forest Home."[26]

In those days, he confided in Henrietta Mears, director of the conference center and director of Christian education at the Hollywood Presbyterian Church. This woman combined a deep knowledge of the Bible with a contagious faith. Bill Bright once said that—with the exception of his family—no one had had a greater influence on his life and ministry than Henrietta Mears. She taught her "boys," as she called the young men, God's Word and together with them founded the Fellowship of the Burning Hearts to prepare them for world-changing ministry. Mears was characterized by an unshakable faith that was based on the reliability of the Bible. This belief of hers was contagious when she explained God's Word to others. Her God was the God of the Bible. This God knew no limits. She was convinced that our vision of the world should resemble his vision of the world: "Youth does not think into the future far enough, therefore we must encourage them to dream of great tomorrows." She described the scope of her ministry with the following words, "There is no magic in small plans. When I consider my ministry, I think of the world. Anything less than that would not be worthy of Christ, nor of His will for my life."[27]

God used this woman to equip several Christian leaders who would eventually have a worldwide ministry, among them Billy Graham. Graham had confidence in "Teacher," as she was commonly called: "Rarely had I witnessed such Christian love and compassion as she had for those students. She had faith in the integrity of the Scriptures, and an understanding of Bible truth as well as modern scholarship. I was desperate for every insight she could give me."[28]

At the same time, his friend Templeton grilled him, "Billy, you're fifty years out of date. People no longer accept the Bible as being inspired the way you do. Your faith is too simple." Whom should he now trust, Henrietta Mears or his friend Chuck Templeton?

Graham went for a walk, deeply unsettled. On impulse, he spontaneously knelt down. A tree stump served as a pedestal for his Bible, as had often been the case when he had attended the Florida Bible college. He opened the Bible at random. But instead of preaching, he began to pray. He poured out his heart to God. There were many things in the Bible he could not understand or that in his opinion did not seem logical. He had many unanswered questions. Several passages in the Bible seemed to contradict others, and some things seemed to be contrary to modern science. He had not found any satisfactory answers to Templeton's intelligent questions.

Graham later recounted how in this situation the Holy Spirit moved him to speak a prayer that would mark his later ministry more than he could have ever imagined at the time. He took his Bible and tearfully prayed, "Father, I am going to accept this as Thy Word—by faith! I'm going to allow faith to go beyond my intellectual questions and doubts, and I will believe this to be Your inspired Word."[29]

Afterward, Graham felt God's presence and power to an extraordinary degree. His questions had not been answered, but he knew that the spiritual battle in his heart and mind had been won. He firmly decided to proclaim the Bible as God's inspired Word and final authority for life and faith and to leave the results up to God. "The Bible says" became his trademark from then on.

As a result of Graham's evangelistic ministry, which lasted more than sixty years, the Holy Spirit convicted people of all ages, walks of life, and ethnic backgrounds of their need for Jesus Christ as Redeemer and Master. Countless people were able to accept forgiveness for their sins through their belief in Christ's sacrificial death on the cross and receive a new, Spirit-wrought life marked by God's fatherly love.

It is interesting to look at the events from Chuck Templeton's point of view. In a biographical retrospective of his life, published in 1996, titled *Farewell to God: My Reasons for Rejecting the Christian Faith*, Templeton writes that despite their basic differences of opinion, he still appreciated his longtime friend Billy for his honesty: "There is no feigning in Billy Graham: he believes what he believes with an invincible innocence. He is the only mass-evangelist I would trust. And I miss him."[30]

At the same time, he felt sorry for Graham: "Forty years after our working together he is saying the same things, using the same phrases, following the same pattern."[31] In view of current scientific findings, Templeton was convinced that it was no longer possible to believe in creation as described in the biblical account.

To Templeton, that kind of blind faith was equivalent to intellectual suicide, as he put it. For Graham, such an attitude was an appropriate expression of his belief in the God of the Bible and the trustworthiness of his Word. Graham felt that faith in God was not anti-intellectual but the consequence of the awareness that we will never comprehend God fully with our five senses. He believed that only by acting in faith do we learn if there is a God and whether the Bible is reliable. According to him, faith is the trademark of a Christian: "The Christian life is dependent upon faith. We stand on faith; we live by faith. Without faith there is nothing."[32]

Graham believed with all his heart that the power is in God's Word alone: "The Bible is the only thing that can combat the devil. Quote the Scriptures and the devil will run. . . . Use the Scriptures like a sword and you'll drive temptation away."[33]

Graham depended on God's Word both in his personal life and in his evangelistic ministry. Again and again, when he spoke to Christian leaders, he emphasized that there is no special promise of blessing on mere human words but on God's Word alone. According to the description of the armor of God in Ephesians, the Bible is the sword the Holy Spirit uses to lead people to the true healer of souls, Jesus Christ.

Graham's faith in the power of God's Word was without limit. From it came his strong conviction that evangelism was about proclaiming God's Word unabridged so that it could unleash its full power:

It is my conviction that if the preaching of the Gospel is to be authoritative, if it is to produce conviction of sin, if it is to challenge men and women to walk in newness of life, if it is to be attended by the Spirit's power, then the Bible with its discerning, piercing, burning message must become the basis of our preaching.[34]

Graham felt that only faith that rests on the unshakable foundation of the Bible is true faith, and only preaching that proclaims the Word of God is true preaching.

In his opening address at the 1974 Congress of World Evangelization in Lausanne, he emphasized that our faith must be able to rest on the absolute reliability of the Bible as the authoritative Word of the living God. If our ministry is to bear fruit, our lives and our message must be founded on God's eternally valid Word. Graham said to the assembled church leaders from around the world:

Absence of a fear of God, loss of moral absolutes, sin accepted and glorified, breakdown in the home, disregard for authority, lawlessness, anxiety, hatred, and despair—these are signs of a culture in decay. In the West we are witnessing societies in trauma, shaken by war, scandals, and inflation, surfeited and bored with materialism, turned off by lifeless religion, turning to the occult.[35]

He then described the missionary movements of the past, stating that evangelism had always been the "lifeblood of the Church":

The missionary and evangelistic movements of the last century were based on the authority of the Scriptures as the Word of God. Because these people were biblically oriented, they had a definite view of salvation. They took seriously what the Bible says about man's lostness and his need for redemption. They also believed strongly in "conversion," convinced that by the regenerating power of the Holy Spirit, men could be forgiven and changed. They believed that evangelism is not an option but an imperative. They were convinced that the primary mission of the Church is to declare the Good News of Jesus Christ. . . . The reason that the great missionary movements of the nineteenth century were able to make a lasting impact on the world was that internally they were strong. They knew what they believed and they were determined to proclaim it to the world.[36]

Graham concluded:

Billy Graham had absolute trust in the authority and transforming power of God's Word.

If there is one thing that the history of the Church should teach us, it is the importance of a theology of evangelism derived from the Scriptures. . . . Biblically, evangelism can mean nothing else than proclaiming Jesus Christ by presence, by word, and by trusting the Holy Spirit to use the Scriptures to persuade men to become his disciples and responsible members of the Church.[37]

Graham finished his message by challenging the Christian leaders to unconditionally trust the Bible as God's inspired, eternally valid Word and to proclaim the Bible's message of Christ's saving grace with new earnestness and deep conviction. With an illustration, he once again underscored the incomparable meaning of faith in Jesus Christ and the importance of telling all humankind that Jesus paid for their sins with his life and offers forgiveness and eternal life:

Many years ago, a man in England on his way to the gallows was being warned by the Anglican chaplain of the "wrath to come" unless he repented. He turned to the chaplain and said, "If I believed the way you believe, I would crawl across England on broken glass to warn people." My fellow evangelists and missionaries, if men are lost, as Jesus clearly taught they are, then we have no greater priority than to lift up the saving Christ to them.[38]

8

Global Responsibility—
Committed Living

The motto I have taken for my life is "to evangelize the world in this generation, that every person might hear the Gospel once before the others have heard it twice."[1]

Billy Graham

I believe God called my mother just as clearly as he called my daddy—called her to world evangelism but she expressed the call by staying home, taking care of us, freeing my daddy up to answer that same call but by leaving home being the evangelist that the world's known. I believe God called them together, the both of them. They expressed their obedience to that call in two different ways and made a complete package.[2]

Anne Graham Lotz, daughter

Jesus taught that we are to take regeneration in one hand and a cup of cold water in the other. Christians, above all others, should be concerned with social problems and social injustices. Down through the centuries the Church has contributed more than any other single agency in lifting social standards to new heights. The Christian must take his place in society with moral courage to stand up for that which is right, just and honorable.[3]

Billy Graham

Melvin Cheatham, clinical professor of neurosurgery, wrote about his experiences while in the company of Billy Graham and his son Franklin Graham. He first wrote in *Make a Difference* about how he and his wife went to East Berlin with Billy Graham, where they met over a thousand church leaders on the steps of the historical Reichstag (House of Parliament) prior to an evangelistic outreach. When they arrived at the Lutheran Gethsemane Church, the church leaders stood up and applauded Graham, who then said:

> Thank you. I feel deeply honored and blessed to be here with you this evening at Gethsemane Church in East Berlin. I know many of you have suffered greatly during the past many years, in part because of your trust in God. Standing here before you now is a very humbling experience for me. I want to invite you to join me in this moment by bowing your head in prayer. I feel humbled before Almighty God, and right now I want to recommit my life to Him. If you will join with me in recommitting your life to Him, as we open our hearts in prayer, I invite you to hold up your hand, in order that each one of us might be counted for Him.[4]

Hands went up all over the church, and people who had suffered for years under the communist regime followed Graham's example and rededicated their lives to Jesus Christ and the fulfillment of the Great Commission. The following afternoon, Graham preached the gospel of Jesus Christ on the Reichstag steps, the same place where Adolf Hitler had once proclaimed the launch of his Third Reich, which he said would last one thousand years. What Hitler announced didn't last more than a dozen years; what Graham proclaimed—namely, Jesus's sacrificial death on the cross—has changed the entire world until the present day.

Under the title *Like Father, Like Son*, Melvin Cheatham wrote about his experiences with Franklin Graham's 1997 evangelistic campaign in Johannesburg, South Africa. He already knew Franklin well because he had participated in several projects of Samaritan's Purse, a relief organization led by Franklin. He had personally experienced how practical needs resulting from famine, epidemics, war, or natural catastrophes had been alleviated. Cheatham had seen how Franklin was "helping others who are hungry, thirsty, sick, or otherwise in need" in many countries. Franklin once said that he and his father were working on the same assignment to change the world with God's love: "But he's going high, and I'm looking low."

One person who markedly influenced Franklin's coming to faith in Jesus and his ministry with Samaritan's Purse was Bob Pierce, the founder of World Vision. Franklin was impressed with the man, his pioneering spirit, his courage, but also his passion for people. Pierce was someone who did his utmost for people in need. His maxim was "Let my heart be broken by what breaks the heart of God!" He was committed to combining practical help with the proclamation of the gospel. Franklin learned from him to offer practical help but to combine it with spiritual help by sharing God's Word and calling people to repentance.

In Johannesburg, Cheatham watched as Franklin followed in his father's footsteps, proclaiming the gospel to an audience of over forty-five thousand people in a packed soccer stadium:

> As Franklin began his message that night, my thoughts returned to the time when he had believed his calling was only to bring medical relief to people suffering in a hurting world. He had no intention of ever preaching like his father. I smiled in amazement as I observed and listened to evangelist Franklin Graham delivering a powerful gospel message to thousands of people.[5]

During a three-day Festival of Hope in June 2009 in Tallinn, Estonia, I ascertained that Franklin Graham's sermons were unsurpassed in their clarity and directness. Franklin spoke frankly about sensitive topics such as sexuality, drugs, and other religions. When asked about this, he said that his goal is always to preach the gospel message as plainly and as practically as possible. He stressed that it is not about our message but about God's message to humankind. And this message should be transmitted in the most understandable way possible.

Franklin has inherited a lot from his mother, especially her directness. In a small group of Christian leaders, he shared that he loves a good battle for people's souls. On the other hand, he is also concerned about not offending his listeners through culturally insensitive remarks. It is easy to recognize that this combination of boldness in preaching and concern for the individual clearly stems from both of his parents. When you see Franklin in action, you can easily recognize both his father's as well as his mother's character traits.

In Tallinn, my wife and I also had the opportunity to speak with the counselor of Franklin's evangelistic team, Ross Rhoads, and his wife, Carol. Rhoads leads a biblical devotional every morning during Franklin's Festivals of Hope. Our son Daniel, himself a youth evangelist, was able to participate in such a time of prayer and spiritual preparation. He was especially touched by the fact that everybody, including Franklin, knelt when they prayed for each other and for the evangelistic outreach. Franklin repeatedly emphasized that this time of listening to God's Word and praying together was the most important time of the day, and everything else depended on it.

These accounts involving the ministries of both father and son make it clear that the Grahams have a holistic vision of Christian missions that focuses on the well-being of the whole person by meeting both practical and spiritual needs. To them, ministry is about bringing Christ's love to bear in all situations. Particularly Franklin inherited his great social concern from his mother. Besides leadership roles with the BGEA and Samaritan's Purse, he seeks to devote at least 10 percent of his time as an evangelist at Franklin Graham

Festivals and similar evangelistic outreaches. He does this although he often rightly remarks that he is no Billy Graham where his preaching abilities are concerned.

This is the same Franklin Graham who for many years rebelled against his parents' faith. He writes about this struggle in detail in his book *Rebel with a Cause*.[6] His mother referred to it at Franklin's ordination:

> Knowing how long and how hard God has worked on this particular servant of His, I had to come out here and, like Moses at the burning bush, stand aside and see this great sight. In case there's some mother out there concerned for a son who is away from the Lord—let me say this morning nobody's hopeless. I mean it. NOBODY.[7]

Ruth herself was rarely active on the missionary front, but she was a missionary at home by combining words and deeds in exemplary fashion, thus creating an authentic testimony of Christ's love. Ruth was characterized by an enduringly positive attitude during her husband's many long absences. She never complained about them. She included her children in her husband's assignment by having them pray together for him as a family and listening to his radio broadcast *Hour of Decision* on Sunday. She shared the global responsibility with her husband. Shortly before the birth of her first child, Gigi, Ruth wrote in her diary:

> My interests are as broad as his, only I view them from the sidelines while he is down in the thick of it. I am so proud of him—so happy to be his wife. And I would like for him to know he has a family to whom he is the most important person in the world. A little family loving him and praying for him, thinking of him always and counting the days till he comes home.[8]

Ruth was a great support to her husband also because she was very interested in what was going on in the world. This interest led her to find books and articles in newspapers and magazines that broadened his horizon. Ruth combined a cosmopolitan worldview with an open heart for individual people's needs.

In later years, when all five children had left home, she accompanied Billy more on his tours, especially abroad. He was able to make use of her in-depth knowledge of the different countries and their customs. A Scotsman once remarked that Ruth knew more about his country than he did himself. Ruth wanted to know everything about people's life circumstances so that she could serve them in the best possible way.

Ruth and Billy were always interested in the well-being of the whole person. In 1956, during a mission in Mumbai, India, Billy wrote in his diary:

> Many of the little children were diseased, many of them had big stomachs from malnutrition. My heart ached as I realized that a little bowl full of rice to these children meant everything. They did not

Ruth saw as her task to care for her family and to assure her husband that the entire family stood behind him and his ministry. The photo was taken in 1960 near Montreux, Switzerland.

have enough to eat. They did not have any doctors to come and help them when they got sick. They were not able to buy any medicine, and I thought of my own children at home and how much they have in comparison to these children here in India. My heart has already gone out to them. I wish that there was something we could do.[9]

In 1976, Ruth and Billy visited Guatemala, where great parts had been devastated by an earthquake. The BGEA helped with food and medical supplies. Ruth and Billy were convinced that if we want to touch the people with the gospel, we have to stand with them in their heartbreaks.

Ruth stood in the world with both feet planted firmly on the ground and eyes wide open. She saw the reality of the lives of people around her and often helped in small yet meaningful ways. People in Montreat and the surrounding area got to know her as a Christian whose faith took action, a person whose commitment stretched the limits of her own strength. Ruth and Billy passed their compassionate attitude on to their children so that all five of them have a great concern for people in need. All of the Grahams are very committed, but this term applies especially to Billy, whose life's work has truly had global dimensions.

Already as a teenager, Billy was very interested in world events. He read not only Tarzan comics but also countless history books. He avidly studied the Civil War and knew all the American presidents. His younger brother, Melvin, a farmer, was convinced that Billy had read more books than anyone else he had ever met. His mother, Morrow, regularly looked for used books that might interest him. Before he was fourteen, he had already read Gibbons's classic *The Decline and Fall of the Roman Empire*.

However, this interest did not translate into enthusiasm for school. Billy was an average student and was told by a teacher that he would not amount to much. Other things were more important to him than a school diploma, such as a career as a baseball player. After he was able to shake baseball legend Babe Ruth's hand (something his father

211

had managed to arrange), he didn't wash his hands for days. Heroes enthralled him from an early age. Already in his youth, he made it his goal to fight for a worthy cause. In those days, no one could have imagined that the young Billy Frank, as he was called at home, who got up early in the morning to milk his father's cows, would personally meet more heads of state during his sixty-year worldwide ministry than probably anyone else in the twentieth century.

During his time at the Bible school in Florida, he told God that he did not necessarily want to become a great preacher but a great soul winner. He still vividly remembers how a student at the Bible school graduation ceremony stated in her graduation speech that it was time for another revival preacher like Wesley, Finney, or Moody. Why shouldn't he be that person? A few years later, at Wheaton College in Chicago, he would meet the one who would share his dedication to reaching the world with the gospel and who would support him in his ministry through sixty-four years of married life. He saw his contribution to changing the world in leading people to believe in Jesus Christ as their personal Lord and Savior and having lives transformed by the Holy Spirit as a result. His credo: Through spiritual rebirth, people become capable of loving not only God but also their fellow human beings, and even their enemies. A growing love for others, according to him, would move these transformed individuals to all sorts of acts of brotherly love. Depending on individual talents and calling, they would support initiatives for the socially disadvantaged or help build structures to promote social justice. According to Graham, societal transformation is always the result of personal transformation through the Holy Spirit and that change always happens from the inside out. This was his lifetime conviction, for which he received both praise and criticism.

At a 2005 press conference in New York, he was asked what he felt was the world's greatest problem. He named poverty and added, "And I believe that the gospel of Christ is the answer, not part of the answer, but the whole answer. We don't have any possibility of solving our problems today, except through Jesus." According to

Graham, the basic problem of social injustice lies mainly in sin, because sin leads to lovelessness and selfish behavior, which have negative consequences for all areas of society.

Throughout his life, Graham was keenly interested in world affairs and in helping relieve society's ills. When I visited him at his home, I showed him a film about the Christ Day in Switzerland, which was held in the St. Jakob Soccer Stadium in Basel in 2004. In this event, flag bearers and their prayer partners from all of Switzerland's 2,786 municipalities committed themselves to praying for their communities and the political authorities on a regular basis. (They still do it to this day.)

When watching the film, Graham's immediate response was, "Couldn't you do something like that as soon as possible in the country of Georgia? They really need united prayer and healing of their land right now." He had just heard about the social upheaval in Georgia on the news that day.

In 2004, in the Basel soccer stadium, flag bearers and prayer partners from all 2,786 municipalities of Switzerland embracing representatives from 119 countries committed themselves to regularly praying for their communities, the residents as well as the authorities.

Graham liked to read several national and international magazines and newspapers to stay on top of the news. If it wasn't possible, he asked Ruth to do it for him and to mark important articles for him to read later.

Billy as well as Ruth represented an interesting mix of profound faith and cosmopolitan interest. They held the newspaper in one hand and the Bible in the other. They did not fear debate with the critical thinkers of their time. Their Bible-based convictions had weathered far too many of life's storms for them to be afraid of losing their faith. On the contrary, they wanted to learn all that was necessary to help them understand people's doubts and fears and be able to give them an answer based on God's Word.

When a student at Montreat College once complained to Ruth about having to learn so many unnecessary worldly things, Ruth asked her, "Who were the two men most used in the Bible?" and promptly answered herself: "It was Moses in the Old Testament and Paul in the New Testament." Ruth then explained that Moses had received the best possible education of the time from the Egyptian scholars, and Paul had been a scholar of scholars, armed with the best teaching of his time. That contributed to their ability to connect with people of all sorts, making them important spiritual leaders in their epoch.[10]

How did Billy Graham live out his global responsibility with regard to the pressing needs of his time? How did he see the relationship between evangelism and social responsibility? How did he define Christian missions based on God's Word?

In August 1948, one year prior to the Los Angeles Mission, a Congress for World Evangelization organized by Youth for Christ took place in Beatenberg, Switzerland. Church historian Garth M. Rosell called it "the most significant mid-century gathering of evangelical youth leaders."[11]

At this gathering, Graham came into contact with an interesting man, the pastor and theologian Harold John Ockenga. Professor of

sociology and Graham biographer William Martin describes Ockenga as "a scholarly man and probably the single most influential
figure of Evangelical circles at the time."[12] We have already discussed
how Ockenga left a lasting impression as a humble intercessor on the
young evangelist Graham at the 1950 mission in Boston, over which
Ockenga presided. Ockenga's influence on Graham's life and ministry, however, went much further. His friendship with this learned
and internationally connected man broadened Graham's thinking
significantly and made his later global contribution as a voice of
God in the second half of the twentieth century even possible. Aside
from Ruth and her father, Nelson Bell, no one contributed as much
to making the small-town Baptist preacher from the American South
a sophisticated ambassador of God as Ockenga. Upon Ockenga's
death in 1985, Graham wrote about his longtime friend and spiritual
mentor, "He was a giant among giants. Nobody outside of my family influenced me more than he did. I never made a major decision
without first calling and asking his advice and counsel." Graham can
be adequately understood only in light of the mind-set and influence
of his closest supporters and friends such as Ockenga.

Ockenga was not only a pastor of the Park Street Congregation in
Boston but also an evangelist and missionary. In his sermon "America's Revival Is Breaking?" he summarized his convictions: "I would
die if we did not have people saved at my church every Sunday. If
we did not have people going into the mission fields; if we were not
supporting scores and scores of new missionaries all the time, I think
I would leave the church. I couldn't stand it."[13]

But Ockenga was also equally concerned about social injustice and
poverty. Ockenga considered poverty to be an even greater problem
than the issue of racism, not least because poverty was the source
of many other, farther-reaching social problems. Both Graham and
Ockenga had personally experienced the horrible effects of the Great
Depression, which began in 1929 and reached its zenith in 1933.
Ockenga had seen people standing in line waiting for work and
bread in Chicago. He saw human dignity being trampled underfoot,

economic misery leading to social misery. Everyone tried to see to themselves and put the blame for the situation on others. He wrote his doctorate on the topic of poverty as a challenge for governments. He concluded that unrestrained capitalism is ultimately doomed to fail and that economic crises cannot be avoided.

More and more experts today would agree with Ockenga. The solution he outlined had to do with his profound faith in God and his commandments, which addressed all areas of life. People had to experience what the living Christ did on the cross, thus liberating them from their hate, aversions, pride, and rebellion. This would have a healing influence on relationships between employers and employees, on social justice and ethnic conflicts. Repression and exploitation would be replaced by love and solidarity between people, similar to the way the first Christians shared everything with one another.

Only when the vertical relationship with God was right could the horizontal relationships between people be healed and devastating selfishness be overcome. The reverse was also true: "What we do to men, we do to God." God will certainly hold us accountable for our actions. Ockenga concluded, "Christianity is the most practical element in life. Embrace Christ and the crux of the social question is removed."[14] Ockenga called Christians to strive for freedom, equality, and brotherly love. These however, according to Ockenga, absolutely required the transforming action of the Holy Spirit upon each individual at the foot of Christ's cross. The solution for all social issues could be found in God's Word: "God has not left us without guidance."[15]

Graham's friendship with Ockenga, who combined a profound walk with God with great learning and a deep commitment to the needy people of this world, made a great impression on Graham. He discovered that evangelistic fervor, thorough theological study, and social responsibility were not mutually exclusive but instead benefited each other. A transformation of the heart leads to a transformation of relationships and finally to a transformation of society. People like Ockenga emphasized that every lasting change in a family or society is the result of a transformation by the Holy Spirit in an individual life. Social endeavors and evangelistic fervor must go hand in hand, otherwise they would result in either dead orthodoxy or sheer humanism.

Graham's perspective on fundamental social ills was clearly illustrated in his radio address on July 17, 1955, during the Geneva Summit of the "Big Four" (the US, the Soviet Union, Great Britain, and France). It is an excellent example of the way he pinpointed the solution for a specific social problem. The topic he dealt with was peaceful coexistence of the nations. The Geneva Summit was the first meeting of the four victorious Allied nations with their government representatives after World War II. The official goal of this conference was to reduce international tensions. The war had been over for more than ten years, yet a Cold War had replaced the armed conflict. This world situation greatly troubled Graham. He therefore saw it as his mission to fly to Geneva once more, after having held a one-day outreach there just two months before. Graham felt urged to point to Jesus Christ as the only true peacemaker.

Just like President Eisenhower and his staff, Graham attended the service at the American Episcopal Church in Geneva on the day before the summit. After the sermon, everyone there, including President Eisenhower, knelt and prayed for God's blessing on the peace talks. The next day, Graham addressed the representatives of the assembled nations

Billy Graham had high regards for President Eisenhower and vice versa. Shortly before the latter passed away, Eisenhower asked Graham to explain to him the way to everlasting life and to pray with him.

as well as the politicians attending the summit in a speech that was widely broadcast:

> There is an air of expectancy here in Geneva. . . . More than 1,500 newspaper reporters are in town from all over the world to cover this event. . . . Of all the historic conferences that have been held in this beautiful Swiss city, this is considered the greatest. The Big Four will wrestle with problems that Sir Winston Churchill has said are too great for the human mind to cope with. . . .
>
> The one cry in Geneva is peace. Some people are ready to sell their soul and conscience for even a temporary peace. I have asked many people here, "How can you have a summit conference and how can you hope for peace without the Prince of peace?" In all the pre-conference meetings at Geneva I have hardly heard God mentioned. Everything is being done on a humanistic level. Christ is forgotten. There is little time for God. There have been other peace conferences in history where God was forgotten and Christ was left out that have ended in war and disaster. . . .
>
> If only the Big Four leaders in Geneva could realize that all of their problems stem from one basic problem, which is the sin of human nature. The problems of the world are not economic or political; they are spiritual. We continue to wrestle with the problems of human iniquity and human failure. Nations have reached agreements only to

Billy Graham is welcomed to the White House on July 18, 1981, by President Ronald Reagan and first lady Nancy Reagan. On February 23, 1983, Ronald Reagan presented Billy Graham with the Presidential Medal of Freedom, the highest civilian honor given to an American.

have them broken time after time. Why? Because they were building their hopes and agreements on the cracked and sinking foundation of human nature. For thousands of years men have failed to take into account the human equation. . . .

The only cure for sin lies at the foot of that cross. The ultimate possibility of lifting human nature to the place where it will love instead of hate and will practice honesty instead of deceit and will keep its agreements with integrity is found only at the foot of this cross. The reason we do not have peace in the world is that we do not have peace in our souls. There can be no peace in the hearts of men without reconciliation to God. All men who will pay the price of repentance and receive Christ by faith can have a new nature and a new heart. We can never build a better world until we have better men and the only way men can be made better is by the transforming and regenerating power of Christ.[16]

In his messages, Graham repeated that pacifism did not lead to true peace, "for the pacifist acts as if men are regenerate and can be appealed to through persuasion and goodwill." This was simply not enough. Peace cannot be created by our own efforts in the same way that a carpenter cannot build a house without a hammer, or an artist cannot paint a picture without a brush. The right equipment is necessary to do the job. The noble calling of a peacemaker can be carried out only if we know Jesus Christ, the true Peacemaker. To promote peace on earth, according to Graham, one needed to personally know the One who is our peace.

Graham was also acquainted with the civil rights leader Martin Luther King Jr. Both men had a great mutual respect for each other. Graham called him Mike, at the latter's request. For Graham, Mike was a prophet of God. Graham invited him to give the opening prayer at his mission in New York in 1957, which was broadcast nationwide on television. He thus showed that he backed King's concerns. Graham repeatedly emphasized that the peace marches King initiated on behalf of the African American population were justified. He had come to an agreement with King to divide their tasks. King fought for racial equality with activities such as peace marches. Graham refused to carry out racially segregated missions and underlined equality in his missions. Jesse Jackson, a Baptist minister and civil rights activist, stated in retrospect that Graham supported racial equality in his crusades. According to Jackson, King led the people out of Egypt's slav-

Billy Graham with civil rights leader Martin Luther King Jr. They appreciated each other, and each felt his ministry enhanced that of the other. This photo is from 1962.

ery into freedom, so to speak, and Graham showed them what that freedom looked like based on God's Word.[17]

From his youth, Graham disdained racial discrimination. There was a black worker on his father's farm whom he appreciated very much. Graham had also known an older black gentleman in Charlotte whom he trusted and with whom he discussed his problems in his younger years. After starting his own family, an African American housekeeper helped ease the burden of his wife's many responsibilities. Bea, as everyone called her, was dearly loved by the entire family and, as a Christian who lived out her faith in everyday life, highly respected.

Early on in his ministry, Graham decided not to permit segregated seating at events in which he participated, even if the organizers specifically called for it, nor did Graham accept any invitations to South Africa as long as the apartheid regime ruled. In 1953, at a mission in Chattanooga, Tennessee, he removed the ropes that separated the whites from the blacks with his own hands as people were entering the hall. The head usher reacted by quitting on the spot.

Some people felt he was going too far with his positive attitude toward African Americans. Among them were many conservative Christians. Already prior to the Supreme Court school decision of 1954, which declared segregated schools unconstitutional, and even before the word *integration* was commonly used, Graham had been convinced by God's Word that any discrimination according to the color of someone's skin did not correspond to God's will. Graham said, "We are made of one blood. The ground is level at the cross of Christ. There are no second-class citizens before God." He referred to the Bible, which clearly states that all are equal: "There is neither Jew nor Greek, neither slave nor free, nor is there male and female, for you are all one in Christ Jesus" (Gal. 3:28).

Graham probably expressed his position on the race issue in greatest detail in 1956 in an article in *Life* magazine. He did not get bogged down in current racial issues but tried to address the roots of the problem. His remarks are still valid today:

The roots of the problem lie deep in the history of our country and they too have spiritual significance. The economy of New England

prospered as the shipping interests fattened on the slave trade. North and South alike are involved in the guilt of slavery and in the responsibility for its consequences. We should not be surprised at the difficulties which we face, for

Bea, the Grahams' housekeeper, was adored by the entire Graham family. She was said to have had the greatest faith of them all.

221

the Bible teaches us that "Whatever a man sows, that he will also reap." We have sown flagrant human injustice and we have reaped a harvest of racial strife. The guilt and the problems are by no means limited to America. . . . I have observed discrimination in almost every country I have visited. Wherever a minority group acts different, looks different, has a different accent or even wears different clothes they are looked upon as outsiders and they are cut off from equal social status with the larger group.[18]

Graham continued by pointing out the view of the Bible:

When Christ died, the veil which separated man from God was ripped vertically from top to bottom and the way was open for all men to have access to God. This is the vertical aspect of the gospel, but it's not the whole gospel. Paul says, "He is our peace, who has made us both one, and has broken down the dividing wall of hostility." The horizontal separation of man was broken at the same time as the vertical. Jesus put no color bar on the Golden Rule (that we should treat each other as we want to be treated ourselves).[19]

Graham then tried to give an answer from the Bible to show how racial issues can be overcome:

We must dare to obey the commandment of love, and leave the consequences in His hands. The whole nation needs a baptism of Christian love, tolerance and understanding. This, alone, in my opinion will solve our problems and ease our tensions.[20]

Finally, he emphasized that the commandment to love one's brother encompasses far more than just overcoming the racial barrier. The Christian must raise his voice in general against society's precarious social situations, but he should also remember that the power to change comes from the Lord alone. One must never forget that faith without works is dead, but the strength and power to carry out the work come from God.

Harvey Cox, former theology professor at Harvard University and author of the bestseller *The Secular City*, recently summarized Graham's contribution to the social issue as follows:

> He pioneered some of the social thinking of the new progressive evangelicals when it was very hard to do so. A "New Testament evangelist" Graham most certainly was, but he was also something of an "Old Testament prophet" sometimes despite himself. . . . If we now see the return in America of an ecumenical, prophetic, and peacemaking evangelicalism, he must certainly be counted among its progenitors.[21]

In the mid-twentieth century, no issue occupied and divided Christians more than the relationship between evangelism and social responsibility.

After World War II, many theologians reduced the gospel to social concern and activities for the world's needy and the establishment of just social and legal infrastructures to benefit people. They often emphasized Christian social responsibility so strongly because many evangelical Christians emphasized individual salvation at the cost of social justice and responsibility for a needy world. Yet Jesus Christ gave us a twofold commandment: We should love God with all our heart and love our neighbors as ourselves.

In focusing on brotherly love, more and more Christian leaders went too far and forgot that brotherly love is nourished by a relationship with God. Without this divine source, none of our good deeds will bear good fruit in the long run. Many even made brotherly love their gospel, but in doing so, they squeezed the message of salvation in Jesus Christ out of the picture. Instead of sharing God's love both in deed and in word, these Christians left out the word of God's salvation in Christ and of the transforming work of the Holy Spirit.

The evangelical camp, including Graham, argued that those who one-sidedly and sometimes even exclusively emphasized the horizontal dimension of the Christian faith represented a social gospel.

They had made social commitment their gospel—a commitment that should not be the gospel but a consequence of it. The evangelicals believed that the World Council of Churches in particular was being increasingly infiltrated by people who advocated a social gospel. Even theologians who did not agree with the evangelical interpretation of the Bible in other areas were speaking out against the growing theological liberalism that was robbing Jesus Christ's gospel of its substance and making it ineffective. H. Richard Niebuhr, professor at Yale Divinity School and brother of the even more renown theologian Reinhold Niebuhr (i.e., someone who was not reputed to be particularly close to the evangelicals), described the doctrine of theological liberalism in his book *The Kingdom of God in America* like this:

> A God without wrath
> brought men without sin
> into a kingdom without judgment
> through the ministrations of a Christ
> without a cross.[22]

Theological liberalism was threatening to become the mainstream doctrine of the churches that had their roots in the Reformation. With it, evangelism and missions lost their importance or were redefined, sometimes even downgraded to mere interpersonal action or dialogue. In this environment, Graham and the conferences he convened played a key role in defining the concept of missions in the twentieth century as including both the proclamation of salvation in Christ and the commitment to provide practical relief through acts of service.

In 1910, for the first time in church history, John Mott gathered missionaries and theologians from different nations and Christian denominations in Edinburgh, Scotland, for an international missionary conference under the catchphrase "The Evangelization of the World in This Generation." Mott had turned to Christ through Dwight L. Moody and was active in the YMCA as a Methodist layman. He was one of the leaders of the Student Volunteer Movement for Foreign Missions founded in 1886, which laid the spiritual foundation for the World Missionary Conference in Scotland: "The ethos of the conference was shaped by the spirituality of the Student Volunteer Movement, which combined zeal for world missions with a consistent emphasis on both private and corporate prayer."[23]

The goal of the Edinburgh gathering was to appeal to the representatives of the different churches and missions organizations to work hand in hand to fulfill the Great Commission. The conference postulated that unity and mission belonged together. Mott was convinced that nothing would contribute more strongly to the unity of the different churches than joint evangelistic action. He believed that the most effective Christian testimony was sharing love and living in unity. In his opinion, it was high time to join forces in the fulfillment of the Great Commission and to proclaim the hope in Jesus Christ in a united front, otherwise Christianity would lose all credibility. Mott said:

> Christ emphasized that the mightiest apologetic with which to convince the non-Christian world of His divine character and claims would be the oneness of His disciples. Experience has already shown that by far the most hopeful way of hastening the realization of true and triumphant Christian unity is through the enterprise of carrying the Gospel to the non-Christian world. . . . It is a decisive hour for the Christian Church. If it neglects to meet successfully the present world crisis by failing to discharge its responsibility to the whole world, it will lose its power both on the home and on the foreign fields and will be seriously hindered in its mission to the coming generation. Nothing less than the adequacy of Christianity as a world religion is on trial. It is indeed the decisive hour of Christian missions. It is the time of all times for Christians of every name to unite and with quickened loyalty and with reliance upon the living God, to undertake

to make Christ known to all men, and to bring His power to bear upon all nations.[24]

Edinburgh 1910 influenced an entire generation of young people who were going out into the world as missionaries to spread the message of reconciliation in Christ. "The Evangelization of the World in This Generation" became a widespread missionary slogan. Bill Bright adopted it many years later while signing his letters.

In retrospect, Edinburgh 1910 can be considered the start of the modern Protestant missions movement. In 1946, Mott received the Nobel Peace Prize for his efforts to bridge the gap of misunderstanding and to bring all people into loving relationship. When asked how he wished to be remembered, he replied, "As an evangelist." Unfortunately, he was not able to unite the majority of Christians under the task of fulfilling the Great Commission of Jesus Christ to make disciples of all nations. The standpoints regarding the inspiration and authority of the Bible were too diverse, as was the basic understanding of missions. Despite the differences, there was an obvious need for missions-minded Christians to get together and to encourage and inspire one another in their global Christian responsibility.

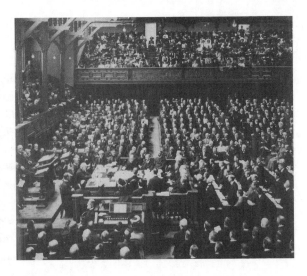

The World Missionary Conference in Edinburgh in 1910 was a unique event in the history of the Protestant missionary movement, as it brought together for the first time Christians from different backgrounds for the purpose of fulfilling the Great Commission of Jesus Christ.

After the World Missionary Conference in Edinburgh in 1910, two world wars showed what disastrous consequences conflict and enmity could bring. A growing consensus that the churches should set a new standard of unity and cooperation emerged among church representatives. In 1948, the World Council of Churches was established in Amsterdam. The Dutchman Willem Visser 't Hooft was its first general secretary. Visser 't Hooft, who was well-disposed toward Billy Graham, invited him, as a representative of Youth for Christ, to participate at the conference as an observer.

One main challenge facing the newly founded World Council of Churches was to respond to Jesus's high priestly prayer in John 17 to contribute to the unity of his disciples and to promote the common effort of Christian missions. The World Council of Churches understood itself as "a world Christian body that would link the churches together in unity, mission, and service." It was Visser 't Hooft's profound conviction that true Christian unity was possible only at the cross of Christ and that Jesus Christ and his work of salvation through the shed blood at the cross must remain the focus of all efforts. At the same time, the search for unity should never become an end in itself but should always serve the Christian mission.

If only these words of caution had been taken more seriously! In the years after the World Council of Churches was founded, a growing trend became visible. More and more, it was no longer Jesus's work of redemption and the mandate of world evangelization that held the various churches together but rather an increasingly diffuse view on missions. Those who led the way did not want to offend liberal Christians or churches who were critical of the mandate to evangelize the world. Efforts to achieve social justice began to take precedence and increasingly removed the proclamation of Christ as God's Son and Redeemer from the picture. Jesus of Nazareth was reduced to a social reformer and a model of fair, just action. A government official in Cuba once told me plainly, "I share many of your convictions. Wasn't Jesus the first social revolutionary?"

Jesus may have been that, but he was certainly much more than that.

Church history shows that if we are not careful, the horizontal dimension of the gospel (loving our neighbor) always has the tendency to replace the vertical dimension (loving

Billy Graham in 1955 speaking to Willem Visser 't Hooft, the Dutch founder of the World Council of Churches, at its headquarters in Bossey, near Geneva, Switzerland.

God). Many people believed this was increasingly the case with the World Council of Churches, whose statements tended more and more toward a social gospel. Its focus became increasingly one-sided, calling societies to repent instead of individuals. The proclamation of Jesus's work of salvation was replaced by initiatives toward peace, justice, and the preservation of God's creation, however important they are. The result was a one-sided emphasis on producing righteous structures. Fulfilling the Great Commission was reduced to combating poverty and injustice.

Christian missions undisputedly include both the proclamation of Jesus's work of salvation and a call to repentance as well as the commitment to provide practical relief through acts of mercy and by promoting justice. According to God's Word, evangelism and global responsibility are inseparable. Yet what happened in the context of the World Council of Churches was not a necessary enhancement of gospel proclamation through practical acts of love but rather a substitute for the preaching of the gospel. In doing so, evangelism often became synonymous with efforts toward making the world a better place.

In his autobiography, Billy Graham describes how he came to invite Christian leaders from all over the world to discuss the topic of world evangelization:

> I came to realize, many churches and leaders had lost sight of the priority of evangelism; some were even ignoring evangelism altogether. This had not always been the case. In the nineteenth century, evangelism was a central concern of the Church, with thousands of missionaries going to the ends of the earth and making Christianity a truly worldwide movement. This explosion in evangelism—the greatest in the history of the Church—was accompanied by the establishment of schools, hospitals, literacy programs, and indigenous churches and denominations.[25]

Graham invited thirty-three Christian leaders from twelve nations to Montreux, Switzerland, in 1960, among them John Stott, the rector of the well-known All Souls Anglican Church in London. Under the heading "God's Strategy in Missions and Evangelization," they discussed the challenges and opportunities of evangelism in an increasingly secularized world. Graham said:

> At the peaceful lakeside setting, we all sensed a deepening spirit of unity among us, and a fresh commitment to do what we could to promote the cause of evangelism. At the same time, no formal document came forth from that gathering, nor were there firm plans for any further meetings.[26]

The necessary impetus for concrete action came from Victor Nelson, a Presbyterian pastor and friend of Graham, who challenged Graham four years after Montreux at a mission in Canada:

> Billy, if you just puddle-jump from crusade to crusade all over the world, you'll never accomplish what you could and should accomplish. You not only need to do this work yourself, but you need to multiply your efforts. You need to train others to do effective evangelistic work also.[27]

Alea iacta est—the die was cast. After consulting with his team, Graham decided to hold a meeting in 1966 in Berlin within sight of the Berlin Wall, which was a symbol of separation. It seemed a fitting venue for the assembly of evangelical leaders who were committed to world missions for the purpose of raising Christ as the universal answer in a world starved for hope and peace.

Graham convinced Carl Henry, editor in chief of *Christianity Today*, to become chairman of the World Congress on Evangelism, as the conference was formally titled. This was a wise decision, seeing that *Christianity Today* had become a worldwide voice for evangelical theology under Henry. As a theologian, Henry was highly esteemed in evangelical circles. Erhard Berneburg, general secretary of the missions department of the German Protestant Church, called Henry "the leading theologian of the new evangelical movement" and "a pioneer of a new contemplation of social responsibility in evangelical theology." Henry was a theologian and a respected scholar who combined in-depth reflection on God's revealed Word with a humble attitude. He therefore always remained acutely conscious of the necessity of the Holy Spirit's illumination for theological study: "If we humans say anything authentic about God, we can do so only on the basis of divine self-revelation; all other God-talk is conjectural."[28]

As the son of German immigrants, Henry had inherited the love of thorough, systematic thinking from his parents; as a friend and co-worker of Graham, the practical winning of souls was important to him. This combination of theory and practice, theological expertise and evangelistic zeal was what Graham needed in a chairman of such a conference. Aside from his relationships with Harold Ockenga and John Stott, it was certainly his friendship and collaboration with Henry that made Graham into a true Christian "statesman" who associated with evangelistic practitioners just as easily as with missiologists and theologians. Without the support of theologians of Ockenga's, Stott's, and Henry's caliber, the Congresses of World Evangelization in Berlin 1966 and Lausanne 1974 would never have been so significant.

While those in charge were preparing the list of participants, the question arose whether members of the growing charismatic movement and Pentecostal churches, who at the time were not part of mainstream evangelicalism, should be invited. Oral Roberts was one of the leading representatives of this group. Graham said:

> I felt that my longtime friend Oral Roberts, world renowned for his preaching and healing ministry as well as for the development of the university bearing his name in Tulsa, Oklahoma, should be included among the delegates. . . . I was convinced that his presence would mark the beginning of a new era in evangelical cooperation.[29]

Roberts afterward emphasized that "there has been more real Christian love expressed here than in any like gathering in which I have been involved."[30] His evaluation was confirmed by Bob Pierce, founder of World Vision, who described the conference as the "warmest display of brotherly affection I have experienced in my twenty-five years of association of evangelicals."

The watchword of the Berlin World Congress on Evangelism in 1966 was "One Race—One Gospel—One Task." Around 1,200 participants from 104 countries participated. To emphasize the urgency of world evangelization, a clock in the center of the conference area showed the world population growth during the time of the meeting. By the end of the conference, the world's population had increased by over 1.7 million people—and all these people needed to hear the gospel. Aside from talks on basic principles and Bible interpretation, one of which was led by Dutch Holocaust survivor Corrie ten Boom, later widely known through BGEA's film *The Hiding Place*, many workshops and podium discussions explored the different facets of evangelism and missions.

The Berlin Congress also had a profound impact on Bill Bright, the founder and longtime director of Campus Crusade for Christ. Graham mentions in his autobiography that Bright once told him that the Berlin Congress had shown him the vision "for Campus Crusade for Christ to become worldwide in its outreach."[31]

Berlin '66 also influenced the launching of Campus Crusade for Christ in Europe. Kalevi Lehtinen, Finnish evangelist and Lutheran pastor as well as interpreter for Graham during his 1987 mission in Helsinki, decided to commit himself to a full-time ministry with Campus Crusade for Christ after observing the podium discussion with Bright on the topic of student evangelism. Lehtinen became the first European staff member of Campus

Billy Graham and his team purposely chose the divided city of Berlin to carry out the first World Congress on Evangelism in 1966. The Berlin Kongresshalle, where the conference took place, can be seen in the background.

Crusade for Christ and later its European director. Later, Lehtinen became Finland's foremost evangelist and preached the gospel all over Russia.

In his opening address, Graham described the conference goal by stating that winning people to a personal relationship with Jesus Christ was the main focus: "Evangelism means to bear witness with the soul aflame. What we need today is a Spirit-anointed passion that comes from a deep conviction that men are lost, and a compassion for them that will not let us rest until we are proclaiming Christ to them."[32]

He then described the Christians' mission as follows:

> Our goal is nothing less than the penetration of the entire world. We are not promised that the whole world will believe. The evangelization

of the world does not mean that all men will respond, but that all men will be given an opportunity to respond as they are confronted with Christ. Most of the illustrations of the Gospel used by Jesus—salt, light, bread, water, leaven, fire—have one common element: penetration. We are not only to penetrate the world geographically, but we are to penetrate the world of government, school, work and home; the world of entertainment, of the intellectual, of the laboring man, of the ignorant man.[33]

Graham continued by explaining the relationship between evangelism and fighting social injustice:

If we want social reform, we must evangelize. The preaching of the cross and the resurrection has been primarily responsible for promoting humanitarian sentiment and social concern for the last 400 years. Prison reform, the prohibition of slave traffic, the abolition of slavery, the crusade for human dignity, the struggle against exploitation—all are the outcome of great religious revivals and the conversion of individuals. The preaching of the cross could do more to bring about social revolution than any other method.[34]

Graham emphasized that evangelism should not result in a neglect of social responsibility. Evangelism and social concern should go hand in hand. He called for a deep compassion in the face of social evil. In his closing message, he reiterated that the efforts toward peace and justice, however important they are, should never replace the preaching of the gospel of Jesus Christ.

Contemporary evangelism is moving away from winning souls one by one to the evangelization of the structures of society. . . . There has been a change from "the church has a mission" to "the church is a mission." . . . We cannot accept this interpretation. Evangelism has social implications, but its primary thrust is the winning of men to a personal relationship to Jesus Christ. Evangelism bears witness with the soul aflame.[35]

He then again summarized what he felt Berlin '66 was about:

In many circles today the church has an energetic passion for unity but it has all but forgotten our Lord's commission to evangelize. One of the purposes of this World Congress on Evangelism is to make an urgent appeal to the world church to return to the dynamic zeal for world evangelism that characterized Edinburgh 56 years ago.[36]

The Berlin Congress gave a face and a voice to those Christians who were committed to Christ's Great Commission to "make disciples of all nations" (Matt. 28:18–20). In later years, this voice was perceived as a counterpart to the increasingly liberal tendencies of the World Council of Churches. Erhard Berneburg summarized the legacy of Berlin '66 as follows:

One can say that in Berlin, "evangelicalism" redefined itself and demonstrated a newly-won unity. It was not a sectarian pattern of evangelical cooperation which was created. The evangelicals' main concern should be the spiritual transformation of individuals and not the political restructuring of society. In this sense, we agreed on a common understanding of evangelization and worked out guidelines for future world evangelization.[37]

Berlin '66 strengthened the awareness that comprehensive mission involving evangelism is and should remain the main task of the Christian church, because the church's identity rests on the fact that it is a "church for others," as the Lutheran pastor and martyr Dietrich Bonhoeffer once stated. It is equally important for the church to be rooted in God's Word as the ultimate authority. The World Council of Churches was increasingly marked by theologians who no longer believed in the divine inspiration of the Bible and who placed their authority above the Bible's. Such theologians increasingly questioned the Bible as the reliable and inspired revelation of God to humanity. Not even the longtime general secretary of the World Council of Churches, Willem Visser 't Hooft, could change that, warning that "our cause lacks convincing power as long as we do not prove that we live under the authority of the same Word of God."[38]

While the evangelical missionary movement grew around the world, academic theological education, particularly in Europe, became increasingly liberal, which served to undermine the missionary endeavors of the body of Christ or interpreted them merely as efforts to fight for a fairer world and peace. With the loss of its focus on making disciples of Christ, the Christian church also lost its power to change society from the inside out. Liberal theologians had thrown out many of the foundational tenets of the Christian faith—such as Jesus's divinity, his sacrificial death for our sins, and his bodily resurrection—as a result of their severe criticism of the authority of the Bible as the inspired Word of God. Consequently, the church lost its evangelistic power as well as its transforming influence.

The fourth plenary meeting of the World Council of Churches in 1968 in Uppsala, Sweden, led to an even stronger polarization between those who saw evangelism as the proclamation of Jesus Christ's divine act of salvation in word and deed and those who understood it as a mandate to promote justice and peace in the world. An attempt was made in Uppsala to make the "theology of secularization," as the World Council of Churches termed it, the authoritative guideline for church and Christian mission. Graham, who attended the World Council of Churches' meeting in Uppsala as an observer, summed up his observation with the following assessment: "Uppsala . . . tended to redefine the good news of the Gospel in terms of restructuring society instead of calling individuals to repentance and faith in Christ."[39]

A lack of biblical foundation led to a growing crisis in missions. At the World Council of Churches' World Missions Conference in Bangkok from December 29, 1972, to January 12, 1973, whose main theme was "Salvation Today," part of the participants altered the definition of the term *salvation*. They dismissed the biblical understanding of salvation as reconciliation between a sinner and his Creator on the basis of personal repentance and faith in Jesus's sacrificial death on the cross. Instead, the conference in Bangkok focused even more seriously than the gathering in Uppsala on social and political justice at the exclusion of the gospel of redemption in Jesus Christ. They equated evangelism with political and social efforts to restructure society. Salvation was defined as "release from a suppressed society to hope." The conviction that personal faith in Jesus Christ was an indispensable prerequisite for salvation came under fire. Peter Beyerhaus, a missiologist from Germany, felt a "deep-seated worry about some of the permeating traits of this ecumenical event, which could be calamitous for the future of missions, and probably even for humanity as a whole."[40]

Beyerhaus correctly interpreted this change of focus as a foundational crisis in missions. The World Missions Conference in Bangkok actually recommended a temporary moratorium on foreign missions. Some no longer saw missions as a matter of supporting pioneer missionaries in areas that had not yet been reached by the gospel. Instead, they promoted a new understanding of salvation and missions to the point of supporting militant liberation movements in Africa.

Fourteen years later, at Amsterdam '86, Billy Graham responded to a question at a press conference by referring to his recent encounter with the Anglican archbishop of Canterbury. When Graham had asked him if the World Council of Churches had managed to maintain the balance between social responsibility and evangelism, the archbishop had replied, "If you call evangelism changing structures and helping the oppressed and the poor, I would say 'Yes,' but if you mean by evangelism, which I think you do, winning people to Christ, I think it has diminished in emphasis," and then he added, "We have to go back to a more balanced point of view."

As a result of the World Missions Conference in Bangkok, held under the auspices of the World Council of Churches, Graham and his staff decided to take a bold stand against the increasing erosion of the meaning of salvation and missions. In July 1974, he invited 2,700 evangelical leaders from 150 countries to a Congress of World Evangelization at the Palais de Beaulieu in Lausanne, Switzerland. Many participants and observers saw the Lausanne Congress as an answer to the World Missions Conference

Under the leadership of the World Council of Churches' general secretary, Philip Potter (shown here with Billy Graham in 1972), Christian missions was increasingly reduced to a commitment to social justice and freedom, which caused Billy Graham to organize a Congress of World Evangelization in Lausanne in 1974.

in Bangkok, which had divided Christians with its moratorium on foreign missions and its new definitions of salvation and evangelism.

The catchphrase of the Lausanne Congress was "Let the Earth Hear His Voice!" *Time* magazine described the event as "possibly the widest-ranging meeting of Christians ever held" and as a "challenge to the prevailing philosophy in the World Council of Churches, headquartered some 30 miles down Lac Leman in Geneva."[41]

When asked about his position on the World Council of Churches, Graham replied, "There was tremendous vision at the [World Council of Churches'] founding in 1948. But the council gradually moved further and further from orthodox ties. The gulf between it and the Evangelicals has deepened. I hope this congress will get the World Council to re-evaluate its theological position."[42] The official goal of the Lausanne Congress was to define "the biblical foundation of evangelization in a time of theological confusion." Because the influence of the evangelical global church had shifted from the First World to the Two-Thirds World, Graham took this into consideration when selecting both the speakers and the participants:

> Care was taken to make it as representative as possible; the days of white, Western paternalism had to end. A committee of 28 people from sixteen nations was finally appointed; about half were from the Third World.[43]

Anglican bishop Jack Dain from Australia was elected chairman. Graham himself acted as honorary chairman. The English theologian John Stott led a team of five who summarized the results of the congress in the Lausanne Covenant.

The congress almost didn't take place due to a lack of funding. It was Ruth Graham who encouraged her husband and his team to stick to the original plan. She was convinced that there would probably never be another opportunity to assemble so many Christian leaders from around the world to work together on the fulfillment of the Great Commission. In the end, the Billy Graham Evangelistic Association paid three-fourths of the budget.

In his opening speech, Graham spoke about the collapse of evangelization in many of the liberal churches. He saw the loss of conviction that the Bible was absolutely trustworthy as the reason for this development, as well as the pursuit of an organizational, artificial unit rather than unity centered on the common task of evangelization. To counteract these dangers, he appealed to the participants to renew their endorsement of the Bible's absolute authority for life and faith and to sign a paper of commitment to biblical evangelism coupled with social action. This declaration was meant not only to serve as an orientation for evangelicals but also to act as a counterpart to the World Council of Churches' one-sided definition of missions that left out biblical evangelism.

In his speech, Graham emphasized the Christians' duty to take care of social hardship, but not at the cost of sharing the gospel of Jesus Christ. He also pointed out the danger of confusing God's kingdom with a specific culture or political program. This wise advice was particularly appropriate in view of the ongoing Vietnam War, which was constantly present in the media during the Lausanne Congress and which also threatened to divide Christians. Was the message of Jesus as the only peacemaker out of place in view of the horrible tragedy taking place? Could a Christian any longer abstain from social responsibility and from dealing with the suffering not only in Vietnam but also in other places? Was Philip Potter, general secretary of the Ecumenical Council, right when, in his opening address in Bangkok, he compared the history of Western missions to the entanglement of colonialism and imperialism and the failure to ease Africa's and Asia's need?

Graham had to reply to that:

> It seems to me that we are always in danger of falling into at least three or four errors on social action. The first is to deny that we have any social responsibility as Christians. It is true that this is not our priority mission. However, it is equally true that Scripture calls us time and again to do all in our power to alleviate human suffering and to correct injustice.
>
> The second error is to let social concern become our consuming mission. Jesus said, "What shall it profit a man if he gain the whole world and lose his own soul?" . . . Without a personal relationship with Christ, man is "lost" in this world and the next. . . .
>
> A third error is to identify the Gospel with any one particular political program or culture. This has been my own danger. When I go to preach the Gospel, I go as an ambassador for the Kingdom of God—not America. To tie the Gospel to any political system, secular program, or society is dangerous and will only serve to divert the Gospel. The Gospel transcends the goals and methods of any political system or any society, however good it may be.[44]

The significance of social responsibility as a part of Christian missions was described even more clearly in the Lausanne Covenant. John Stott and a team of five under his leadership worked late into the

night, summarizing
the findings of each
day's meetings. The
result of their work
became the Lausanne
Covenant. Graham
himself reviewed each
individual point in de-
tail together with his
brother-in-law, Cana-
dian theologian Leigh-
ton Ford. According to

John Stott from Great Britain was the key architect of both
the Lausanne Covenant and fifteen years later the Manila
Manifesto.

Graham, Ford made a contribution to the formulation of the Lausanne Covenant equal to that of Stott, who was officially in charge.
The Lausanne Covenant is probably the most important result of
the Lausanne Congress. (The full text of the Lausanne Covenant
can be found at www.lausanne.org.)

Contrary to the World Council of Churches' increasingly liberal
and nebulous view of missions, the Lausanne Congress held up the
banner for a biblical understanding of evangelism and missions. It
gave evangelical mission-practicing Christians an identity and thus
also a voice. It also contributed significantly to the unity of evangelical
Christians from both the Old World and the New, from established
as well as younger churches.

Despite initial opposition from Graham, a permanent organization was created after Lausanne '74 to continue to promote
the Lausanne issues throughout the world: the Lausanne Committee
for World Evangelization. It was later called the Lausanne Movement for World Evangelization or simply the Lausanne Movement
or even just Lausanne. Graham transferred the leadership of the
Lausanne Committee to his brother-in-law, theologian Leighton
Ford. Ford once emphasized how much the Lausanne Movement
meant to Graham:

I think Lausanne represents Billy. I don't think it represents his organization, which is centered on actually doing evangelism. Billy's broad
view of evangelism and social issues and theology and churchmanship
are not represented as much in the organization as in Billy himself.[45]

For obvious reasons, Americans see Billy Graham mainly as the
evangelist of the masses who proclaimed the gospel all over the world,
even behind the Iron Curtain. They also see him as "America's pastor"
and the spiritual advisor of twelve presidents. For non-Americans, he
is also the evangelical voice of the second half of the twentieth century. He defined evangelical concerns and contributed enormously to
the worldwide fulfillment of the Great Commission, not the least by
equipping others for their evangelistic mission. The former director
of the Baptist World Alliance, Nilson Fanini from Brazil, confirmed
the Lausanne Movement's enormous worldwide impact. According to him, God used the Lausanne Movement to revive the spirit
of evangelism and missions throughout the world. Fanini has been
ministering in over eighty countries, and he points out that he has
seen the impact of Lausanne all over the world.

The Lausanne Movement helped to prevent the theology of evangelical Protestantism from becoming clouded by God's enemy. Graham believed that the best defense against a liberal theology was an
intellectually profound biblical theology. Such a theology is conscious
of its limits and therefore always aware of the need of the illuminating
work of the Holy Spirit. By combining theology that is faithful to
the Bible with evangelistic practice, the main thrust remains intact,
which is to get to know God better and deeper and not merely to
accumulate knowledge about God. The Lausanne Movement made
it possible for heart and mind to come together again. Today, Graham stands for Lausanne, at least outside of North America, and
Lausanne represents a view of Christian missions that includes social
responsibility but without losing sight of the christological center
and the evangelistic focus.

Time and again, I have experienced how broad-based initiatives, such as the missionary network Hope for Europe or the two international conferences EXPLO '91 and EXPLO 2000, held in Lausanne and televised internationally, did not waste time trying to formulate a common theological foundation but quickly agreed to use the Lausanne Covenant as their basis. The Lausanne Covenant has truly become something like a summary of what evangelical faith and missions comprise.

In my opinion, the Lausanne '74 Congress, together with the Lausanne Covenant, is one of Billy Graham's most significant legacies. Thanks to Lausanne '74, the increasing erosion of the meanings of salvation and missions was halted and God's Word was again proclaimed as the trustworthy foundation for all activities of the body of Christ. Thanks to Lausanne '74, the evangelicals received a common identity. Lausanne '74 connected the most diverse Christians. Representatives of the established churches got to know the enthusiastic representatives of the newer churches, and the representatives of the newer churches, mainly from the Two-Thirds World, came to know members of the established churches who were just as committed to evangelize the world and help the needy as they were. The long-time president of the German branch of Trans World Radio, Horst Marquardt, stressed the importance of this fact in his booklet "25 Years of the Lausanne Movement":

Most everyone seems to have found it enriching that all of a sudden, people from established churches were sitting next to

Anglican bishop Jack Dain, chairman of the Lausanne '74 Congress, and Billy Graham signing the Lausanne Covenant.

members of free churches, Charismatics next to Anticharismatics, Pentecostals next to people from various evangelical fellowships, representatives of the Missions' Department of the Protestant Church with delegates from the Conference of Evangelists together with representatives of the German Evangelical Alliance and the so-called parachurch ministries—a variety never before experienced. . . . The Congress in Lausanne pointed out that the task of evangelization is never finished. It is great to see how many heard this. . . . Quite a few people made themselves available to the Lord again in Lausanne. They prayed for forgiveness of their sins. After Lausanne, many evangelists evangelized with new authority, preachers preached with new joy, theologians discovered the value of the Holy Scriptures, missionaries found new courage.[46]

The Lausanne Movement served as a worldwide catalyst for evangelistic strategies and projects. As a result of Lausanne '74, many Lausanne branches in countless countries, often in cooperation with national Evangelical Alliances, sprung up in order to implement the decisions of Lausanne '74.

The Lausanne Congress left its mark on my country, Switzerland, too. The Swiss delegation's report concluded with the following remarks: "Congregations of different denominations should learn to cooperate in evangelistic undertakings. . . . The lostness of Switzerland must grip our hearts. Switzerland, hear his voice!"[47]

All over the world, national Lausanne Movements were initiated as a result of Lausanne '74. Their goal was and still is to coordinate and promote the evangelistic efforts in their countries. In many countries, so-called mass evangelism was again advocated in addition to a renewed emphasis on personal and church-based evangelism using a variety of methods and tools. Horst Marquardt had the following to say about this:

We recognized anew that evangelistic events, including mass evangelism, have a particular importance. We ask our churches and communities to plan and help support such events. At the same time, we must also go new and unusual ways. Imagination and creativity help to make Jesus' testimony easier to comprehend.[48]

In 1989, fifteen years after the Lausanne Congress, another International Congress on World Evangelization was held in Manila in the Philippines. Manila '89, or Lausanne II in Manila, as the congress has also been called, tried to show more profoundly why a holistic understanding of missions must include both evangelism as well as practical efforts to ease suffering. The main theme, "Proclaim Christ until He Comes: Calling the Whole Church to Take the Whole Gospel to the Whole World," already made it clear that not only the word of love but also acts of love are part of the gospel. Social concern was unquestionably an integral part of a comprehensive view of missions. Manila was also the right place to show participants from the Western world the need for practical action and social change. Even on the way from my hotel to the conference building, I passed by people clothed in rags sitting on the sidewalk and begging for the most basic necessities of life.

The Manila Congress was also significant in terms of the diversity of its participants: 4,300 delegates from 173 countries, including Eastern Europe and the Soviet Union, with a larger percentage of women and younger leaders than at previous gatherings.

The fact that 60 percent of the participants came from developing countries contributed to a greater sensitivity toward human suffering. It was impossible to remain blind to their urgent needs without losing credibility as Christians. The speech of the newly elected director of the Lausanne Committee, Tom Houston, was groundbreaking. He emphasized that the world would only be fully evangelized once the gospel was brought to the poor, whereby the word *poor* was a collective term for all kinds of needy people.

A major way in which we can make the Good News of Jesus convincing in a hostile or reluctant world is to show by our compassion its relevance to the poor and their needs. We will also be able to combat secularism in the West if we restore this kind of authenticity to the Good News of Jesus Christ.[49]

In an interview I conducted with Houston, he emphasized the importance of ministry authenticated by signs of God's presence, such as practical deeds of love and affection but also spiritual gifts such as healing and deliverance. These signs of God's presence would authenticate our message of God's love and transforming power.

In Manila, there was a widespread consensus that we should aim for a broad transformation of all domains of society according to fundamental Christian values. But it was equally emphasized that the transformation should happen from the inside out in the form of spiritually renewed people who live in renewed relationships. Only by connecting with Jesus, the "Prince of Peace" (Isa. 9:6), can true peace be accomplished. Only in close communion with him can a just society be formed. Jesus's command that we should be the earth's salt and light includes both evangelistic preaching and a call to personal repentance as well as actions that promote solidarity and justice in society. Both the proclamation of eternal salvation in Jesus Christ and efforts toward social justice must draw their strength from God's power and love. These were no longer regarded as contradictory but instead as harmoniously enhancing one another.

More than twenty years after Manila '89 and exactly one hundred years after the World Missionary Conference in Edinburgh, the Lausanne Movement organized another congress in cooperation with the World Evangelical Alliance. The Third International Congress for World Evangelization (Lausanne III) took place in Cape Town, South Africa, in October 2010. A total of 4,200 delegates from 197 countries attended. Unfortunately, most delegates from China were unable to attend, as the Christians from nonregistered churches were prevented from leaving their country.

In a written welcome to the participants, Billy Graham under-scored the necessity of analyzing the changes that had taken place since Lausanne '74 and of evaluating their impact on the missionary mandate given by God. At the same time, he emphasized that the gospel and our Christian mission never change:

> But in all your deliberations, I pray you may never forget that some things have not changed in the last 36 years—nor will they ever change until our Lord returns. For one thing, the deepest needs of the human heart have not changed—the need to be reconciled to God, and to experience His love and forgiveness and transforming power. Nor has the Gospel changed—the Good News that God loves us and sent his only Son, Jesus Christ, into the world to forgive us and save us by His death and resurrection. Nor has Christ's command to His disciples changed—the mandate to go into all the world and proclaim the Gospel, urging men and women everywhere to put their faith and trust in Jesus Christ as Savior and Lord.
>
> I am praying that during your time in Cape Town the Holy Spirit will not only continue what has been done in previous conferences, but that He will increase your burden for a lost and dying world, and cause you to rededicate yourself to the priority and urgency of evange-lism. May He also encourage and refresh you as you gather together in Bible study, prayer and fellowship. As you leave Cape Town, may you go with a renewed commitment to live for Christ, and a fresh deter-mination to walk humbly

At Manila '89, Leighton Ford, brother-in-law of Billy Graham and chairman of the Lausanne Commit-tee, thanks Thomas Wang and his wife for their leadership role in Manila '89 and in the Lausanne Movement as a whole.

with Him every day. Never lose sight of your calling, but keep your eyes on Christ every day as you take time to be with Him in prayer and personal Bible study.

For eight days, representatives from all over the world discussed what it means to fulfill the Great Commission today. Special emphasis was placed on personal interaction in small groups at the tables, where the topics addressed in the lectures could be discussed in greater depth in multicultural groups. Workshops offered delegates opportunities to examine current problems in various social contexts and tried to define a Christian response based on God's Word. It was repeatedly pointed out that the word of love often only becomes credible when coupled with loving action.

Pranitha Timothy, director of Aftercare, International Justice Mission (IJM) in Chennai, India, urged her listeners to carry Jesus's light into the darkness of the world: "We must stand committed to bringing the light of Christ into the hidden darkness. We must demonstrate that our God is just, that our God sees the suffering and hears the cries." She emphasized that we can count on God's blessing only if we are passionate about the well-being of our fellow human beings, as God is. Other sessions discussed social problems such as human trafficking, the suffering of a broken world and broken families, and the corruptive influence of megacities.

Speakers repeatedly emphasized the importance of developing equal partnerships at an equal level in order to respond effectively to human needs. Increasingly, Christians from the Two-Thirds World carry out cross-border missions and send ambassadors of Christ to the First World. Many countries that formerly received missionaries from the First World have recognized their missional responsibility to help reach the increasingly secularized industrial countries of the West. Especially Christians who must live out their faith under oppression and persecution have a lot to offer the "soft" Western Christians who tend to avoid suffering at all costs. Christians whose lives are shaped through pain and trials are a powerful testimony to the comfortable Christians in the affluent Western world. Many delegates acknowledged that personal encounters with Christians from other cultures were just as valuable as the messages and workshops. Friendships were made that might someday result in ministry partnerships.

The so-called Cape Town Commitment (see the full text at www.lausanne.org/ctcommitment) attempted to recall and refresh the key points of the Lausanne Covenant and at the same time address the great challenges brought on by rapid global change. The Cape Town Commitment specifically emphasized that the content of the gospel remains unchanging even as our world is constantly changing: "The Gospel is not a concept that needs fresh ideas but a story that needs fresh telling." The Cape Town Commitment clearly rejected purely human attempts at transformation by pointing out the centrality of the Holy Spirit in all forms of missionary endeavors:

> Our engagement in mission, then, is pointless and fruitless without the presence and power of the Holy Spirit. This is true of mission in all its dimensions: evangelism, bearing witness to the truth, discipling, peace-making, social engagement, ethical transformation, caring for creation, overcoming evil powers, casting out demonic spirits, healing the sick, suffering and enduring under persecution. All we do in the name of Christ must be empowered by the Holy Spirit.

At the same time, the commitment emphasized the importance of trusting in the credibility and authority of God's Word illuminated by the Holy Spirit:

> We receive the whole Bible as the word of God, inspired by God's Spirit, spoken and written through human authors. We submit to it as supremely and uniquely authoritative, governing our belief and our behavior. We testify to the power of God's word to accomplish his purpose of salvation. We affirm that the Bible is the final written word of God not surpassed by any further revelation, but we also rejoice that the Holy Spirit illumines the minds of God's people so

that the Bible continues to speak God's truth in fresh ways to people in every culture.

In her session titled "A Fresh Approach to Witness in the Twenty-First Century," Rebecca M. Pippert, international speaker and author, stressed the importance of living authentic relationships when sharing the gospel: "The problem with evangelism is often not that we lack information; it is that we have failed to be ourselves." The Cape Town Commitment put it similarly: "There is no biblical mission without biblical living. Nothing commends the gospel more eloquently than a transformed life."

Far more than in previous statements by the Lausanne Movement, the Cape Town Commitment upheld the Christian responsibility to preserve creation, borne by the conviction that if we love God, we also love his creation and are bound to preserve it:

> Such love for God's creation demands that we repent of our part in the destruction, waste and pollution of the Earth's resources and our collusion in the toxic idolatry of consumerism. Instead, we commit ourselves to urgent and prophetic ecological responsibility.

In his closing speech, Lindsay Brown, executive manager of the Lausanne Movement, emphasized the importance of a holistic Christian witness carried out at the expense of neither loving action nor evangelistic proclamation:

> Some of us are word-centered; our challenge is to balance that with empathy and care for the needy and broken. For those in ministries of compassion, our challenge may be to ensure that we sensitively, compassionately, and wisely, but also verbally, communicate the gospel. Our model is Jesus, who both spoke to and fed the five thousand.

Doug Birdsall, the executive chairman of the Lausanne Movement, reminded the congress participants never to forget their foundations. Quoting Graham, he admonished the delegates, "Keep evangelism at the center. Make Christ your focus. Base everything on Scripture. And pray, pray, pray."[50]

Lausanne III in Cape Town not only extended and deepened the legacy of Berlin '66, Lausanne '74, and Manila '89 but also reinforced the impact of the three Conferences for Itinerant Evangelists, Amsterdam '83/'86/2000 convened by Billy Graham and the BGEA. At the three conferences in Amsterdam, thousands of evangelists from all over the world, particularly the developing countries, were equipped for their evangelistic ministry.

Lausanne III brought church leaders and missiologists together with evangelistic practitioners just as the previous congresses in Berlin, Lausanne, and Manila had done. This combination of theory and practice characterized these gatherings perhaps more than anything else. Evangelistic passion was linked with profound theological reflection and missiological research, revealing that the challenges of the future require both a sound mind and a passionate heart. Effective holistic missions require a collaboration of people with different giftings, as the apostle Paul put it in his letter to the Ephesians:

> So Christ himself gave the apostles, the prophets, the evangelists, the pastors and teachers, to equip his people for works of service, so that the body of Christ may be built up until we all reach unity in the faith and in the knowledge of the Son of God and become mature, attaining to the whole measure of the fullness of Christ. (4:11–13)

9

Empowerment—Spirit-Led Living

Come Holy Spirit, convict, consecrate, convert, blow as the wind, reveal as the light, burn as the fire, and may we see no one but Jesus tonight![1]

Billy Graham

As a staff member at many of Billy Graham's crusades, I was always impressed anew by his great sensitivity towards the Holy Spirit's leading. Billy Graham had a special gift of hearing God's soft voice and therefore always knew when the right time had come for a particular matter.[2]

Viktor Hamm, director of BGEA Europe

One of the most striking things in my view about Mother's spiritual life has been her attitude of obedience to God. If Mother believes the Lord is directing her to do something, then there is no question as to whether she will do it. . . . Mother seems to yield immediately. Her attitude is, and has been since I can remember, "My Commander has spoken; it is my joy to follow."[3]

Ruth "Bunny" Graham, daughter

B ritish prime minister Benjamin Disraeli (1804–81) once wrote, "The greatest good you can do for another is not just to share your riches, but to reveal to him his own."[4]

The most important task of any leader is to develop the God-given potential in the people he or she leads. A leader must see people through God's eyes. He should focus more on what a person can become by God's grace and the enabling of the Holy Spirit than on his or her present condition. A good leader encourages his followers constantly by pointing to their gifts and potential. At the same time, a good leader reminds his associates of the fact that spiritual giants are not born and that big shots are small shots who kept on shooting. A true leader continually affirms his trust in the people he is leading. He urges them to pray and recognize their dependence on the Lord by laying out a faith-inspired vision that goes far beyond what they have ever achieved. He instills faith in the unlimited power of the Holy Spirit to change people and situations. The leader himself acts as an example by not giving up before reaching his own God-given potential.

Billy Graham always wanted those around him to become all the Lord intended them to be. He therefore gave his co-workers great freedom to develop their God-given gifts to the fullest, even if it meant they would leave the BGEA. When Dick Jenson turned down Graham's offer to become press secretary in order to have more time for his family, Graham wrote that he felt Jenson would have been a wonderful press secretary. Then he continued:

> I think you have made the right choice. I really want you to do what the Lord would have you to do. I have never given orders to the members of my Association. I want them to have great freedom within the boundaries of the Association to do what the Lord would have them to do.

Graham was not a directive leader but a leader who empowered his colleagues. V. Raymond Edman, president of Wheaton College during the years when Billy and Ruth were students there, was certainly a role model for Graham in this area. Billy Graham spoke of him "as the most unforgettable Christian" he had ever met. In the foreword of Edman's biography, *In the Presence of the King*, by Earle E. Cairns, Graham describes the reason why he felt this way: Raymond Edman took an interest in Ruth Bell and Billy Graham. He always addressed them by their first name, as he did all the other students. He always had a word of encouragement for them. Graham said:

> During the early days of my own ministry as an evangelist, he encouraged me at every level. . . . On several occasions he called me to his office for prayer. . . . Often he gave me little gospel outlines because he knew I was struggling to prepare new sermons while taking a full school load. I always was amazed at how much time he seemed to have for everyone.[5]

Edman saw great potential not only in Billy but also in Ruth. When Billy and Ruth were dating, "Proxy," as President Edman was called by the students, passed Billy on campus one day and commented to him, "Bill, Ruth is one in a million." According to Billy, that short sentence helped him to confirm that Ruth was to be his life companion. When Billy was later criticized, by both the extreme right and the extreme left, Proxy would always smile and have a word of encouragement. "Billy, pay no attention. You have only one person to please, and that's the Lord." Edman later became a charter member of the BGEA board of directors and was known for his ability to always put some spiritual framework into a business meeting. It was his habit to go to bed early, saying, "You cannot accomplish anything after nine o'clock." But he also got up early so he could be empowered by the Lord in prayer, worship, and by studying the Scriptures, which allowed him to empower others in turn.

Edman is the author of the classic *They Found the Secret*, in which he describes how various people were fundamentally changed by the transforming power of the Holy Spirit by clinging to Jesus day in and day out. Few books have helped me as much as this one to understand the importance of not relying on my own strength but of being empowered and led by the Spirit of God. Everyone experiences this empowerment and transformation by the Holy Spirit in a different way and might use different words to describe it. But the principle is always the same, as the short biographies of various people in Edman's book show: when people give up trying to lead their lives in their own strength and entrust the leadership of their lives to the Lord Jesus, he in turn empowers and leads them by his Spirit. One result of this transformation is a peace beyond human understanding and a deep knowledge that God's favor does not have to be earned. We receive a deep foundation for our lives when we realize that we are children of the King of kings. Such a life cannot be easily shaken.

Billy and Ruth Graham have fascinated me ever since I was a teenager. I admired Billy Graham's big vision, which included the whole world. Heads of state came and went. Graham stayed, seemingly unaffected by what was happening around him. The Grahams did not seem to be the typical pious sort of people. I marveled at how they managed to remain so normal and modest, so approachable and authentic despite all the public attention they received and all the fuss that was made about them. What is the reason why all the attention didn't go to Billy's head? How did the stage team (Billy Graham, Cliff Barrows, and Bev Shea) manage to stay together all those years? Why did they never deviate from their evangelistic commission? I wanted to find what gave this couple and their closest co-workers such stability. I was convinced that knowing this secret would be helpful not only for me but also for countless leaders, future evangelists, and even Christians in general.

Many assumptions were confirmed during my study of their lives and ministry. Yet I also made several surprising discoveries that didn't fit the picture I had of the Grahams. One underlying principle was the importance they placed on the Holy Spirit. While Billy more strongly emphasized the Holy Spirit's ability to empower, it was important for

Ruth that the Spirit stands beside us every day as a divine Counselor and Helper. Ruth spoke less of the Holy Spirit than Billy did, but she experienced him in everyday life just as much. This increased the more she submitted her entire life to God, praying that God would speak to her. As it was her goal always to be "online" with God, she experienced how he repeatedly revealed his good intentions toward her, even through small, everyday things. Ruth often spoke about how important it is to listen to God's soft voice in the midst of our everyday lives and to follow his instructions. She wanted her life and actions to be in tune with God's will. Once when she was visiting friends, she had an unusual experience:

> I was in our bedroom. The phone rang. Instantaneously our TV set came on. Since I'm not electrically or mechanically minded, such things are beyond me. But I could wish that I, as a Christian, could be so spiritually attuned to God that when someone is hurting or in need, He could, as it were, by remote control (an impulse, a suggestion from a friend, a Bible verse recalled, a divine "nudge") turn me on.[6]

Many who were in contact with Ruth, not least Billy himself, testify to her special gift of instantly recognizing people's needs. During my visits to Montreat and the surrounding area, I heard two main comments about Ruth over and over again. First, she was a very humorous, spirited person with a sharp wit and spirit—one store owner called her a "firecracker"—and second, she was often the first person to appear when someone was living through difficult times. She had just the right word or expression of love and interest for each person. Billy benefited from Ruth's help more than anyone else. He emphasized that she often drew from her vast store of knowledge to point out the right Bible verse for a certain topic or to provide the corresponding illustration for a sermon.

Ruth was an attentive observer of current events and an avid reader of books and magazines. God often spoke to her through the things she read or through daily events. She used this gift with the people she met as a way to make biblical truths come alive. Ruth's greatest role model was Jesus Christ himself, who often used common occurrences to explain spiritual truths. Ruth's first and foremost source of inspiration was the Word of God. She often compared several versions and translations of a biblical text and tried to understand the original wording of a text with the help of Bible commentaries. Her question was always, "Lord, what do you want to tell me?" Ruth once said, "We . . . need to keep carefully studying our Book of Instructions, listening attentively when our Instructor speaks, and promptly following His instructions."[7]

Ruth encouraged others to listen to and take heed of what God was telling them:

> When we were in school, we always kept a notebook handy to take notes on the professor's lecture. How much more important it is to take notes when God is teaching us. If a busy housewife has to clear off a spot for Bible study during a crowded day, she is likely to put it off. But if she has a place where her Bible is always open and handy, whenever there is a lull in the storm she can grab a cup of coffee and sit down for a few minutes or more of pure refreshment and companionship. Now, while working around the house, driving the car, ironing, shopping, or whatever I may be doing, some verse I have memorized will slip into my mind at an unexpected moment, and may be exactly the word I need.[8]

The Bible verses she learned by heart were Ruth's assets. When she could no longer remember Bible verses as a result of her accident, she felt totally destitute: "Suddenly I felt as a man must feel who learns the bank has failed and he has lost his life savings. 'Lord,' I begged, 'You can have anything I've got, but please give me back my Bible verses.'"[9] The first Bible verse she then recalled was, "I have loved you with an everlasting love; I have drawn you with unfailing kindness" (Jer. 31:3). Ruth said, "It was there, given back when I most needed it."

256

Billy Graham was brought up in a Calvinistic Presbyterian church, and the Graham family later attended a Calvinistic Presbyterian church in Montreat. John Calvin emphasized the Bible as God's authoritative Word and the only guideline for faith and life. But he equally stressed that the Spirit acts through the Word and the Word is confirmed by the Spirit. In *Institutio* II.3.10., Calvin explained the guiding role of the Holy Spirit:

> The Lord by his Spirit directs, bends, and governs our heart and reigns in it as his possession. . . . It is obviously the privilege of the elect that regenerated through the Spirit of God, they are moved and governed by his leading.

In the Geneva Catechism (Q 128/OS II 96), Calvin defined repentance as the hatred of sin and the will to please God through a holy life. He then put it in relation to a life led and governed by the Holy Spirit:

> These things lead us to denial of self and mortification of flesh, so that we yield ourselves to be ruled by the Spirit of God, and bring all the actions of our life into obedience to the divine will.

Calvin is often acknowledged as the "theologian of the Holy Spirit" among the reformers of the sixteenth century.

The Holy Spirit speaks to us through the Bible as his instrument. Being familiar with God's Word is the best prerequisite to being filled and led by the Holy Spirit himself. This partnership of Word and Spirit is illustrated by the apostle Paul in his letters.

> Let the message of Christ dwell among you richly as you teach and admonish one another with all wisdom through psalms, hymns, and songs from the Spirit, singing to God with gratitude in your hearts. (Col. 3:16)

> Be filled with the Spirit, speaking to one another with psalms, hymns, and songs from the Spirit. Sing and make music from your heart to

the Lord, always giving thanks to God the Father for everything, in the name of our Lord Jesus Christ. (Eph. 5:18–20)

According to Calvin, the more we live out God's Word, the better the Holy Spirit can fill our lives with his presence and shape our lives. The more we absorb the biblical truths and "metabolize" them, the closer our relationship with Jesus Christ is and the more spiritual fruit our lives will bear! Let us recall Jesus's words in the parable of the vine and the branches:

If you remain in me and my words remain in you, ask whatever you wish, and it will be done for you. This is to my Father's glory, that you bear much fruit, showing yourselves to be my disciples. (John 15:7–8)

Ruth was a good disciple of John Calvin, especially where the role of the Bible was concerned. She challenged women to honestly examine themselves and to ask the question, "Are we building our homes according to God's building code? Is our blueprint the Bible?"[10] She then added, "The Bible is the most relevant, the most exciting, the most marvelously practical book in the world today."[11]

Ruth considered her entire life as a service to God. In Romans 12:1–2, the apostle Paul connects this attitude of total commitment with the capacity to discern God's will:

Therefore, I urge you, brothers and sisters, in view of God's mercy, to offer your bodies as a living sacrifice, holy and pleasing to God—this is your true and proper worship. Do not conform to the pattern of this world, but be transformed by the renewing of your mind. Then you will be able to test and approve what God's will is—his good, pleasing and perfect will.

According to Ruth, we can only discern and carry out God's will to the extent that we have relinquished our own selfish will at the foot of Christ's cross. Ruth was by nature very strong-willed, and she had firm convictions, which was also one of her great gifts. She

258

described herself as someone who tended to be stubborn. But because she always submitted her thoughts and opinions to God's examination and accepted his correction, she was capable of recognizing the Holy Spirit's leading and was able to do what God wanted her to do at any given moment. She could also leave things whose time had not yet come.

In times of increasingly rapid change, the ability to react quickly is essential. Discerning God's will in a given situation and carrying it out will become even more important as the pace of life accelerates. We must learn to listen to the still, small voice of the Holy Spirit in order to assist him in his plans and not misuse him simply to fulfill our own plans. We must practice to discern God's voice among the many other voices that seek our attention.

My very practically minded paternal grandfather, an embroidery manufacturer by trade, once gave me a valuable tip. I had read through old letters from my grandparents' German friends during World War II and afterward. I noticed sentences like, "Hans, how happy you made us! How could you possibly have known that we can't get any suspenders right now?" Or, "The potatoes arrived just at the right time." So I asked Grandpa to explain. His answer has remained forever in my memory because of its simplicity: "When something good that we could do to other people crosses my mind or my wife's, then we just do it. It could be from the Lord."

Ruth was convinced that God normally speaks to us through everyday circumstances. He leads us to do things simply by guiding our thoughts in his preferred direction. When she felt something needed to be done, she did it.

Jesus emphasizes in John 10 that sheep can distinguish between their shepherd's voice and the voices of others to whom the sheep do not belong. However, our problem is often that we do not listen: "For God does speak—now one way, now another—though no one perceives it" (Job 33:14). For this reason, it is crucial for us to regularly get away from the hectic pace of life to slow down and intentionally "tune in" to God's frequency.

Ruth was someone who tried to align her inner antenna to God throughout her life. She wanted to pick up the Holy Spirit's faintest signals. Ruth's sensitivity and readiness to obey God in all things made it possible for him to continuously give her both large and small assignments, which she willingly carried out. Ruth's constant endeavor was not to be ruled by her own emotions but by the truths of the Bible and by the Holy Spirit.

Why is it so important to be constantly filled with the Holy Spirit?

On January 1, 2012, my wife and I exchanged deliberations concerning the future. We discussed the need to keep an attitude of faith and a positive attitude in an increasingly uncertain world in which we are daily bombarded with negative news. How are we ourselves able to keep our thoughts on the Lord and his will for our lives, and how can we help others not to become depressed but to be a strong light in a world that needs orientation and strength more than ever?

It must have been God who led my thoughts to a small booklet that I have kept in the drawer of my bedside table for many years. It's a German translation of an article Nelson Bell first published in *Christianity Today* in 1973. In this article, he points out how important it is to guard our hearts and to keep clean thoughts. He quotes Romans 12:2: "Do not conform to the pattern of this world, but be transformed by the renewing of your mind." Bell points out that even the most pious Christian is constantly challenged to shut the entry door to his heart from unholy intruders who steal our joy and strength and make us say things that are not helpful, to say the least. "Above all else, guard your heart, for everything you do flows from it. Keep your mouth free of perversity; keep corrupt talk far from your lips" (Prov. 4:23–24). Bell continues to emphasize our need to be cleansed, which is possible as soon as we realize our need and bring it to the Lord, as David did: "Create in me a pure heart, O God, and renew a steadfast spirit within me" (Ps. 51:10).

Bell then points out that God's enemy always attacks the weak points in our lives, be it a low self-image, rejection, self-pity, jealousy, sexual impurity, pride, or fear. Realizing that our thoughts do not reflect God's truth in our lives, we have to renounce them and bring them under the control of the Holy Spirit. "We demolish arguments and every pretension that sets itself up against the knowledge of God, and we take captive every thought to make it obedient to Christ" (2 Cor. 10:5). Then we have to fill our hearts with things that are true and uplifting: "Finally, brothers and sisters, whatever is true, whatever is noble, whatever is right, whatever is pure, whatever is lovely, whatever is admirable—if any thing is excellent or praiseworthy—think about such things" (Phil. 4:8).

Bell emphasizes that we need to keep our entry doors closed to the destructive thoughts inspired by the enemy. And this enemy especially likes to fill our hearts with negative thoughts regarding fellow Christians, by this sowing division in the body of Christ. His name is diabolos, which means someone who divides and creates disunity. We have to be careful to recognize quickly when God's enemy, who by nature is a liar, tries to infiltrate our thoughts with his lies. We have to respond in an opposite way. We are able to do this if we constantly let our thoughts and lives be cleansed and filled by the Holy Spirit and the Word of God. Walking in the power of the Holy Spirit and constantly keeping the biblical truth in our hearts, according to Bell, is the only remedy against all kinds of destructive whispers, whether they stem from our carnal self, the world, or Satan. And it is a lifelong learning process to discern the sources of our thoughts and fill our hearts with what is true and noble. Bell concludes that as a result of disciplining our thoughts and aligning them with the truth of the Bible, we are truly healthy, for our hearts and thoughts are filled with love, joy, peace, patience, and spiritual alertness.

Bell had an enormous influence on his daughter Ruth and her husband, Billy, as well as the wider Graham family. He was held in the greatest esteem by all who knew him. I'm sure one of the reasons is that he learned to let his thoughts, words, and actions be governed by the Holy Spirit.

One of the greatest challenges today to keeping spiritually alert is handling modern technical equipment in a wise way. Personal blogs and social networks such as Facebook and Twitter can reach thousands of people instantly and allow us to give testimony of our lives with Jesus Christ. One example: our French Facebook page, La Bible, has close to five hundred thousand "friends" who daily receive a Bible verse with a corresponding question to help apply the biblical content to everyday life. Yet we can also fill our precious time with trivial matters, making it nearly impossible to perceive God's quiet voice. Television is not identical with a wide vision. Too much time on Facebook can hinder us from facing the Book, the Bible. And we need smartness to deal smartly with smartphones. With cell phones and instant messaging, we can save time and energy and connect with others. But we can also waste time and energy that we could have used to build God's kingdom. It often takes time to leave the world's distractions fully behind and arrive in the holy of holies in prayer. Intentionally removing a source of diversion can make all the difference. Thus, it is important to shut out any disturbance in advance. It helps me personally to take long walks with God. In her younger years, Ruth sometimes climbed a tree to be alone with God.

Because she regularly took time out from the hustle and bustle around her, Ruth experienced the Holy Spirit as a Counselor in her life who helped her both to recognize God's will and to carry it out. He was also the one who gave her strength for each day and filled her with love for others. And when she was weak, he was beside her, renewing and restoring her.

Ruth and Billy's youngest son, Ned, experienced God's liberating and restoring power in a special way. Ned had suffered for a long time from the consequences of some painful events during his school years. He tried to fight the pain on his own. Let him tell how he found deliverance and new freedom in Christ: "I'm a rock climber and mountaineer, and I'd always pushed past pain in my life through sheer strength and willpower."[12] But he was unable to get rid of the pain in his life and became increasingly depressed: "I came to a point where I gave up everything. I stopped caring. I no longer feared death or life. I no longer feared failure or success. It was at that point that God could interact with me." Someone advised him to seek guidance from a pastoral counselor with experience in the area of inner healing.

With this counselor, he worked through his past, finally inviting Jesus to come with his healing power into all areas of his life. Completely free and with great joy and thankfulness, he was able to praise God for his restoration. When his mother was asked what changes she had noticed in her son, she replied, "Ned has been so much more thoughtful and attentive, and he exhibits more of the Spirit of God."

In another interview, Ned emphasized how that experience had shown him the importance of putting on the spiritual armor of Ephesians 6 every morning and ensuring that his thoughts and actions are based on God's promises in his Word. He realized the need to be daily empowered by the Holy Spirit in order to live a free and fruitful life.

⌒⸓⌐

What did the Holy Spirit mean to Billy Graham? How did he define the Holy Spirit's role in his personal life, as well as in his evangelistic ministry?

I was honestly surprised when I first heard that Billy Graham was going to write a book about the Holy Spirit. Graham was not generally considered a charismatic in the narrow sense of the word; at most, he could be considered an "other-type charismatic," as I would like to call it. Nevertheless, Graham's book *The Holy Spirit* opened the eyes of many Christians to the key significance of the Third Person of the Trinity in Christian life and ministry.

It is indisputable that Graham's heart was very close to God's heart. He often heard God's voice more distinctly than many around him. In such moments, this rather apprehensive man demonstrated absolute determination and fearlessness because he knew that God had spoken and that God would carry out everything just as he had planned. One impressive example of Graham's spiritual sensitivity was indicated in a *Time* magazine report of October 25, 1954:

> Billy's fondest hope is to spark a real religious revival in the US; and if any one person can do it, he is a likely candidate. He can prophesy: "The greatest sin of America is our disregard of God. . . . God has allowed evil nations to be destroyed by other wicked nations. . . . It may take persecution and humiliation to bring America to God. . . . When I see a beautiful city such as New York, I also have a vision of crumbling buildings and dust. I keep having the feeling that God will allow something to fall on us in a way I don't anticipate unless we return to Him."[13]

Perhaps *Time* was not too far off target by alluding to his prophetic gift. What was Graham's opinion of other spiritual gifts, such as healing?

Graham did not feel called to the ministry of healing. When asked about healing ministries, such as that of Oral Roberts, he said that he was thankful for people who were able to help others with such gifts but added, "My only specialty is soul-winning. I'm not a great philosopher, not a theologian, not an intellectual—God has given me the gift of winning souls."[14]

In light of his calling, discovering how highly Graham valued the Holy Spirit in his life and ministry takes on even more significance. Graham was convinced that the Holy Spirit is the true evangelist and that he himself was at most his mouthpiece. This mouthpiece, as he expressed it, would become a dead piece of clay if what was said no longer glorified Jesus alone. As he once stated, "Any activity that is not of the Holy Spirit is just a bunch of busyness." So he then waited many years before God gave him the okay to accept the New York churches' invitation to carry out a major mission there. In 1957, when *Newsweek* ran a detailed report on Graham and wanted to know the secret of his success in New York, he pointed to the Holy Spirit's power:

> Reporters can't understand how an intelligent university graduate can get up out of a crowd and come down front and commit himself to Christ. But while I'm talking there is another force at work—the Spirit of God. For many weeks maybe, the Spirit of God has been preparing that person. I have no power to convert anybody— that is the work of the Spirit of God.[15]

Billy sought to become a Greek to the Greek and a Naga to the Naga. This picture was taken during a mission in Kohima, Nagaland, in the northeastern part of India, in 1972. Graham spoke about being a warrior for Christ.

Graham always counted firmly on the Holy Spirit's powerful presence at his missions, and, as a result, he also experienced how God in his sovereignty drew large numbers of people to himself through the events. Sometimes the movement of the Holy Spirit was so strong that people began coming forward even before being asked to do so.

One married couple once had a particularly moving experience. They were initially disappointed and upset over having been seated in the middle of a group of noisy teenagers who were constantly whispering to each other. When Graham started to preach, Morgan and his wife were distracted by all the commotion around them. Suddenly, about halfway through the sermon, a hush fell over the entire group. What Morgan remembers most is the response of the teens around them. "Weeping, lots of weeping," he says. "All around us,

265

teens were weeping. Then just before the invitation a lot more were weeping and dozens got up and walked down the stairs—before the invitation had even been given. Hundreds left their seats to go forward to receive Christ that evening." This experience had a lasting effect on the couple. They had seen how the lives of thousands of people, including many teenagers, had been changed: "We were amid the power of God that night and saw him move."[16]

Such obvious evidence of the impact of the Holy Spirit confirmed Graham's conviction that the Spirit was the true evangelist and that he was at most his assistant. During his speech to church leaders prior to his 1954 mission in Dusseldorf, Germany, Graham described it this way:

> I want to repeat once again that I want to give all honor to God, the Holy Spirit, for what we experienced in our gatherings. I often stepped back in the meetings because I felt that I was put aside to let the Holy Spirit do the work. We need to be totally dependent on the Holy Spirit.[17]

At the 1952 annual meeting of the National Association of Evangelicals in Chicago, Graham spoke about the role the Holy Spirit plays in evangelism and revival. He first spoke about God's holiness:

This picture was taken at the 2005 New York mission and shows Dahlia Moxen of Brooklyn, New York, worshiping the Lord.

Every great Revival that ever came in the history of the world, or in the history of the Church, laid great emphasis on the holiness of God. Study the nature of God. Get every Scripture that you can find on the holiness and righteousness and purity of God, and study it and breathe it on your knees and you will be a different man or a different woman. Study it! Breathe it! Digest it! Read it!—until it grips your soul. God is a holy God.[18]

He then mentioned the role of personal sanctification: "It is time for personal consecration—holy living." Graham mentioned that, as a sign of a holy, revived life, we have to apply Jesus Christ's and the New Testament's teachings in everyday life. He then gave some practical examples:

We'll begin to forgive seventy times seven. We'll begin to turn the other cheek. We'll begin to go the second mile. We'll give our cloak as well as our coat. We'll begin to live by First Corinthians Thirteen and we'll love one another.[19]

He continued by emphasizing that love must be put into action as the firstfruits of the Holy Spirit in all areas, even toward those who do not share our opinions. Finally, he spoke directly to pastors and leaders present:

I want to ask you something. Are you filled with the Holy Spirit? . . . If you are not filled with the Holy Spirit then the things that you say and the decisions you reach may be led of the Spirit, or they may not be. You may be totally wrong in your whole life unless you are filled by the Spirit, and moment by moment led by Him. You are not a victorious Christian unless you are filled with the Spirit. You cannot be used of God unless you are filled with the Spirit.[20]

Stanley High, former publisher of *Reader's Digest*, wrote in his biography of Billy Graham, *The Personal Story of the Man*, about the secret of Graham's great and long-lasting influence. After following Graham closely for some time, he came to the conclusion that it was the redeeming power of the Holy Spirit that made the simple message so effective. High attributed the moving of the Spirit at Graham's missions to Graham's constant desire not to taint God's honor. High stated, "The fear he lives with is not that outwardly he may fail but that inwardly he may fail the Almighty." High mentioned that Graham once referred to the story of Samson and Delilah, saying that it could happen to him too. Just like Samson, he could lose his strength as a result of sin without even noticing it. Then High quoted Graham:

> I've been asking myself, sitting here: "Billy Graham, are you filled with the Holy Spirit?" My only claim to power is the Holy Spirit. Without that, whatever I do is of the energy of the flesh and will be burned up before the judgment seat of Christ. I don't care how big the crowds are and how big the reported results are; it's all "sounding brass and tinkling cymbal" unless I am filled with the Holy Spirit.[21]

After evaluating Graham and his ministry, High was convinced that Graham's resoluteness never to undertake anything without the help of the Holy Spirit contributed more than anything else to the great effectiveness of his ministry.

How did Graham come to understand the Holy Spirit's key importance?

While still on staff with Youth for Christ at the end of World War II, he got to know the young Welsh evangelist Stephen Olford in Great Britain. After Graham heard Olford speak about the importance of being filled with the Holy Spirit, he became conscious of the fact that he himself was lacking that experience. Of course, Graham knew he had received new life through the Holy Spirit and that as a result of his believing in Jesus Christ the Holy Spirit indwelt him. At the same time, he realized that he lacked the spiritual empowerment Olford so obviously possessed. Graham described it like this: "He had a dynamic . . . exhilaration about him I wanted to capture."

Graham approached Olford and said, "You've spoken of something that I don't have. . . . I want the fullness of the Holy Spirit in my life too." In a small hotel room, Olford went through all the biblical steps with Graham that led Graham to the discovery of a Spirit-filled life and to the renewal of his ministry. Olford explained to Graham how he had claimed this fulfillment and empowerment through the Holy Spirit by trusting in God's Word. Yet this would not happen without a prior inner brokenness. The vessel must first be emptied in order to be filled with God's Holy Spirit. Olford said, "As I talked, and I can see him now, those marvelous eyes glistened with tears, and he said, 'Stephen, I see it. That's what I want. That's what I need in my life.'" Both men then knelt and prayed that Graham would be filled with the Holy Spirit, just as the Bible promises. "I can still hear Billy pouring out his heart in a prayer of total dedication to the Lord." Together they praised God and thanked him with overflowing joy.[22]

As a result of his being filled with the Holy Spirit, more people than ever before responded to Graham's call to accept Jesus Christ into their lives as their Lord and Savior. More and more he learned to walk in the power of the Holy Spirit. Years later, Graham emphasized that being filled with the Holy Spirit enabled him to better understand what it meant to constantly live in an attitude of victory, because Jesus, the Victor, lives in us through the Holy Spirit.

Olford became a well-known evangelist himself and proclaimed the gospel from Great Britain to the nations on his international radio program *Encounter*. As an excellent Bible teacher, he became the spiritual mentor of many younger Christian leaders. Graham once said that Olford influenced his ministry like no other man. I heard Olford for the first time in 1983 at the first conference for evangelists organized by Graham in Amsterdam. Olford spoke there about the need for a holy life and the importance of absolute trust in the authority of God's Word. The power of a sermon, he said, was based on our being able to say with conviction, when quoting the Bible, "Thus says the Lord." We should always remind ourselves that under normal circumstances the Holy Spirit works in response to God's proclaimed Word, something of which many preachers unfortunately are not fully aware.

At the same Amsterdam conference, Graham called to the assembled evangelists from around the world: "May God set us ablaze with the fire from off the altar—may the Holy Spirit descend on us in mighty Pentecostal power. This is the word of the Lord. '"Not by might nor by power, but by my Spirit," says the Lord Almighty' (Zech. 4:6)." At the end of his presentation, he asked us to say three times aloud with him, "Not by might nor by power, but by my Spirit, says the Lord Almighty."

In Amsterdam, it is worth noting how Graham continually tried to draw the attention away from himself toward God. If the audience applauded him, he demonstratively applauded with them to demonstrate that God alone deserved all the praise.

The sixty years after World War II mark the period of Graham's public ministry. During those sixty years, two trends could be observed among the Bible-based, mission-minded Christians, or evangelicals. First, they returned to their pietistic and Puritan roots, where personal piety was always connected to responsibility for addressing society's miseries. Second, they went back even further, two thousand years, to the coming of the Holy Spirit, who turned fishermen into effective fishers of men. Graham always emphasized that the secret to the early Christians' power was the Holy Spirit and that we needed this power just as much as the early church. Both topics—the role of social responsibility as well as that of the Holy Spirit—were hotly debated by the evangelicals in the second half of the twentieth century.

I have already described how Graham and the missions congresses, especially those in Lausanne and Manila, reemphasized the holistic responsibility to meet the needs of the world. But what was the situation with the equally debated topic of the Holy Spirit, with his gifts and manifold fruit? What follows are Graham's main statements on this topic, beginning with his time at Youth for Christ, before he was known to a greater public.

In 1947, Graham described the Holy Spirit in his first book, *Calling Youth to Christ,* as a powerful ally standing by our side in spiritual battles:

> He demands Lordship. Thus, when you are entirely yielded to Him, He fills you with His Spirit, and His powerful dynamo called the Holy Spirit will enable you to stand against every onslaught of Satan. . . . It is not a battle with flesh and blood; it is a spiritual battle against principalities, against powers, against rulers of the darkness of this world, against spiritual wickedness in high places. The Holy Spirit is absolutely the only one who can give you the ability to "hold the line." Are you holding? Are you standing? Only as you "stand" against every attack can you say you are living above the clouds in glorious sunlight on the mountain slopes of God's love, peace, joy, happiness and pleasure. "In thy presence is fullness of joy; at thy right hand are pleasures forevermore."[23]

As part of the evangelistic campaign of 1949 in Los Angeles, Graham devoted an entire evening to the question of how people can be filled by the Holy Spirit. At first glance, it might seem inappropriate to speak about the Holy Spirit at an evangelistic event. But many Christian believers who had never heard about the empowerment of the Holy Spirit also attended such events. Bill Bright once described the message concerning how we can be continually filled and empowered by the Holy Spirit as the most important truth for people who want to lead a blessed life as a Christian. Here is an excerpt from Graham's sermon in Los Angeles on the role of the Holy Spirit:

> Are you filled with the Spirit? I am persuaded that our desperate need tonight is not a new organization, nor a new movement, nor a new method—we have enough of those. I believe the greatest need tonight is that our men and women who profess the name of Jesus Christ be filled with the Spirit. Are you filled with the Spirit? I do not believe it is possible to teach a Sunday school class with power unless you are filled with the Spirit. It is not possible to preach with power unless you are filled with the Spirit. It is not possible to reproduce the

life of Christ daily unless you are filled with the Spirit. "Be ye filled with the Spirit!" . . . I have asked God if there were ever a day when I should stand in the pulpit without knowing the fullness and anointing of the Spirit of God and should not preach with compassion and

"Be filled with the Spirit! It is not possible to reproduce the life of Christ daily unless you are filled with the Spirit."

fire, I want God to take me home to heaven. I don't want to live. I don't ever want to stand in the pulpit and preach without the power of the Holy Spirit. It's a dangerous thing.[24]

Several years later, in his weekly radio broadcast, *The Hour of Decision*, Graham highlighted certain aspects in his talk on "The Fruit of the Spirit":

The Bible teaches that the Holy Spirit is co-equal with God the Father and co-equal with God the Son. The Bible also teaches that the Holy Spirit is a Person. He is never to be referred to as "It." He's not just an agent, He's not just an influence. He is a mighty Person, the Holy Spirit of God. . . . The moment you come to Christ, the Spirit of God brings the life of God into you and your being to live. For the first time you begin to live with a capital "L." There's a spring in your step and a joy in your soul and a peace in your heart, and life has taken on a new outlook. There's a whole new direction to your life because the Spirit of God has given to you the very life of God, and God is an eternal God—that means you'll live as long as God lives. The Bible also teaches us that the Spirit of God produces the fruit of the Spirit. "But the fruit of the Spirit is love, joy, peace, longsuffering, gentleness, goodness, faith, meekness and temperance." Now these things, these nice things, nine clusters of fruit, are to characterize the life of every Christ-born child of God.[25]

A few years later, in an article titled "The Spirit of Pentecost" in the May 1961 issue of the magazine *Decision*, Graham again highlighted the connection between personal awakening by the Holy Spirit and a nationwide awakening:

Church history reveals that far more people are brought into the church during periods of revival than during eras of so-called normality. So many more, in fact, that I am convinced that revival is the normal condition of the Christian Church. The Church was born in a supernatural revival at Pentecost. It was nourished and invigorated by the revivals of the first century. It has been sustained by revivals down through the years. . . . The prophet Habakkuk once stood in the midst of a people who had been showered with every blessing conceivable, but who had lost their spiritual sanity, and he cried, "O Lord, revive thy work in the midst of the years" (Hab. 3:2). That is the heart-cry of consecrated people everywhere. Revival is America's greatest lack. It is the world's greatest lack. We need a revival of Christian faith, of Christian experience and God-consciousness. . . . God has said, "If my people . . . shall seek my face . . . " if they will rediscover that He is holy, real, actual, absolute and personal, then the reality of the truth will be transferred to the world and revival will ensue. It has worked through the centuries. It has worked in American history before. It will work again.

The New Testament Church has been told to "be filled with the Spirit." John the Baptist said concerning Christ, "He shall baptize you with the Holy Spirit and with fire." It is one thing for us to be born of God, and it is another thing for us to be aflame with God. I am convinced that it is possible for every child of God to become ablaze with God—to be in a spiritual sense like that bush in the wilderness which Moses saw aflame with God.[26]

It is quite striking to hear these words from the mouth of an evangelist. It clearly shows the importance Graham gave to God's sovereign action throughout his life.

In the opening speech of Berlin '66, Graham called the audience to expect a new outpouring of the Holy Spirit. He countered the idea that revivals belonged to the past and were no longer on God's agenda:

> In my travels I have met many sincere Christian leaders who believe that it is impossible to have a worldwide revival. Brethren, I do not believe that the day of miracles has passed. As long as the Holy Spirit abides and works on the Earth, the church's potential is the same as it was in the apostolic days. The great Paraclete has not been withdrawn; he still waits to work through those who are willing to meet his conditions of repentance, humility and obedience. Let us not limit God in his working, and let us not fail to be ready for new and great outpourings of the Holy Spirit in this critical period of history. We are now living in a generation when nothing will avail to break through the overwhelming power of Satan except supernatural power beyond what most Christians have known anything about.

These statements and the desire for spiritual revival are more relevant today than ever.

In his article "Why Lausanne?" in *Christianity Today*, Graham wrote extensively about the relationship between evangelism and the work of the Holy Spirit:

> There can be no adequate evangelism without the Holy Spirit. It is the Holy Spirit who convicts of sin, righteousness, and judgment. It is the Holy Spirit who performs the work of regeneration. It is the Holy Spirit who indwells believers. It is the Holy Spirit who guides, teaches, instructs, and fills the new believer. The great communicator of the gospel is the Holy Spirit. He uses ordinary people such as us as instruments—but it is his work![27]

In his closing speech at Lausanne '74 under the title "The King Is Coming," Graham dealt with the question of whether we could expect a revival of the Holy Spirit in view of the increasing spiritual darkness in the world:

> I believe there are two strains in prophetic Scripture. One leads us to understand that as we approach the latter days and the Second

Coming of Christ, things will become worse and worse. Joel speaks of "multitudes, multitudes, in the valley of decision!" The day of the Lord is near in the valley of decision. He is speaking of judgment. But I believe as we approach the latter days and the coming of the Lord, it could be a time also of great revival. We cannot forget the possibility and the promise of revival, the refreshing of the latter days ("the latter rains" of Hosea), or the outpouring of the Spirit promised in Joel 2:28, and repeated in Acts 2:17. That will happen right up to the advent of the Lord Jesus Christ. James seems to associate the "latter rains" with the return of Christ. Evil will grow worse, but God will be mightily at work at the same time. I am praying that we will see in the next months and years the "latter rains," a rain of blessings, showers falling from heaven upon all the continents before the coming of our Lord. There is a mystery of iniquity, but there is also a mystery of righteousness, and both are working simultaneously.[28]

Nine years after Lausanne '74, in 1983, the International Conference for Itinerant Evangelists took place in Amsterdam. In his welcome address, Graham emphasized how the disciples used all methods at their disposal to spread the faith and then continued:

We, too, need to explore every legitimate method for reaching our world for Christ. New challenges call for new methods and new strategies. But methods and organization alone are not enough, important as they may be. The reason is that we are involved in a spiritual battle. The evangelist and the work of evangelism are opposed on every hand by Satan and his forces. When the seed of the Gospel is being sown, he is always there sowing the tares (weeds) and blinding the minds of those whom we seek to evangelize. Let us not underestimate the strategy of Satan. He uses every kind of deception, force and error to try to destroy the effectiveness of the Gospel. He certainly will be opposed to this Conference, and we will sense his presence here.

But we know that greater is He that is in us than he that is in the world. We need to trust the Holy Spirit to guide, lead, and direct this Conference, just as we trust the Holy Spirit for the results in our evangelism, because He alone can give success. And that is why prayer is such a critical part of evangelism. There can be no discussion about methods unless we recognize that God's method is men and women. There is no doubt that the heart of the method of God is men and women who have been filled and anointed and called by the Holy Spirit, and are in turn witnessing for Him wherever God sends them. That is one reason why the greatest need of the hour is the revival of the Church of Jesus Christ. We are now living in a generation when nothing will break through the overwhelming power of Satan except the supernatural power of the Holy Spirit.

If the Church was supernaturally blessed of God at its birth, who will say that in the closing days of its witness here on Earth it will not be blessed in an even mightier way? Our prayer should be, as we leave Amsterdam ten days from now, "Oh, Lord, stir the flames of revival and begin in me!"[29]

Graham referred to people who are filled with the Holy Spirit as *the* evangelistic method used by God.

David Yonggi Cho, leader of the Assembly of God church in Seoul, South Korea, spoke at the same conference on the topic "The Evangelist and the Life of Faith." Cho stressed the importance of daily communion with God's Spirit.

We need to have a close, intimate fellowship with the Holy Spirit, to give Him time to reveal the Word to us and make Jesus Christ more real to us. As we live in close fellowship

Billy Graham emphasized at Amsterdam '83 that God's methods are Spirit-filled men and women.

with the Holy Spirit, our faith will grow. . . . We will believe that Jesus Christ will do all He promised He will do, and that you can do all He said you can do! If you believed that now, you would start out tomorrow to set your part of the world ablaze with the message of God's Word! Fellowship with the Holy Spirit will set your life ablaze for His glory.[30]

The fact that an evangelical leader like Graham invited a leading figure of the Pentecostal-charismatic movement to give one of the main messages signaled a turning point in evangelical thinking. Already at the Lausanne '74 Congress, Graham had invited the founder and leader of the charismatic movement Youth with a Mission, Loren Cunningham, to lead a workshop on "Mobilizing Young People for World Evangelization," which was very well received by charismatics and non-charismatics alike. Cunningham emphasized that especially young people are sensitive to the genuine and quickly turned off by the superficial and that one should never use gimmicks to mobilize young people into such serious work as world evangelism. He stressed that many have become permanently alienated from service through such practices.

Leighton Ford, codirector of Amsterdam '83, said that evangelicals and charismatics meeting with one another and learning to appreciate one another was one of the most important contributions of the conferences called by Graham. For the Pentecostals and the charismatics, acceptance into the evangelical mainstream had a healing effect. For many conservative evangelicals, such acceptance helped them rediscover a biblical truth that had often been neglected in the past. Cho later expressed his thanks to Graham for bridging this gap:

> As for me personally, I'm greatly indebted to his life and magnanimity because when we were celebrating one hundred years of the Korean Church, some didn't want to accept me into the celebration because I am from the Assemblies of God. Billy Graham was invited to speak at the convocation and he strongly insisted that I should be included. So they accepted his recommendation and I was adopted as one of the

speakers at the celebration. Since that time I have very close fellowship with all the denominations—especially Presbyterians. I have a feeling that has come about through the love and ministry of Billy Graham.[31]

Oral Roberts, one of the most influential Pentecostal-charismatics at that time, expressed it in a similar way:

> Within my ministry of healing and fulfilling God's call upon my life, Bill has been a friend who at the right moment has said or done the thing that made a major difference in the thoughts of the public leaders toward me. Only he could have done these memorable deeds so lovingly and fearlessly. His willingness to dedicate Oral Roberts University in April 1967 before eighteen thousand Tulsans and others, all covered by national television, was the incomparable deed that gave Oral Roberts University life in its infancy. Billy's totally unashamed stand for the Gospel of Jesus Christ, our Savior and Lord, without ever wavering or compromising, has been a tremendous encouragement to me to stand tall in my own witness and ministry.[32]

Graham esteemed spiritual leaders with other spiritual gifts, such as healing. At the same time, he was against the so-called prosperity gospel, in which the meaning of prosperity was often reduced to material wealth. Graham pointed out that while God truly loves to bless us, even with material things, he mainly blesses us spiritually so that we can bless others in turn. He emphasized that God has given us two hands, one to receive and one to give. According to Graham, an abbreviated prosperity gospel would only promote egoism. According to God's Word, the Holy Spirit and his gifts are not given primarily for our own lives as Christ's disciples but rather to help us bless others and fulfill the Great Commission given by Jesus to his disciples: "But you will receive power when the Holy Spirit comes on you; and you will be my witnesses in Jerusalem, and in all Judea and Samaria, and to the ends of the earth" (Acts 1:8).

Graham felt it necessary to point out that empowerment through the Holy Spirit must go hand in hand with loving our fellow men and holiness in all areas of life. We need humility and God's wisdom to handle the authority and power granted to us. Outward success could otherwise easily become a drug and lead us astray.

In the opening speech of the second International Conference for Itinerant Evangelists in 1986 in Amsterdam, Graham said that an evangelist's life should radiate God's holiness. He quoted Robert Murray McCheyne: "It was nothing you said that made me wish to be a Christian; it was rather the beauty of holiness which I saw in your face." Graham told the assembled evangelists from around the globe that God was looking for workers who had crucified their selfish desires and continued to put them at the foot of the cross. Only in this attitude could they powerfully proclaim the crucified Redeemer.

In his closing address in Amsterdam, he reminded the participants that the Holy Spirit uses God's Word to speak to people. He emphasized that we are God's mouthpiece. Evangelism is not about proclaiming the mind of man but instead the mind of Christ. It is about passing on the timeless biblical truths by proclaiming with conviction, "Thus says the Lord."

> Such preaching is hard to find these days. We must remember that the Holy Spirit only answers the Word; souls are born again, "not of corruptible seed, but of incorruptible, by the Word of God, which lives and abides for ever" (1 Pet. 1:23). Paul urges Timothy to "preach the Word" and "do the work of an evangelist" (2 Tim. 4:2–5).

At the Lausanne II Conference in Manila in 1989, the topic of the Holy Spirit was given even more space. Remarkably, evangelicals and charismatics, such as Vonette Bright and Jack Hayford, at times shared the same podium. Seminars and workshops dealt with controversial topics such as spiritual warfare, often unleashing stormy debates, particularly among German-speaking delegates. The majority of the delegates shared the conviction that in the future the Holy Spirit must be given greater importance in evangelistic proclamation. According to Jesus's parting words, the Holy Spirit is the one who opens people's eyes to their need of forgiveness and reconciliation with God through faith in Jesus Christ.

The Manila Manifesto summarized the important outcome of the gathering and described the Holy Spirit as the real evangelist. At the same time, people were called to repent in those areas in which they had built on their own strengths in their evangelistic efforts.

I would like to close this chapter dealing with the significance of the Holy Spirit in the Grahams' lives and ministry with the following passage from the Manila Manifesto:

> The Scriptures declare that God Himself is the chief evangelist. For the Spirit of God is the Spirit of truth, love, holiness and power, and evangelism is impossible without Him. It is He who anoints the messenger, confirms the word, prepares the hearer, convicts the sinful, enlightens the blind, gives life to the dead, enables us to repent and believe, unites us to the Body of Christ, assures us that we are God's children, leads us into Christ-like character and service, and sends us out in our turn to be Christ's witnesses. In all this the Holy Spirit's main preoccupation is to glorify Jesus Christ by showing Him to us and forming Him in us.
>
> All evangelism involves spiritual warfare with the principalities and powers of evil, in which only spiritual weapons can prevail, especially the Word and the Spirit, with prayer. We therefore call on all Christian people to be diligent in their prayers both for the renewal of the church and for the evangelization of the world.
>
> Every true conversion involves a power encounter, in which the superior authority of Jesus Christ is demonstrated. There is no greater miracle than this, in which the believer is set free from the bondage of Satan and sin, fear and futility, darkness and death.
>
> Although the miracles of Jesus were special, being signs of His Messiahship and anticipations of His perfect kingdom when all nature will be subject to Him, we have no liberty to place limits on the power of the living Creator today. We reject both the skepticism which denies miracles and the presumption which demands them, both the timidity which shrinks from the fullness of the Spirit and the triumphalism which shrinks from the weakness in which Christ's power is made perfect.

We repent of all self-confident attempts either to evangelize in our own strength or to dictate to the Holy Spirit. We determine in the future not to "grieve" or "quench" the Spirit, but rather to seek to spread the good news "with power, with the Holy Spirit and with deep conviction" (1 Thess. 1:5).[33]

10

Grace—Compassionate Living

Over the years, I have met literally thousands of wonderful Christian men and women and families. I have never met anyone more humble, gracious, and, in a word, "real," than Ruth Graham and the members of her marvelous family.[1]

Jim Bakker, TV evangelist

Ruth Bell Graham is the embodiment of grace. She has nothing to prove, no one to compete with, and she's wholly at peace with herself.[2]

Guy Kawasaki, businessman

I can candidly make the statement that Billy Graham is the kindest, most compassionate person I have ever known.[3]

Grady Wilson, team member

Two months after Billy Graham's last major mission in New York, hurricane Katrina devastated New Orleans and a large number of the coastal towns on the Gulf of Mexico. Graham couldn't talk about anything else but the needs of the people who had been affected by this catastrophe. He told his daughter Ruth how helpless he felt. He and his wife decided to let a family from New Orleans who had become homeless as a result of the storm use their former home, now empty. Their son Franklin had met the family during a relief operation in the area.

Shortly thereafter, the Martinez family, who was originally from Honduras, moved into the Grahams' former home in Montreat. The family consisted of five people from three generations. The grandmother, Ernestina Martinez, in her late seventies, had been injured while attempting to swim through the debris-laden floodwaters. Daughter Ruth Graham describes visiting the Martinez family at the former Graham home and finding her father there as well. "Mrs. Martinez was talking as I entered the living room. Daddy sat next to her on the couch holding her hand." Ruth reports how, with the help of an interpreter, Mrs. Martinez told Billy of her experiences during the flood and the injuries she had suffered. After listening, Billy prayed for her. In his prayer, he summarized the gospel. In her

Franklin Graham with his father in New Orleans in March 2006, where they spoke to the victims of the hurricane and also provided practical help through Samaritan's Purse.

book *Legacy of Faith*, Graham's daughter Ruth later reflected on the situation:

> I looked at my father sitting there on the couch, holding Mrs. Martinez's hand, and I thought about the times he had led us in family devotions here in this very room when I was a little girl. My first childhood memory is of kneeling by the fireplace in the Old House during family devotions and fiddling with a loose brick on the hearth while the adults prayed. Now, some fifty years later, Daddy was still praying here.

Ruth added pensively:

> He was being himself at home, as authentic as ever, loving those in his midst. The big platform might have gone, I thought, standing there

In 1954, in New Orleans, Billy Graham preached the gospel in an overcrowded stadium. More than half a century later, he again visited the town, this time to help in practical ways and to encourage the people to seek the Lord in their misery.

in the Old House looking on. The vast crowds, the arenas—the time for that is over now. But the little platform, the one-on-one, is still available to Daddy. And he will use it for God. As long as he is with us, he will use it. Because that is who he is.[4]

Ruth and Billy Graham did not serve others because that's what good Christians are supposed to do or because it was part of the greater Christian mandate; they did it because God's love and the mercy they experienced moved them to tell others of his grace.

They taught their own children early on to give generously. Gifts given to the family were often passed on to needy neighbors, something the Graham kids were not always happy about. The Grahams often drove out in their Jeep before Christmas, stopping at the home of a needy person to sing Christmas carols and to deliver a gift that Ruth had carefully and beautifully wrapped.

Whenever Billy heard that someone had problems or was in need, he wanted to help. It was not unusual for him to drop everything to help someone in need, even during preparations for his weekly radio message, *The Hour of Decision*. If he heard that someone in trouble was at the gate and wanted to see him, he was happy to take the time. It was not always easy for his family to shield him from this kind of visitor. One time a desperate person begged to speak to Billy Graham, listing the reasons why it was necessary in a very assertive tone. Ruth replied with equal determination that it was not possible at that time. However, the intruder did not give up. "I would still like to see him for a few minutes!" whereby Ruth, quick-witted as always, replied, "So would I."

Billy often needed to be protected from himself. After he jovially issued an invitation to his radio audience to come see him in Montreat, his listeners came in droves. When he and his ministry became known nationwide, busloads of tourists wanted to take a look at this "holy family." The Grahams' children, however, did not always behave in a very holy way, sometimes replying to the inquiries of tourists looking for the Graham house, "Billy Graham? No idea,

For more than fifty years, the Grahams lived in this log cabin, which they named "Little Piney Cove," on the mountain overlooking Montreat.

never heard of such a man." Or they did business by selling lemonade to the curious trespassers.

Ruth once said that you could tell which Christian denomination people belonged to by the degree of their pushiness. The Baptists were definitely the boldest. The Baptists felt particularly close to Billy, whom they considered their colleague. Ruth generally appreciated courageous people, but when it reached the point that her husband could only move from one room to another by crawling on the floor, to avoid being seen, it was too much for her. She decided it was time to move up onto the mountain overlooking Montreat to be as unreachable as possible to the masses of tourists.

They needed this place of retreat. And over the years, countless visitors of "Little Piney Cove," as they named it, benefited from their hospitality there, not only well-known and successful people but also the socially disadvantaged. Many of these people were stranded, their lives ruined, they themselves rejected and in need of encouragement.

286

Their trust in God needed to be renewed and their souls needed to recuperate.

A particularly impressive example of someone who benefited greatly from the loving hospitality of the Graham family during a difficult time in his life was the "fallen" former

Billy Graham shared the gospel with influential people as well as people who lived at the edge of society. In 1950, he addressed twelve hundred inmates at a state prison.

TV evangelist Jim Bakker. A sex scandal led him to resign his leadership of a thriving television ministry. Subsequent revelations showing that he had intentionally misled people with promises he would not have been able to fulfill (mail fraud and wire fraud) brought about his imprisonment.

In his book *I Was Wrong*, he recounted in detail how first Franklin Graham and then his father, Billy, visited him in prison. Bakker wrote that Franklin stood by him despite all his failures and treated him as a friend after most of his "friends" had dropped him: "No gift Franklin could have given me was greater than his affirming friendship. Franklin Graham demonstrated risky, genuine Christian love."[5]

Billy Graham's visit meant a great deal to Bakker. Bakker says that Billy was genuinely interested in how he was doing and even passed on greetings from Ruth, who was unable to come because she was in the hospital. They discussed both good and difficult matters, and at the end of their meeting, Billy prayed for him, which left an indelible impression on Bakker:

> I will never forget that the man who had just been voted one of the most influential men in the world and who has ministered to millions of people took time out of his busy schedule to come minister to one

prisoner. Amid my depression, flu, filth, and hopelessness, Billy Graham had come. I felt as though Jesus Himself had come to visit me.[6]

The story of Jim Bakker and the Grahams continued. While Bakker was completing his sentence in a halfway house, he received

Jim Bakker with his second wife, Lori, together with Ruth and Gigi Graham after Bakker's rehabilitation.

an invitation from Ruth to spend a Sunday with their family, which the prison authorities approved. Together with the Graham family Bakker attended the Sunday worship service at the Montreat Presbyterian Church, the Grahams' parish. Bakker recalls that the family, with all the children and grandchildren, filled two entire rows of seats. Ruth entered and sat down right next to him. Franklin gave the sermon and introduced Bakker as his personal friend. When the congregation applauded, Bakker was overcome by emotion. Just forty-eight hours earlier he had been in jail, prisoner 07407-058, and now he had the honor of worshiping in the midst of the Graham family. Afterward, they drove to the Grahams' home, where Ruth served a delicious meal:

> I felt as though I was sitting in the midst of a family reunion. We talked and laughed just as any family might during the Sunday afternoon meal. We talked a great deal about one of Ruth's favorite subjects, as well—how we could better get Bibles to inmates and their families.[7]

Ruth wrote a letter for Bakker to give to the warden in which she thanked the warden for treating Bakker well and for giving him the opportunity to spend the day with her family. This day was very important to Bakker because he was able to experience God's love and acceptance through the Graham family, which initiated a profound healing process. Bakker later gave a wonderful testimony about the Grahams, who were true, authentic Christians living out God's unconditional love.

⌒⌒⌒

Ruth was convinced that most people failed because of a lack of encouragement. To her, discouragement was the main reason for obvious cases of misconduct. That's why she wanted to be an encourager first and foremost, especially toward her children. She once wrote in her diary:

> Never let a single day pass without saying an encouraging word to each child. Particularly wherever you have noticed any—even the slightest—improvement on some weak point. Some point at which you have been picking and criticizing. And never fail to pass on any nice thing you have heard said about anyone, to that child. In David's prayer for Solomon, he said, ". . . prayer also shall be made for him continually; and daily shall he be praised" (Ps. 72:15). "More people fail for lack of encouragement," someone wrote, "than for any other reason."[8]

It was during her time in high school in today's North Korea that Ruth first became acutely aware of what it meant to receive God's grace. Her parents had told her early on that God had sent his Son to die for the world's sins, but she doubted whether Jesus had really died for her too. She could not believe that God cared enough about an insignificant teenager to forgive her own personal sins. She asked her older sister, Rosa, who was also attending the same boarding school in Pyongyang, what she needed to do to be completely certain that God had sent Jesus into the world to die for her sins. Rosa told her to read Isaiah 53 and to replace the words *we/our/us* with her own name:

Surely he took up Ruth's pain
   and bore Ruth's suffering. . . .
But he was pierced for Ruth's transgressions,
   he was crushed for Ruth's iniquities;
the punishment that brought Ruth peace was on him,
   and by his wounds Ruth was healed. . . .
The LORD has laid on him
   the iniquity of Ruth. (Isa. 53:4–6)

As Ruth spoke those verses aloud, a deep assurance that God cared about her personally entered her heart. She was now convinced that Jesus Christ had given his life for her personally so that she could stand blameless before God. He no longer saw her flaws; he saw a person who was pure and perfect through her belief in Jesus's shed blood for her.

After this, Ruth became more and more aware of the need to see others through God's eyes. She did not want to focus on the outward dirt but the crystals behind the dirt that begin to sparkle when cleansed by the blood of Jesus. Her ability to see people through the eyes of a crystal hunter was a great encouragement to all who met Ruth. Many of them opened up their lives to Jesus as a result, claiming his forgiveness and cleansing personally. Ruth thus helped many people around her because she felt true compassion for them. What Ruth did one-on-one is exactly what Billy did from the podium for thousands: help to give people back the dignity and value bestowed on them at creation so they could shine once again. In this way, those people became lights to guide many others to faith in Jesus Christ.

Because both Ruth and Billy were so conscious of their own failures and called on God's grace daily, they were capable of being gracious to others. Nothing made them more indignant than seeing a person criticized ruthlessly. If even God does not judge someone, who are we to judge others? Ultimately, we are all cut from the same cloth and deserve judgment.

One telling example of Ruth's awareness of her own sinfulness is her request to be buried in a coffin that had been made by a death row inmate. The words she wanted on her gravestone were equally characteristic: "End of Construction—Thank you for your patience." She applied these words, which she had read following roadwork, to her own life, which she viewed as a construction site supervised by God.

Because Ruth felt she was attending God's school throughout her life, she extended grace to the people around her whom she felt needed some extra lessons at God's school. She compassionately backed a young gang leader whom others had long given up on as "a hopeless case." When the phone woke her up early in the morning on New Year's Day, she regarded it as a beautiful New Year's present. The "hopeless case" just wanted to let her know that he had registered for a Bible college and wanted to become a pastor. Ruth asked, "Can you think of a better way to start a new year?"[9]

She especially felt compassion for people who could not cope with life or were seen as no longer having any earthly use. When Ruth heard about an old man who had been treated heartlessly by his neighbors, she invited him to live in a cabin she had furnished just below the Graham home. Although he was able to cook for himself, she often prepared meals for him. When the Grahams went on weekend family outings, he was invited along. Naturally, they took him to church too, and Ruth made sure he got some good Bible teaching. With tears in his eyes, the man later told a friend of Ruth's that he had finally found a home. Long after his death, Ruth had his photograph hanging in a prominent place in her home.[10]

There was also the prostitute Ruth had gotten to know during the first mission in London in 1954 and with whom she exchanged letters for many years. She continued to write to the woman even when it seemed that all her efforts were in vain.

A man who had been very close to Ruth for many years told me in a trembling voice how much he missed her. She had helped him to believe in a God of love because she had lived out that love and mercy herself. As a result, he had begun attending church again.

Sometimes things were a bit less idyllic—such as when Ruth had the impression that a person needed to be cured of an enlarged ego. In these situations, Ruth was mercilessly hard because she considered self-pity and self-righteousness extremely dangerous and destructive. Jesus's harsh tone with self-righteous people was her model. Ruth especially had a hard time with Christians who took themselves too seriously, and she let them know it. She communi-

Ruth was a good observer, loving but occasionally quite mischievous. Many of those around her got a taste of it!

cated her conviction to them in very unique ways, but it always hit home.

One day while Ruth was entertaining friends, one of them dominated the conversation by talking about her poor health, sharing that her blood pressure was too high and her doctor had forbidden her to eat sweets. When Ruth offered the guests a piece of her wonderful blueberry pie, the woman immediately forgot all her problems. This guest asked for a piece of pie with lots of whipped cream, just like everyone else was having. Ruth gave her a piece, but before serving it, she substituted plenty of Billy's shaving cream for the whipped cream. The lady eagerly took a bite and then was quiet for the rest of the evening.[11]

Ruth felt that people often complained for no real reason. In her opinion, complaining only made a situation worse, whereas a positive attitude could solve many problems or at least make them easier to bear. Once on a long overseas flight, Grady Wilson did not stop complaining to Ruth about not being able to fall asleep. She gave him some capsules of sleeping pills, which she had prepared beforehand—by filling them with mustard! After Grady woke up, he said he had slept well but now needed some help with his stomach.

There may be kinder ways to make people aware that they take themselves and their problems much too seriously, but there are not many ways that are more creative.

For the Grahams, loving others never came at the cost of speaking the truth and making people aware of areas for growth. I know of no better example of people who combined truth with love than Ruth and Billy Graham. Truth and love are mutually dependent. Truth spoken without love cannot be taken in. It makes us deaf. Love without truth blinds us to reality and is therefore equally dangerous. So it is with God's grace. Grace gains its full meaning only against the background of imminent judgment. Yet truth spoken without love is damaging because it negates the most important truth in the Bible that God loves us even though we do not deserve it.

What is our appropriate response to God's unconditional love? Jesus himself gave the answer in his commandment to love God with all our hearts and to love our neighbor as ourselves (see Matt. 22:39). When speaking about the end times, Jesus mentioned a lack of adherence to God's commandments and put it in relation to the decreasing love in society: "Because of the increase of wickedness, the love of most will grow cold" (Matt. 24:12).

Billy Graham often reminded his listeners of God's love for them. However, during the early years of his ministry, he just as often pointed out the horrors of the last judgment, which we deserve when we break God's laws and give sin free reign in our lives. He then presented God's merciful offer against the background of the last judgment: God forgives all who repent of their sins and ask God for forgiveness, for Christ's sake, and gives them new life.

The Bible verse Graham probably preached about more than any other was John 3:16: "For God so loved the world that he gave his one and only Son, that whoever believes in him shall not perish but have eternal life." Interestingly, it was during my visit with Graham that the consequences of sin became obvious to me through a personal experience; I also experienced what grace means in such a situation.

Before traveling to the US for the visit, I was bitten by a tick while out looking for mushrooms. The skin around the bite turned red, but I did not pay any attention to it, even though the ring-shaped redness became more prominent over the next few days. My wife and I flew to the US, where we were to meet Gigi Graham for a visit with her father. Between our two visits with Billy, I realized that the red ring around the bite had expanded. I still did not take it seriously, but my wife, who is a trained nurse, felt differently. But there was no time to see a doctor.

After arriving at the Graham home, I showed the bite to the nurse who was there, who advised me to see a doctor as soon as possible. During lunch with Billy, the subject of my tick bite came up. He was very concerned and advised me to see his own doctor, who lived twenty-five miles away in Asheville. He literally bragged about his doctor, describing him as the best doctor imaginable. After lunch, as we drove down the steep mountain road, I thought to myself, "That's exactly what Billy Graham did throughout his life. He pointed out the disastrous consequences of sin and showed people the best doctor, Jesus Christ." Just like the many thankful people who streamed forward to the stage at his missions to confess their sins and to experience forgiveness and healing, I was equally thankful that I could be examined and treated by Billy's personal physician. And just like with Jesus, the treatment was "gratis," or free of charge. *Gratis* is Latin, and literally translated it means "out of grace." The antibiotics I received worked quickly and killed the bacteria that had caused the Lyme borreliosis disease. I later learned that, left untreated, Lyme disease can lead to severe and chronic damage of the body, including signs of paralysis. Severe symptoms often only occur after several months or even years.

What a fitting picture of the consequences of sin that is not dealt with—for example, resentment and bitterness. Although insignificant at first, such consequences hinder our spiritual growth and damage our spiritual health until our entire spiritual life is paralyzed. Should we not be thankful to accept the healing from the great Physician that stops the insidious yet ultimately fatal effects of sin in our lives? And the treatment is free; all we need to do is admit our need and go to the doctor to receive healing.

Many evangelistic sermons today offer grace without judgment. This could explain why so many conversions are superficial and have no long-term impact. If we neglect the sin in our lives and let our egos continue to rule our lives instead of Christ, then we will never experience the joy of being a child of God. Of course, the Good News must never become bad news, but it is not really good news if we are not aware of the imminent judgment hanging over us if we go on living selfish, egotistical lives.

Graham was able to act as God's mouthpiece not least because he didn't hide the serious side of the situation. Yet he shared the gospel in an incomparably gracious way, presenting not only God's holiness but also his unconditional love. A member of our men's prayer group who was often on business trips in America expressed it this way: "Although the Christian faith didn't really interest me at the time in my hotel room in the US, I just had to listen to Graham, because he transmitted the gospel in such a gracious, noble way."

The apostle Paul exhorts us to convey the biblical truth in a gracious way: "Let your conversation be always full of grace, seasoned with salt, so that you may know how to answer everyone" (Col. 4:6). Paul uses the Greek term *charis*, which literally means "grace." *Charisma*, "gift of grace," and *character*, "a lifestyle of grace," have the same etymological origin. The word *character* could also be derived from the Greek term *chará*, which means "joy." Is joy not closely connected with a lifestyle of receiving and extending grace?

Grace and truth are inseparable. The disciple John writes in his Gospel, "For the law was given through Moses; grace and truth came through Jesus Christ" (1:17). Jesus never hid the truth about the judgment resulting from sin. But he, by his grace, always showed a way out, ultimately making forgiveness, healing, and new birth possible through his death.

Grady Wilson, himself an evangelist, pointed out in his autobiography, *Count It All Joy*, that it was wrong to view Graham one-dimensionally as a preacher of judgment or of grace. He was always trying to preach the whole counsel of God, not just a part of it:

> Those who are not close to Billy have never seen all of his facets. . . . According to where they're coming from, they view Billy differently. Because of his preaching the whole counsel of God, and his emphasis on judgment and hell, some may think of him as stern, even harsh. Because of his equal emphasis on grace and God's redeeming love, others may think of him as too lenient. It's all according to where the person is positioned.[12]

Graham confirms that in the beginning he placed more emphasis on God's holy judgment, whereas in later years he underscored God's undeserved love for sinners. With the years, he increasingly emphasized the cost of discipleship and obedience. The main problem, in his view, is our desire to live our lives separated from God, not wanting him to intervene. This attitude of indifference or even rebellion is called sin in the Bible. Graham did not see it as his task to set up a ranking of sins and to determine which were worse and which were not so bad but instead to call people to loving obedience. Overcoming sin (singular), an attitude of indifference and separation from God, would then awaken the desire and strength to no longer commit sins (plural). That is why in his messages Graham concentrated on overcoming sin in general and did not highlight specific individual sins, no matter how severe they were. After forty years of preaching the gospel, Graham confided:

I am preaching the same Gospel I have always preached. If anything, I am stressing more and more the cost of discipleship. I do not know of a single moral issue that I have not spoken about at one time or another—everything from racism and apartheid to nuclear armaments and peace. However, I do not feel it is my calling to get out in the streets and lead demonstrations. Nor am I singling out one sin from the scores mentioned in Scripture and riding a hobbyhorse—although I have had a lot of pressure across the years to do so.[13]

Graham then added another very practical reason for this focus: "If I spent all of my time on sins (plural) I might never be able to get at the root cause, which is sin (singular)."

People felt drawn to the Grahams because they saw them as sincere people who conveyed truth with grace. The Grahams opened not only the way to God for them but often also the way to church after having been disappointed by other Christians. They attracted the successful and also the broken and those living on the fringes of society.

The late singer and actress Ethel Waters often enhanced Graham's missions with her presence and her moving songs. She once told a *New York Times* reporter, "Ruthie feels exactly the way her husband does. I learned what love really is from that precious child." Waters continued:

I'll never forget the night when I was with the crusade in London. At that time I had a bad foot and was trying to leave before the huge crowds started pouring out. That's when I ran into her on the stairway. She was holding on to a teenaged girl who was so drugged, her eyes were rolling—she was really on a trip. Somehow the girl had gotten into the meeting and had almost passed out. There was delicate little Ruthie, half carrying, half-dragging this girl who was twice her size. She was a dirty, hippie type—smelled like she hadn't taken a bath in months. But that didn't seem to bother Ruthie. She was soothing this girl. Embracing her. Showing her the love of God. Showing her that someone cared.[14]

People do not care what we believe until they believe that we care. Billy and Ruth truly cared about people. They didn't just proclaim God's unconditional love; they lived it. And people were drawn to them, just like suffering people and outcasts were drawn to Jesus. Jesus did not primarily see the Samaritan woman at the well as an adulteress (see John 4) but as a human being who was thirsty for love and true life. Similarly, the Grahams saw their fellow human beings, no matter how deeply marred by sin, as people hungry and thirsty for true love, profound joy, and a meaningful life.

Peter speaks of God as the "God of all grace" (1 Pet. 5:10), and Paul talks about the "good news of God's grace" (Acts 20:24). *Grace* is a key word in the New Testament. The transforming power of God's grace makes us different from the people around us and is not found in any other religion. Graham always believed that transformation happens from the inside out. Swiss theologian Emil Brunner, whom Graham held in high esteem, influenced Graham heavily in this area, as Brunner was very outspoken on the subject. In *Christianity and Culture*, part 2, Brunner states, "The Christian knows that all changes that begin from without are no real changes."

The famous jazz and gospel singer Ethel Waters was a close friend of the Grahams. She often sang one or two songs and gave a short personal testimony during the crusade meetings. Here she is between Billy and Ruth Graham at the wedding of President Nixon's daughter Tricia.

Christians are people who have received grace and have the mandate to live the gospel of grace and to pass it on to others. Jesus even commanded his followers to love their enemies. Next to loving God, loving one's enemies is at the heart of Christian faith and is a unique characteristic of Christianity. We Christians should not be known for what we think is wrong but rather for being gracious and merciful people who radiate God's unconditional love. If we Christians live this love, not least in the way we treat one another, then the unchurched will stream into churches because they will receive something they do not get anywhere else: love and acceptance. These people in turn will open their hearts to the proclamation of the gospel and receive Jesus Christ as their personal Savior and Lord. They will be convinced that if his representatives are full of grace and love, then God is too. And once people have a personal encounter with the God of all grace, they feel compelled to please him more and more in all things. Christians who are filled with the Holy Spirit hate sin but love the sinner. They know that they themselves are also sinners, but sinners who have received grace or, as Martin Luther once put it, beggars who have found bread and who now show others where they can find bread too.

I dream of a church that is known for its love and yet conveys undiluted biblical truth in a gracious and merciful way, where it is considered a privilege to bring one's broken past to the cross and where one is allowed to start anew. Philip Yancey, author of *What's So Amazing about Grace?*, describes the difference between a merciless world and a loving Christian church. In light of the following lines, it is easy to understand why Billy Graham said he appreciates no other author in the evangelical world more than Yancey:

> If the world despises a notorious sinner, the church will love her. If the world cuts off aid to the poor and the suffering, the church will offer food and healing. If the world oppresses, the church will raise up the oppressed. If the world shames a social outcast, the church will proclaim God's reconciling love. If the world seeks profit and

self-fulfillment, the church seeks sacrifice and service. If the world demands retribution, the church dispenses grace. If the world splinters into factions, the church joins together in unity. If the world destroys its enemies, the church loves them.[15]

Yancey adds that this is at least the vision of the church found in the New Testament.

Ruth and Billy Graham represent God's grace but not a cheap grace that allows for a careless and disobedient life. On the contrary, they charged people to radically direct their lives toward Jesus. Billy repeatedly emphasized that Jesus was no weakling, the way he is often depicted in paintings. He was a revolutionary leader and called for a revolution of the heart that would change the very roots of society. He demanded 100 percent from his followers. Graham once described the revolutionary qualities of Jesus the following way:

> While He was gentle, quiet and meek, He was also a militant leader whose influence and teaching took the shackles off the slaves, lifted women to a new position and shook the foundation of the Roman Empire, and whose influence has caused the fall of dictators even up to the present. I have often said that Jesus Christ was a composite man, made up of heaven's best and earth's best; and

God's unconditional love, demonstrated by the sacrificial death of his Son on the cross, was Billy Graham's main theme all his life. Here he is shown speaking to the participants of the Southern Baptist Convention in Dallas, Texas, in 1974. In his message, he challenged the delegates to share God's love and be "firebrands" for Christ.

that I did not think He was like the effeminate, emaciated conceptions of some artists.[16]

Time and again, Graham emphasized that following Jesus meant denying oneself and being prepared to take up the cross. As followers of Christ, we may be ridiculed or harassed because of our faith, perhaps even persecuted. If Jesus was persecuted and died on a cross, shouldn't his disciples be prepared to suffer as well? Graham repeatedly expressed his regret that people often preached a weak version of Christianity, a faith that required no sacrifice. This resulted in conversions that were often superficial and had little impact. In an interview he gave to *Guideposts* magazine, Graham illustrated why the costs of being a disciple should not be left out when preaching the gospel.

A famous man had approached him, deeply moved and ready to accept Christ. He was married but at the same time kept a mistress. Although he prayed and wept, he was not prepared to break off the extramarital relationship. Graham made it clear to the man that this was a test of whether he was serious about obeying God. Without a clear willingness to give up sin, there could be no true conversion and no forgiveness of sin. Graham himself had undergone a similar test when he had decided to follow Christ, so he could sympathize with the man. Graham then told the man what it had cost him to do God's will.

When I first came to Christ I was going with a girl who was not a Christian, and she was unwilling to become one. I was very much in love with her, or so I thought, but the Lord seemed to be telling me that this was my big test—was I willing to give the girl up, or was I not? I remember the night I went over and told her that we had to stop seeing each other. We'd been going together for three years, and I'm sure we both had intended to be married. And I remember that when I drove home that night, about ten miles, I wept all the way. But I was doing it for Christ. Of course, I didn't realize then that the Lord had somebody else in mind who would turn out to be the ideal wife for me.[17]

In the same interview, Graham expressed regret that many people were no longer prepared to make commitments at all:

People are just apathetic, interested in their own pleasure, not committed to any cause. And the cause I'm talking about is Jesus Christ. Some people are not willing to say, "I'll burn all my bridges behind me and surrender totally—my will, my mind, my heart, my family, my business or whatever—all my goals to Jesus Christ." And that is what Christ asks of us: to burn our bridges behind us and say, "Christ, you and you alone are the One I'm going to depend on for my eternal salvation and for my daily personal relationships. You come before everything, and I don't do anything without asking Your guidance and help."[18]

In his old age, Graham's complete trust in God was once again tested, this time when he developed several illnesses, including Parkinson's disease. He saw his illness and the accompanying weakness as a means to grow closer to God:

Someone asked me recently if I didn't think God was unfair, allowing me to have Parkinson's and other medical problems when I have tried to serve Him faithfully. I replied that I did not see it that way at all. Suffering is part of the human condition, and it comes to us all. The key is how we react to it, either turning away from God in anger and bitterness or growing closer to Him in trust and confidence.[19]

Ruth was also weak in advanced age. Her worsening arthritis, accompanied by stiffness, primarily in her neck, gave her a great deal of pain. Perhaps because of her personal frailness, she felt even more drawn to everything that was useless in the world's eyes. She once bought a broken vase, to the potter's great astonishment, remarking that God loved broken things. Her great passion was fixing damaged items that others thought were trash. Didn't Jesus have the same passion to fix broken people by his grace? She wanted to have the same attitude of grace toward the people of her day. Her daughter Ruth testifies that her mother always saw the good and beauty in people, qualities that were meant to be set free.

> Mother sees beauty, too, in people whom others might ignore or overlook, like the elderly, the poor, and the helpless. All of my life, I have watched Mother treat with dignity and respect those whom others might dismiss as worn-out; and I have watched Mother encourage hurting people, insisting that their lives were far from over and their contribution valuable.[20]

When Ruth saw a need, she tried her utmost to relieve it, especially when she had the impression that the person in need was not at fault. When a fellow student at Wheaton College lacked the funds to continue his studies because he refused to take on a well-paying job that required him to work on Sundays, Ruth paid the money anonymously. She had saved part of the money herself and got the rest from her father. The student was Paul Freed, who went on to launch Trans World Radio. Freed experienced God's grace thanks to Ruth and her father.[21]

In his evangelistic sermons, Graham wanted to stick to conveying basic biblical truths and pointing to the consequences for the individual. Graham was often criticized, mainly during the first part of his ministry, by people who believed that he one-sidedly emphasized individual ethics—the private sins—at the cost of social ethics—society's sins. The American theologian Reinhold Niebuhr was one of the most strident proponents of this opinion.

Niebuhr was a widely respected professor at Union Theological Seminary in New York and throughout his life voiced his opinion not only about theological questions but also about social concerns. As founder of the magazine *Christianity and Crises*, Niebuhr was often referred to as the "crisis theologian." He battled against both religious liberals, with their idealism of the social gospel, and religious conservatives, with their separation of personal faith and social responsibility. Niebuhr, himself influenced by Karl Barth, influenced many generations of students, including Dietrich Bonhoeffer, German Lutheran pastor and founding member of the Confessing Church who was martyred for his opposition to Adolf Hitler's totalitarian regime.

Niebuhr felt that Billy Graham made it too easy for himself when he deemphasized social sins and focused nearly exclusively on personal sins in his messages. In Niebuhr's opinion, Jesus had been not only the Redeemer but also a social revolutionary. One could not persist in an individualistic pietism and block out America's cultural sins, especially in view of the many who had been exploited by them.[22]

Niebuhr later reproached Graham for what he considered to be an indiscriminate familiarity with the American presidents. In his essay "The King's Chapel and the King's Court," he described Graham as "domesticated" and "tailored," as he lacked the critical radicalism that had distinguished Jesus. Niebuhr put his finger on a delicate issue here. In fact, Graham himself later regretted that despite all his efforts to stay out of party politics, he had occasionally let himself be used politically and had sometimes tended to equate the American culture with God's kingdom.

Not only Niebuhr but also Graham would certainly have endorsed the following words of Jon Meacham:

> Experience shows that religious authorities can themselves be corrupted by proximity to political power. . . . There is much New Testament evidence to support a vision of faith and politics in which the church is truest to its core mission when it is the farthest from the entanglements of power. The Jesus of the Gospels resolutely refuses to use the means of this world—either the clash of arms or the passions of politics—to further his ends.[23]

The most complex relationship Graham had was with Richard Nixon, whose family Graham had known since the 1949 mission in Los Angeles. Nixon had warned Graham early on not to let himself be abused for political purposes, as if foreseeing later events, reminding Graham that his evangelistic ministry was more important than his own political career. The tapes of Nixon, which were released during the Watergate scandal, opened Graham's eyes to the truth of Nixon's statement. He was sorely disappointed in his friend: "Those tapes revealed a man I never knew. I never saw that side of him."

But Graham himself also had to apologize for some negative remarks he had made about Jewish Americans. In a conversation with Nixon, he had shared, or at least not objected to the latter's judgment, that the Jews in the US eventually wanted to gain control of everything. Yet Graham had always supported the Jewish cause in public. According to Ruth, the time surrounding Nixon's impeachment and the disclosure of Graham's remarks about Jews was the most difficult time her husband had experienced in his whole life, especially as his remarks did not reflect his generally positive feelings toward the Jews and the country of Israel. He felt he was a failure who at least in this case had tried to please man more than God. He was also very disappointed in Nixon and especially his use of vulgar language, revealed on the Watergate tapes. Nevertheless, even after Watergate, Graham stood up for his longtime friend and preached at Nixon's funeral.

Nixon and Graham felt close to each other because they both had a truly global perspective. When I visited Graham, he mentioned that Nixon was one of the first to point out China as an upcoming world power. Graham always took Nixon's advice very seriously, as he saw in him a statesman of exceptional quality. He also saw in him a man who held up his Christian convictions. Yet this very closeness to Nixon caused Graham the greatest problems of his life.

Graham should nonetheless be credited for almost always getting around to speaking about key points of the gospel when meeting political leaders, a fact that is unanimously verified by his closest staff members, who accompanied him on visits to various heads of state. He saw himself always as God's ambassador and considered it a holy mission to bring the gospel of Jesus Christ not only to simple people but also to the power brokers of this world. When doing so, he repeatedly emphasized the need for a basic change of heart, which was possible only if people prayed for forgiveness of their sins and trusted their lives to Jesus Christ.

Throughout the years, Graham prayed with many world leaders, among them the Queen of England, to whom the Grahams had a very special connection. Over the years, Graham met the queen at least ten times.

Since the time of the first mission in London in 1954, the Grahams had close ties to the Queen of England.

She often sent him greetings on his birthdays.

Several of the American presidents counted Graham as their personal friend and counselor and were glad to have a man of his caliber of faith come alongside them in times of trouble. One of these was President George Bush Sr. In April 2006, he bestowed on Graham the George Bush Award for Excellence in Public Service—an award previously bestowed on statesmen such as Mikhail Gorbachev. It was a very emotional moment when the former president of the United States spoke. "If I knew the task fell to me to try to explain why we are honoring Billy tonight, I could not get through it. What he has meant to me and to my family is too personal, and too emotional," he said, his voice cracking. Recalling Abraham Lincoln, he noted that every president was driven to his knees by the demands of the job. Then he added, "But sometimes even that is not enough. No matter how deep one's faith is, sometimes you need the guidance and comfort of a living, breathing human being. For me, and for so many other Oval Office occupants, that person was Billy Graham. When my soul was troubled, it was Billy I reached out to, for advice, for comfort, for prayer."[24]

What about his son George W. Bush? George W. Bush had been strongly influenced in his faith by Graham in his youth, but during his presidency he had little contact with Graham due to the latter's age. However, he did personally take Graham on a tour of the White House, pushing him in his wheelchair. After his presidency, in an interview with *Fox News*, Bush shared what attracted him to Graham:

> Billy Graham is such a gentle soul. His humility and obvious love for God and Christ can overcome any cynic. Here is one of the most famous people in the world, a great historical figure, and in his presence you realize how humble he is. He is a very humble, very disarming man. His humility overpowers you. I truly was captivated, was amazed. He helped change my life. I was a cynical person at the time. I was a questioning person. I was drinking a lot. He helped me to understand the redemptive power of the risen Lord.[25]

George Bush Sr. was very close to the Graham family. He is shown sitting between Franklin and Billy Graham in a crusade in Texas.

And then Bush gave an interesting explanation for Graham's effectiveness:

> He is an unaffected messenger because of his charisma and his heart. He has no political agenda. He has an agenda of the Lord. He is a magnet, but the interesting thing is that he is not a magnet to Billy Graham. He is a magnet to a higher authority.[26]

Billy Graham was a regular speaker at Presidential Inaugural Prayer Services. Here President George W. Bush shakes the hand of Billy Graham at the 2005 Inaugural Prayer Service, where Graham gave the opening prayer.

The Clintons also admired Graham because he did not treat them as celebrities but as normal people. They confided, however, that despite his well-mannered approach, he also addressed sensitive issues.

In April 2010, President Barack Obama visited Billy Graham at his home in Montreat. They had planned the meeting when Obama had called Graham to congratulate him on his birthday the previous November. While meeting in Graham's home, Obama and Graham spoke about their common roots in Chicago, about golf, but also about very personal matters. Obama confessed, like other presidents before him, how lonely, demanding, and humbling

Barack Obama was the twelfth American president in a row who respected Billy Graham as a prophetic Christian voice. This picture shows the two meeting at Graham's home in Montreat in April 2010.

the presidency can be. Graham encouraged the president to always draw on spiritual resources and to seek the advice of the Lord. He gave him two Bibles, one for himself and one for his wife. The two concluded by praying for each other. According to Franklin Graham, his father prayed for the nation and that God would give Obama wisdom in his decisions, and the president prayed to thank God for Billy Graham.

Celebrities loved Billy Graham because, as Johnny Cash put it, "he is the kind of friend who like my mother loves me the same regardless of what I've done." And he added, "That's what friendship is all about."[27]

The famous movie star Steve McQueen, nicknamed "The King of Cool" and once the highest-paid movie star in the world, asked Billy Graham to visit him shortly before his death from cancer in 1980. During the visit, Graham gave McQueen his personal Bible with the inscription, "To my friend Steve McQueen, may God bless you and keep you always. Billy Graham, Philippians 1:6. November 3, 1980."

Barbara McQueen writes about the encounter in *Steve McQueen: The Last Mile*: "Graham's visit comforted Steve tremendously and prepared him for the inevitable. The Bible became Steve's proudest possession and it never left his side." A few days after the visit, McQueen died, on his chest the Bible Graham had given him. His wife, Barbara, recalls:

> The first person I called was Billy Graham, who consoled me for the next half hour. He basically told me that Steve was in a much better place. Billy said that he constantly prayed for Steve, but also prayed that whatever happened, it was God's will and that there was a reason why he took Steve. His words comforted me greatly, and I've never forgotten his kindness in my time of need.[28]

Graham himself described the meeting with McQueen in the foreword of the biography *Steve McQueen: The Final Chapter* by Grady Ragsdale:

I look back on that experience with thanksgiving and some amazement. I had planned to minister to Steve, but as it turned out, he ministered to me. I saw once again the reality of what Jesus Christ can do for a man in his last hours.[29]

Graham was often asked if he would do anything differently if he could go back in time. He did his best to answer the question in January 2011:

Yes, of course. I'd spend more time at home with my family, and I'd study more and preach less. I wouldn't have taken so many speaking engagements, including some of the things I did over the years that I probably didn't really need to do—weddings and funerals and building dedications, things like that. Whenever I counsel someone who feels called to be an evangelist, I always urge them to guard their time and not feel like they have to do everything. I also would have steered clear of politics. I'm grateful for the opportunities God gave

Billy Graham regretted that he had not spent more time with his children and grandchildren when they needed him most. Here he holds up Stephan Nelson, his first grandchild.

me to minister to people in high places; people in power have spiritual and personal needs like everyone else, and often they have no one to talk to. But looking back I know I sometimes crossed the line, and I wouldn't do that now.[30]

Contrary to many other spiritual leaders, Graham never kept silent about his failures. When asked in the same interview about the most important issues facing evangelicals today, he answered:

I'm grateful for the evangelical resurgence we've seen across the world in the last half-century or so. It truly has been God's doing. It wasn't like this when I first started out, and I'm amazed at what has happened—new evangelical seminaries and organizations and churches, a new generation of leaders committed to the gospel, and so forth. But success is always dangerous, and we need to be alert and avoid becoming the victims of our own success. Will we influence the world for Christ, or will the world influence us? But the most important issue we face today is the same the church has faced in every century: Will we reach our world for Christ? In other words, will we give priority to Christ's command to go into all the world and preach the gospel? Or will we turn increasingly inward, caught up in our own internal affairs or controversies, or simply becoming more and more comfortable with the status quo? Will we become inner-directed or outer-directed? The central issues of our time aren't economic or political or social, important as these are. The central issues of our time are moral and spiritual in nature, and our calling is to declare Christ's forgiveness and hope and transforming power to a world that does not know him or follow him. May we never forget this.[31]

Graham was able to preach with authority about God's grace and forgiveness because he claimed the gospel of grace for himself on a daily basis. Despite all his achievements and the honors he received, he never became haughty. He could bear both applause and criticism because he saw himself first and foremost as a disciple of Jesus, similar to Henry Dunant, the founder of the Red

Cross, who once said, "I would like to be a disciple of Jesus, nothing else." Ruth and Billy Graham were, without a doubt, good disciples of Jesus.

When I hear all the different testimonies shared by people who met Ruth and Billy Graham during their long lives and ministry, I have to agree with the remarks of their daughter Anne:

> That's been a blessing to watch—the reality of my parents' faith lived out on the anvil of those day-to-day experiences of things that go wrong. To have done it so well and to maintain the consistency of their faith and their joy in the Lord and their love for the people—it's amazing. That's God's grace.[32]

Ruth and Billy judged their lives in the light of their divine calling and the One who gave it. In his presence, they remained conscious of their daily need for God's forgiveness and mercy. Not only the seekers whom they served or the clearly sinful people around them but they themselves, the world-renowned preacher and his wife, needed God's forgiveness.

Ruth and Billy treated their fellow believers with the same grace and generosity. A great number of people—old, young, and from various backgrounds—received new life and will someday populate heaven because of their lives and ministry. This group includes a surprisingly large number of spiritual leaders who not only came to faith in Christ at or resulting from one of the missions but also received a vision "to do something courageous in God's name," to put it in the words of the Swiss Reformer Huldrych Zwingli. All this and many more things that will only be fully known in heaven happened because Ruth and Billy remained faithful to their divine calling throughout their lives. They proclaimed the gospel of Christ's grace simply and clearly, trusting in the power of God's Word and the Holy Spirit.

The late German pastor and well-known youth evangelist Wilhelm Busch writes in his foreword to the German edition of Billy Graham's book *Peace with God*:

Perhaps Billy Graham's influence rests on the fact that he so unrestrainedly proclaims the power of Jesus Christ's grace. And he does so in a language that Hänsel and Gretel can understand. Here is the Gospel, clear, biblical, wonderful Gospel! . . . Billy Graham tells us how to "grasp salvation."[33]

The well-known German theologian Helmut Thielicke wrote in a letter to Graham after attending one of his missions in Los Angeles:

The evening was a profound experience of repentance for me. . . . When I was asked for my opinion from time to time about the type of preaching, I was certainly not too modest to transmit one or two theological observations. The evening with you made it clear to me (and the Holy Spirit must have helped me), that the question must be asked the other way: What am I and my colleagues in the pulpit and at the university lectern missing that make a Billy Graham so necessary? . . . On that evening with you, it became clear to me once and for all, my dear Dr. Graham, that you are sharing biblical bread and not intellectual tidbits and sophisticated propaganda. I would like to thank you for that.[34]

In his autobiography, *Notes from a Wayfarer*, Thielicke described his encounter with Graham and his team this way:

The encounter with Billy Graham, who was holding his gigantic crusade event in the Los Angeles Stadium, was important. At first, I had some misgivings to accept his invitation to sit next to him on the balustrade. When I did actually do it upon my friends' urging, I kept my eyes critically wide open. When thousands came forward for the invitation, I then noticed that his crew showed only collected meditation, no signs of triumph. His message was good homemade bread. I was quite taken by his warmhearted, unpretentious humanity.[35]

Time and again while writing this book, I had to put down my work to thank Ruth and Billy Graham and the wonderful team around them and plead to God, "Please, do it again! We need biblical prophets and voices like Billy Graham more than ever."

We desperately need warriors like Ruth and Billy who in a vibrant partnership drive God's kingdom forward into all areas of society, battling in the power of the Holy Spirit. Let us pray that God will raise up authentic, Spirit-filled leaders again. Let us ourselves be people who stand up and are obedient to Jesus's Great Commission and the Great Commandment to love God and people deeply! I dream of an increasing number of believers whom God can entrust with important assignments—faithful people whom he can trust to carry out their God-given tasks humbly and to his glory.

In the midst of increasing chaos and confusion, we are standing before a major spiritual harvest throughout the world. In view of the growing economic, social, and political crises and the increasing enmity against all monotheistic religions, this harvest work will not take place without blood, sweat, and tears, to put it in Churchill's words.

We Christians have to work hand in hand in the harvest. We have to sharpen our sickles in order to proclaim the gospel with clarity, with hearts full of love and mercy and with helping hands to meet practical needs wherever possible. In addition to sharing the gospel one-on-one, we need large-scale evangelistic outreach events to bring in the great spiritual harvest in the coming years.

Using a variety of tools, Graham proclaimed the simple Bible message of salvation found in Jesus Christ and him alone. Jesus saved us by paying the ultimate price, giving his life on the cross. He died that we might live, and live eternally. God wants to give us a new eternal life when we put our trust in him. This message, which characterized the lives and ministry of Ruth and Billy Graham, must again be spread far and wide. Now is the time for many new Ruths and Billys and Cliffs and Bevs whom God can send out into the world with this wonderful message. It is time for couples to see their marriages and families in the light of helping fulfill the Great Commission. Healthy families and teams will be a powerful witness in a decaying world.

It was moving to hear Billy Graham, marked by illness and lying in bed during one of our visits, remark with regret that it was now impossible for him to continue to proclaim the gospel: "You see, I just can't preach the gospel anymore." But we can. We can carry on his task to share the good news of Jesus Christ.

"This is good, and pleases God our Savior, who wants all people to be saved and to come to a knowledge of the truth" (1 Tim. 2:3–4). Our reply to the words of the apostle Paul must be, "God wants all people to be saved, and we want it too!" Is there any calling more beautiful than to share the best possible news that through his Son God forgives our sins and offers us a new start—yes, a totally new, eternal life?

Our individual contribution to fulfilling the Great Commission may vary. Some form the spearhead and are active on the front lines of missions. Equally important, however, are the people who form the shaft, keeping the spearhead on course through prayer, advice, and financial support. Some have the gift to provide organizational support. All of us have the task as well as the privilege to be a witness for Christ where we live, be it in our family, our community, or our profession. To do this, we must strive to maintain daily contact with Jesus, following Ruth and Billy Graham's example.

Growth normally takes place slowly, nurtured by God's Father-love. Our heavenly Father does not love us because we help to fulfill the Great Commission; he loves us for ourselves, even when we fail him again and again. If we lose sight of this fact, life and ministry become a joyless and fruitless struggle.

Partnership, authenticity, humility, intimacy, focus, integrity, faith, global responsibility, empowerment—all these core values, no matter how important they are—find their true relevance only in combination with God's grace. God, the Father, loved us first, and he continues loving us, regardless of our behavior. What a wonderful message to share with others!

Let us conclude by quoting a sister in the Lord who lived in a different part of the world and whose assignment was different from that of the Grahams' but whose life equally reflected God's heart to the world. Mother Teresa from Calcutta encourages us to share God's love and goodness wherever we are:

> Spread love everywhere you go: first of all in your own house. Give love to your children, to your wife or husband, to a next door neighbor. . . . Let no one ever come to you without leaving better and happier. Be the living expression of God's kindness; kindness in your face, kindness in your eyes, kindness in your smile, kindness in your warm greeting. . . . Do not think that love in order to be genuine has to be extraordinary. What we need is to love without getting tired. Be faithful in small things, because it is in them that your strength lies.[36]

And speaking about our mission on this earth, she said:

> What I do you cannot do; but what you do, I cannot do. The needs are great, and none of us, including me, ever do great things. But

This private photo of Ruth and Billy Graham shows a married couple who lived in an active partnership and who throughout their long lives never lost sight of their main goal of passing on the saving gospel of Jesus Christ to others.

we can all do small things with great love, and together we can do something wonderful.[37]

So far, I have met few people who had such a high perception of Christ and at the same time such a low one of themselves as Ruth and Billy Graham. They were always conscious that people and things can only be lastingly changed "not by might nor by power, but by my Spirit" (Zech. 4:6). At the same time, they also believed that nothing is impossible for God (see Luke 1:37). God used Ruth and Billy Graham as his instruments because they combined truth and love in such an inimitable way and never relinquished their God-given mission to lead people to Jesus Christ. They loved their heavenly Father from the bottom of their hearts and were thus able to make him so attractive to others.

The Bible encourages us to learn from those who have gone before us and who have been faithful to their calling: "Remember your leaders, who spoke the word of God to you. Consider the outcome of their way of life and imitate their faith" (Heb. 13:7).

Conclusion

I would like to summarize what is, in my opinion, Ruth and Billy Graham's legacy. Looking at their lives, we can learn many things to help us stay on course throughout our lives and fulfill our God-given calling. This exceptional couple highlights important principles for receiving God's blessing for one's life and ministry.

Awhile ago, my wife and I were speakers at a WEC event. WEC (Worldwide Evangelization for Christ) is a missions organization founded prior to World War I by C. T. and Priscilla Studd of England and now involves several thousand missionaries working in over one hundred countries. We had lunch with a retired WEC staff member, who had served as a missionary in Senegal for nineteen years. She told us how she had only truly understood the gospel of Jesus Christ for the first time during an evangelistic crusade by Billy Graham in Zurich. As a result of that presentation, she entrusted her life to God. Later, she sensed a call to missions work in Africa with WEC. There she saw a similar effect of Graham's message on the Africans as she had experienced in Switzerland. That convinced her that his was not a Western or even American gospel but simply the gospel of Jesus Christ, who was crucified and rose again for people of all races and cultures.

Billy and Ruth believed deep in their hearts that the message of love and forgiveness in Christ must be preached all over the world, irrespective of local culture or political system. They never deviated from their calling. They saw themselves as ambassadors of Christ and not of the United States, and they constantly sought to maintain the integrity of the message of the cross, not weakening or watering it down by trying to be "relevant." They believed that the gospel of Jesus Christ is already relevant to all people in the most diverse circumstances; it does not need to be made relevant through adaptation or by compromising its challenging message of personal forgiveness, salvation, and transformation.

Billy remained focused on only one thing throughout his life: that the gospel be passed on as simply and as comprehensibly as possible so that people could lay down their burdens of sin at the foot of the cross of Jesus Christ and begin a new life in the strength of the Holy Spirit. Graham's mother had counseled him more than once, saying, "Billy Frank, preach the gospel and keep it simple!" and his wife, Ruth, had prompted time and again, "Preach the Word! God has not promised to bless our words but the Word of God!"

Today more than ever, amid all the important efforts to proclaim God's love in both word and deed, there is a danger of neglecting the key Christian message that Jesus Christ bore our sins on the cross and offers us forgiveness of our sins and a completely new life.

Graham's mission can be compared to Jesus's mandate to the apostle Paul:

> I will rescue you from your own people and from the Gentiles. I am sending you to them to open their eyes and turn them from darkness to light, and from the power of Satan to God, so that they may receive forgiveness of sins and a place among those who are sanctified by faith in me. (Acts 26:17–18)

The Christian mission focuses on nothing less than a complete reorientation and a fundamental transformation, similar to the metamorphosis of a caterpillar to a butterfly. People who have been transformed by the Holy Spirit have in turn an increasingly transformational impact on their environment and light up many dark areas in the world with the light of God.

At international Congresses on World Evangelization, Graham particularly emphasized that any transformation must first begin with the individual. Each person must first repent and be transformed by God's Spirit in order to have a transformational influence on family and society. God's method of changing society is through transformed people who become channels for his transformational love. People who have been changed in this way are empowered to champion the needs of their fellow men and to seek fairness and justice in society. Many social institutions around the world have been initiated by Christians filled with God's love and compassion for others. God's love changes individuals as well as the people and situations around them. We too should take seriously Graham's admonition to link words of God's love with acts to demonstrate that love. Today, love in action is more important than ever. Christians must be known by their love.

Nevertheless, in our commitment to ease human suffering and create just societies, we must always remain alert to the danger of favoring social activism over clear and bold evangelism. In our own missionary work in Switzerland as well as abroad, we receive high acclaim for our humanitarian outreach, even from those who do not share our Christian beliefs. However, with the proclamation of Jesus as "the way and the truth and the life" (John 14:6), often applause abruptly ends. How quickly we then stand in danger of merely offering a social gospel in which Jesus is at best a role model for a revolutionary lifestyle. Jesus, however, is much more than a social revolutionary. He is foremost the Savior and Redeemer who sacrificed his life so that we can receive forgiveness of sins by faith in him. A gospel without the call to repentance is no gospel at all. Mission without proclamation of the gospel of Jesus Christ is no mission in the Christian sense. This is what Graham always emphasized in one way or another. It also served as the primary focus of criticism against him.

The Bible makes it clear that we are not saved by good works but are saved to do good works. Only our trust in Jesus's completed act of salvation makes us righteous in God's eyes and empowers us to be instruments of God's transforming love. Hardly any other person in the twentieth century was as committed as Graham to staying true to the core Christian message, never compromising the key truths of the Christian faith.

Both Billy and Ruth were conscious of the fact that they were at best instruments used by the Holy Spirit to be channels of God's love. For this reason, they strove to connect with their heavenly Friend on a daily basis, knowing full well that all blessings come from him. In their opinion, their God alone deserved all praise. They had a deep aversion to being given credit for something they felt they did not deserve. This was not false modesty but rather a sober estimation of their position in Christ. The awareness of their daily dependence on the Lord kept them grounded, both in times of great applause and admiration, of which there were certainly many, and in times of criticism, whether justified or unwarranted. In the end, the only thing that counted was what God thought about them.

Ruth and Billy were forever in love with their divine Friend. When you are in love, it makes no great difference what others think of you. In my conversations with him, Billy constantly emphasized that it was not about him but about Jesus Christ. All the fruit in his life was to God's glory alone. His words revealed a holy fear of ever taking credit for something he did not deserve.

I recently received a copy of Graham's publication *Nearing Home*, with a personal dedication from the author. Graham added the Bible verse Philippians 1:6, which includes Paul's encouragement to the Philippians. He continued to claim this promise for himself in his old age and also used it to encourage others: "Being confident of this, that he who began a good work in you will carry it on to completion until the day of Christ Jesus."

At the venerable age of ninety-three, Graham summarized his lifelong convictions in this book, interspersing it with personal experiences and anecdotes. It is a very honest book that does not gloss over the challenges Graham has faced in his later years. It is primarily a book with God at the center. It also clearly depicts the essential role Ruth played in her husband's life and ministry, both in younger years and in later life. To Billy, Ruth was the great role model of how to maintain joy in the Lord in the midst of weakness and pain due to illness. Billy said:

> The Bible's words are true: "Neither death nor life, neither angels nor demons, neither the present nor the future . . . nor anything else in all creation, will be able to separate us from the love of God that is in Christ Jesus our Lord" (Rom. 8:38–39). In the weeks before her death, my wife, Ruth, repeated these verses over and over to us. Ruth was always thinking of others. This was her secret of getting through so much of life with joy. She never focused on her problems, she turned her attention to Christ, and He always led her to someone who needed a word of encouragement or a listening ear.[1]

Ruth's life resembled the experiences of Priscilla Studd, founder of WEC, in many ways. While serving as a missionary in China, Priscilla lost a child at birth and was contemplating ending her missionary career. She opened her Bible, seeking God's wisdom, and then decided otherwise: "I made a covenant with my God that I would never let any worry come into my life, which could ruin my life as a missionary."[2]

Ruth tried to view everything from God's eternal perspective. Thus, even death and dying took on new meaning. In a 1991 interview with CBN, she shared her views on this process: "We look at death from the wrong point of view. We think of how much we are missing the one going home. We are not looking at it from God's point of view: a child is coming home, and all the excitement in heaven when one of God's children is coming home."

As Billy was faced with the limitations of age and illness himself, one might wonder how he coped with the fact that he could no longer regularly proclaim the gospel to thousands of people. When I showed

Billy the film about Christ-Day in Basel with a soccer stadium full of people, he could not hold back his excitement. Still, I sensed a bit of sadness that his career as God's public ambassador had come to an end. At the same time, my wife and I felt how much he had learned to value the small things even more, like one-on-one encounters with people. We benefited from the time he spent with us, listening to

Hanspeter and Vreni Nüesch visited Billy Graham shortly after his ninety-fourth birthday in his home in Montreat with three of their Jesus.net staff members. From left to right: Simon Loffel, Matthias Langhans, and Dominic Fontijn.

and answering our questions. After so many years filled with appointments and events in his younger days, we felt his desire was to get the most out of this stage of later life by keeping the Word of God active in his heart and spending time with his Lord.

When Vreni and I had the privilege of visiting the ninety-four-year-old Billy for a third time in his home together with three of our Swiss Jesus.net staff members, we still felt his passion to share the Good News of the Lord Jesus to the world. Together we prayed that he might once again have the opportunity to share the gospel via the internet through the My Hope America with Billy Graham Campaign around his ninety-fifth birthday.

Several years ago, I asked Billy what Jesus meant to him personally. His answer was, "Everything!" Now I asked him the same question again but with the request that he expand his answer for the readers of this book. After taking some time of reflection, Billy responded, "I am sorry. I cannot say anything more, because Jesus just means everything to me."

Then he blessed us with the following words:

Father, we thank you today that these people are available to be used as witnesses to teach your Word and ministry. Jesus Christ, we thank you that you were willing to come to this earth and go all the way to the cross for our sins. Some of it is a mystery to all of us, but it happens; we see lives changed and transformed by his life and ministry. Bless each one of these, I pray, as individuals and as a group. May the Holy Spirit empower them. We thank you that you gave us the Holy Spirit to help us with our daily lives and to speak through us and produce the love and the fruit of the Spirit. Bless each one as they go back to their own responsibilities. In Jesus's name, amen.

Before leaving, the three younger men asked him for a word of advice on how they could keep their passion for the Lord until the end of their lives, just as he had. Billy mentioned three things:

1. Pray often, several times a day.

When he said this, his daughter Gigi added that her dad prays right on the spot for things that are brought to his attention.

2. Study the Word of God and memorize key verses.

He added that his wife was a role model for him in this area: "She impressed me deeply with her love for the Bible."

3. Trust the Lord always.

His current challenge when we met him was trusting the Lord that he would be able to share the gospel once more despite his declining health. In his book *Nearing Home*, Billy summarized his fundamental attitude toward the period of his life after active public ministry:

The Lord blesses people who bless others, and He gives grace to those who focus on the things that please Him. Life is seldom easy as we grow older, but old age has its special joys—the joy of time with family and friends, the joy of freedom from responsibilities we once had, and the joy of savoring the little things we once overlooked. But most of all, as we learn to trust every day into His hands, the golden years can be a time of growing closer to Christ. And that is life's greatest joy.[3]

⟨⟩

Billy and Ruth Graham were able to step out of the limelight with gratitude because they drew their value not from their ministry activities but from their relationship with God, the source of their self-worth and identity. Being God's children meant more to them than anything else. Throughout their lives, they were more impressed by the King of kings than by any of the earthly kings of politics, culture, and finance they met. This enabled them to interact with earthly "kings" on equal footing. In return, many "celebrities" who met the Grahams expressed their appreciation at meeting people who treated them like normal human beings for a change.

Ruth was drawn more to the needy, those marginalized by society and people living with handicaps. People who had the privilege of knowing Ruth personally experienced her as a very down-to-earth and helpful person who had a good word for everyone. She showed genuine affection for others, not artificially puffed up piety. When she came in contact with the weak and brokenhearted, those who had lost their self-esteem, she practically radiated God's grace. She showed them the appreciation they needed and helped them believe in a heavenly Father who loved them boundlessly, even more than she herself loved them.

Both Ruth and Billy were steadfastly conscious of the fact that they needed God's grace on a daily basis just as much as anyone. They knew their daily survival depended solely on God's merciful help. The blessings of the past in the service of their Lord were no guarantee of continued blessing in the present and the future. Even in their later years, they still memorized Bible verses in order to align their thoughts and deeds with God's Word.

The Grahams consciously chose not to dwell on the past. When my wife and I first visited Billy in his cabin home, we were given a tour of various rooms. We noticed that there were no photographs from the glory days, not a single picture of a packed stadium or of meetings with heads of state or other important public figures. Instead, we saw many photos of their big family. On the wall above Ruth's desk hung a crown of thorns from Jerusalem with a large nail as a reminder of Jesus's crown of thorns and his sacrificial death for our sins. During the latter years of her life, Ruth lived in great pain. Whenever she was tempted to complain, she looked at the thorny crown and said to herself, "If Jesus suffered so much because of my guilt, who am I to complain about the comparatively minor pain that God expects of me?"

The One crucified for man's sins was the center of Billy and Ruth Graham's life and ministry. They thanked him unceasingly. They wanted to make him known and to glorify him with their lives. They drew strength for their lives and ministry from a daily relationship with the crucified and risen One. Allowing themselves to be filled and satiated by his love on a daily basis enabled them to faithfully present him to others with an appealing genuineness. It gave them authority to help others receive Christ as the Bread of Life for themselves.

Billy's main conviction was that we should align our entire thinking and actions with God until our last breath. He warned against acting on our own authority, which tempts us to release ourselves from our dependency on God. He warned, "Don't try to fight the battle of the Christian life in your own strength. Instead turn to God in submission and faith, and trust His Holy Spirit to help you."[4]

Ruth and Billy were evangelists through and through, but they were equally committed prayer warriors. They strove to remain connected to their heavenly Father throughout each day, cultivating God's presence, as Ruth described it. Billy repeatedly emphasized the important fact that prayer is more than simply presenting God with a list of requests:

Prayer isn't just asking for things we want. Prayer is for every moment of our lives, not just for times of suffering or joy. Prayer is really a place, a place where you meet God in genuine conversation. True prayer includes thanking and praising Him for who He is and all He does. The Bible tells us in 1 Thessalonians 5:17 to "pray continually"—and not just when we are facing a crisis or want God to do something for us. No matter how dark and hopeless a situation may seem, never stop praying. Prayer should be an attitude of life. We cannot afford to be too busy to pray.[5]

Ruth and Billy knew they could not hide anything from God but also that they did not need to because they knew him as a loving, merciful Father who accepted them despite their weaknesses and sinfulness. This personally experienced mercy was their incentive and the source of their desire to please God in every way and to keep their motives pure. Billy remembers, "My mother always told us, 'The important thing is to be right in the eyes of God, God sees into our hearts. He reads our motives.' This has followed me through life."[6]

Billy and Ruth did everything humanly possible to ensure that their lives as God's ambassadors did not dishonor the Lord or tarnish the message of new life through the power of the Holy Spirit, which they proclaimed. One important contribution to the reputation of integrity Billy enjoyed was made early in his career when he decided

For over sixty years, George Beverly Shea (left) enriched Billy Graham's campaigns with his songs. Here they are at the 1973 crusade in Seoul, South Korea, where an estimated 1.1 million people attended the last service.

together with his closest team members to conduct themselves beyond reproach in four sensitive areas. Throughout their lives and ministry together, this group of men held one another accountable to these guidelines.

Even in their later years, Billy Graham, Cliff Barrows, and George Beverly Shea occasionally entertained the Christian leaders assembled at the BGEA retreat center, the Cove near Asheville, North Carolina, with stories and memories of their sixty years of service together. One participant said that there had been lots to laugh about, especially when the over one-hundred-year-old Shea talked about "his young friend" Billy, who was over ninety at the time. Joyful stories abounded because they had placed themselves not only under God's protection but also under that of their fellow Christians. They were constantly aware that "going solo" in God's kingdom is very dangerous.

Asking for help is always humbling. Graham became such a great Christian statesman because he always asked advice of people whose expertise exceeded his in a particular area. Working with people who combined the heart of a missionary with profound theological insight, such as Harold John Ockenga, Carl Henry, and John Stott, expanded his horizon and gave him credibility even in theological circles.

However, the key to Graham's genuine modesty was his daily exchanges with Ruth. When traveling, he phoned her daily, mostly at 5 p.m. his time, to pour out his heart. In these calls, Ruth encouraged him to hold fast to the fact that a loving God had everything under control. Ruth had the gift of wise counsel and the gift of pinpointing a problem in order to find a solution. In addition to her profound Bible knowledge, her faith that God has only good thoughts about his children allowed her to exude almost supernatural calm and peace. The partnership Ruth and Billy exemplified is certainly one of their most important legacies. During their entire life together, they remained aware of their joint calling to ministry and that God had asked each of them to contribute their unique gifts to complete the picture.

During my study of the history of evangelism and revival in the twentieth century, I became acquainted with another side of Graham. Mainly while reading books by J. Edwin Orr, the noted revival historian, I became more clearly aware of how Graham saw his evangelistic proclamation ministry as part of a greater revival initiated by God. Orr served as an important role model for Graham during his initial public ministry and continued to be someone Graham greatly respected. In the foreword to Orr's book *Full Surrender*, Graham writes of the author, "I know of no man who has a greater passion for worldwide revival or a greater love for the souls of men."[7]

The same book relates an important experience when Orr showed Graham the dormitory rooms where John Wesley and his friends lived at Lincoln College in Oxford when they founded the "Holy Club." "That's John Wesley . . . and that's Charles Wesley . . . that's George Whitefield." Upon the question of how old John Wesley was at that time, Orr replied, "About twenty-six." Graham said, "You mean that all that began with a group of students on their own?" Before they left Lincoln College, they knelt down, and Graham prayed for a great spiritual revival like the one at the time of the Methodist revival: "O Lord, do it again!"[8]

Shortly thereafter, Orr and Graham ministered together at the Forest Home Retreat Center near Los Angeles, led by Henrietta Mears. Night after night, they discussed the meaning of revival in a practical sense and what they could do to help prepare for it. Aside from God's Word, Orr particularly emphasized the significance of the Holy Spirit. In the following excerpt, Orr gives a personal account of what happened afterward:

> In discussing historical revival and the deeper life, this consecrated and widely travelled young man was altogether an eager inquirer or listener. I think that the climax was reached after midnight one Wednesday night, when he opened his heart and told me of his desire for a renewal of his consecration and an anointing of the Holy Spirit.

330

At two in the morning, he returned to my cabin to tell me that he had received not only the sought-for blessing but an assurance that he was going to see real revival in his forthcoming campaign. Little did I know what was to follow, but I did learn that his ministry began to change from good to better.[9]

That was indeed the case, as the subsequent evangelistic outreach in the autumn of 1949 in Los Angeles became a turning point in Graham's ministry, making him famous overnight.

Graham's book *Revival in Our Time* contains transcripts of several of the messages he gave at that time in Los Angeles. Two things stand out. First, Graham quotes the Bible very often. As we have already seen in an earlier chapter, it was at the same conference at Forest Home that Graham decided in faith to accept the Bible as God's inspired, authorized Word and to proclaim it as such. Second, he emphasized that the empowerment through the Holy Spirit was absolutely essential for a fruitful spiritual life. In messages given during the first two weeks of the evangelistic outreach in Los Angeles, he spoke twice about the necessity of being filled and empowered by the Holy Spirit. This topic, which is typically reserved for Christians, is atypical for an evangelistic meeting. However, Graham was aware, most certainly as a result of his talks with Orr, that only when believers have been spiritually renewed will the eyes of unbelievers be opened to their own spiritual condition and their need of repentance. He was convinced that the lack of dependence on the work of the Holy Spirit by God's ambassadors was the true problem preventing the full blessing over evangelistic proclamation.

Personal history and background typically lead people to emphasize either the biblical Word or the Holy Spirit as core prerequisites for blessing in ministry. However, both are equally necessary according to Paul (see Eph. 6:17). Graham combined the Word and the Spirit in exemplary fashion: 100 percent God's Word supported 100 percent by God's Spirit. Herein lies one of the greatest secrets of Graham's authoritative and powerful proclamation ministry over the years. In this way, he was 100 percent evangelical as well as 100 percent charismatic. He was convinced that the Word without the Spirit leads to dead orthodoxy and heartless legalism. At the same time, he was conscious that the Spirit without the Word leads to a subjective, experience-oriented faith that fails the test of time because it lacks a biblical foundation. The presentation of God's Word empowered by God's Spirit and reinforced by a life of integrity was the key to Graham's success in ministry. This lifestyle was only possible, however, because both he and Ruth communed daily with God and devoted a significant amount of time to prayer and the meditation of his Word.

In the future, it will become increasingly important to establish technology-free areas in the midst of our hectic everyday lives, in order to spend extended time with our heavenly Father. We must learn to kneel before God and his Word to be able to stand up and change the world in a positive way. Ruth and Billy are examples for this kind of personal devotion to God.

In *Stories That Feed Your Soul*, American pastor and professor of sociology Tony Campolo recounts an event that reveals one secret why Graham's preaching ministry was so powerful.

Mike Yaconelli, one of the key leaders in developing youth ministries in America, once told me about finishing up an evening of meetings in Nashville, Tennessee, just before Billy Graham was to conduct an evangelistic crusade there. It was a rainy, foggy night as Mike and a friend were driving back to their hotel. Driving past the steps of a building constructed to look like the Parthenon, they noticed a man sitting on the steps, his head between his knees, and his coat pulled over his head to keep out the cold rain and the wind. The man looked so pathetic that Mike stopped his car, and he and his friends got out and climbed the steps to where this sorry figure was huddled. Thinking him to be a homeless man, Mike said, "Hey, mister, you don't have to sit here in the rain like this. We've got enough money to put you up in a hotel. Come on with us. We'll provide what you need for a good night's sleep." The man looked up, and Mike was shocked to realize that the one whom they thought to be a pathetic derelict was none other than the great Billy Graham himself. "It's okay," replied the evangelist. "I just want to sit here for a while and pray for this city." Mike and his friends retreated back to the car, and just sat there for a long moment. Then Mike said, "So that's it. That's why Billy Graham is able to win so many people to Christ. That's why he's so effective in the pulpit. Before he ever preaches, he prays over the city, just like Jesus once prayed over Jerusalem."[10]

Ruth and Billy knew their God was big enough to solve all problems. When he gave them a job to do, he also gave them everything they needed to carry it out. This God was not only capable but also willing to bless his children. God's desire to bless his children was even greater than their own desire to receive blessings. His passion to help was unlimited. Because Billy and Ruth had such an intimate and trusting relationship with God, they were able to do great things both for him and with him. "But the people who know their God will firmly resist him" (Dan. 11:32).

Ruth and Billy had a God for whom nothing is impossible, a God who loves people with a passionate love, and a God who had done everything to gain their trust. This impacted their lives more than anything else.

Let me share a personal account of how God once brought the same truths that so impacted Ruth and Billy home to me in an impressive way through an encounter with a person whose spiritual status was not even clear to me.

At the end of 1989, I was watching the Romanian uprising in Timisoara on television. This popular revolt ended in the downfall of the Romanian dictators Nicolae and Elena Ceausescu. Spontaneously a thought came to mind: the people in Timisoara know what's bad. But they don't know what's good. I prayed, "Lord, grant that next year's EXPLO conference will make it possible for people in Romania and the entire Eastern bloc to hear about you. I don't know how that will happen concretely, but you're the miracle expert." As a result, we experienced some very obvious signs and wonders. The European Space Agency (ESA) viewed this as a pilot project for their Olympus satellite and offered their services to us free of charge. The Swiss national telecommunications company PTT surprised us by offering a specially equipped mobile satellite control center, including the technical staff, also free of charge.

Although we already experienced God beyond measure, I got scared one day before the EXPLO began in Lausanne, Switzerland. I wondered what would happen if the technology did not function properly and the people in Romania, Czechoslovakia, Poland, Hungary, East Germany, and the Soviet Union could not receive the satellite signal from Switzerland. The thought alone of several thousand people in Timisoara being left stranded troubled me deeply. With these questions in mind, I asked the woman responsible for maintaining the connection to the satellite if she had everything under control. She replied, "No," adding that she had lost contact with the satellite. She then added with a knowing smile, "But with your God, things will work out just fine!"

Honestly, I would have preferred an answer like, "Mr. Nüesch, don't worry. We're experts in this area." I was not sure whether to be happy about this woman's faith or not. At any rate, I became conscious of the fact that she had a greater God than I did.

Everything then did truly work out just fine, but our faith was put to the test when the link to Budapest was still not established only ten minutes before the start of the broadcast. In those anxious moments of waiting for the connection to go online, the simple statement of faith by the satellite technician rang in my ears like a personal sermon from the Lord. "With your God, things will work out just fine!"

Nearly ten years later at EXPLO 2000, I recalled that woman's statement of faith when the live connection to Bethlehem for the millennium event refused to work. This was to be the conference highlight, and seventy-five subsidiary conferences around the world along with several TV networks were also linked in, waiting to see live believers gathered at Jesus's birthplace to celebrate the New Year and the new millennium. Someone shouted, "Put in the emergency cassette!" (We had previously filmed a clip in Bethlehem for exactly this situation!) At that moment, I remembered those words of faith of the satellite technician at the previous EXPLO conference. We interrupted the program and asked everyone present in Lausanne as well as all the locations connected to Switzerland to begin praying for the Bethlehem link to work. We had hardly begun to pray when the link was established. As a result, we had every reason to thank God that his Son, who was born in Bethlehem two thousand years ago, still takes our prayers seriously and answers them in such wonderful ways.

Perhaps, after reading this book, some of you may be thinking, "It's clear that God can use people like Billy and Ruth to fulfill the Great Commission. They are so talented and model Christian discipleship. They are much better examples of Christianity than I will ever be. How can I be of any use to God?"

I would like to reply to you in the following way: Ruth and Billy were also people like you and me, and they failed time after time. They openly shared about their mistakes time and again. Billy was not always the "tower of strength" he appeared to be from the outside. Without God, without Ruth, and without his closest co-workers, who always encouraged him, he would not have been the steadfast voice of faith he was for an entire generation.

God used the Grahams as his tools, not because they were perfect Christians but because through them he was able to meet people as the Redeemer who forgives sins and as the loving Father who welcomes new children into his family with all the rights and privileges that accompany that new status.

I also have to remind myself regularly that God can use me, despite my failures and lack of discipline, as long as I do not hide them. I became truly aware of this fundamental truth for the first time while in Argentina on a sabbatical leave. Among other things, I attended an evangelistic outreach hosted by the Argentinean evangelist and businessman Carlos Annacondia. Carlos is a man who combines humility with great faith in God and his Word, and I wanted to learn as much as possible from him.

So there we were, out in the Argentinean pampas in the middle of nowhere. Several thousand people had listened attentively to this evangelist, and several hundred had answered the altar call to entrust their lives to Jesus Christ. Then something completely unexpected happened. Carlos announced to everyone present that there was a brother from Switzerland at the event who was going to pray for healing in the name of Jesus for anyone in the audience suffering from an illness. I went to the evangelist in a completely perplexed state and muttered something like, "I don't have a church background where prayer for healing is common practice. I have little experience in healing prayer." Just then a condemning thought shot through my mind as I remembered how I had once again not kept my resolution to watch what I ate and had indulged in too much ice cream. How was God supposed to use a failure like me to heal sick people? Carlos didn't seem to be particularly impressed by my arguments. He blessed me for the task and made a simple statement that would impact my ministry for the rest of my life: "Brother, God will use you because he loves people." And to my great surprise, this proved to be true, as many were healed on the spot from various diseases. God wants to use us as a blessing to others, not because we are such model disciples but because he loves people and wants to bless them through us.

In my mind, the Grahams were revolutionaries of love, although they never would have used such words to describe themselves. But they believed deeply that God's love working in and through our lives and ministries would finally convict people of their need of a Savior and make them ready to accept Jesus as their Lord.

Ruth and Billy had not only the gift of leading people to Jesus, the Redeemer and Physician of souls, but also the gift of setting people free to start influential ministries. Several national and international missions initiatives were started because Billy encouraged the founders to take a courageous step with God's help. The lives of countless full-time ministry workers were decisively impacted through participation in Graham's evangelistic campaigns.

While writing this, divine providence led to a meeting with a woman whose husband had come to faith at Graham's 1960 evangelistic crusade in Basel, Switzerland. It turned out that no less than three of our staff members had received foundational biblical training through the ministry of this couple. As an indirect consequence of Graham's ministry, we as a missions organization have received three biblically grounded and Spirit-filled staff members. When I thanked God for this, the parable of the sower came to mind again. In this story, we read that some seed fell on good soil. It produced a crop one hundred, sixty, or thirty times more than what was planted (see Matt. 13:8).

Graham trusted that the proclaimed Word would fall on good soil in some of his listeners and would bring forth manifold fruit over the course of time. Seen from this perspective, all personal sacrifices became worthwhile.

Ruth had to bear at least as great a sacrifice by not having her husband around, but she did it willingly, seeing how others were greatly blessed as a result. Ruth said:

Mine has been the task of staying home and raising the family. No higher calling could have been given me. At the same time, it has been loads of fun. Also, I've had a vicarious thrill out of my husband's travels around the world in his unceasing attempt to carry the Good News to all who will listen. . . . Looking back, if I had insisted on having my way, I would have lasted in Tibet four years at the longest. Then that part of the world closed to foreign missionaries. And I would have missed the opportunity of a lifetime of serving God with the finest man I know.[11]

What would Ruth and Billy pass on to people who have just finished reading a book about their lives and ministry? The following are words of encouragement and caution shared by them in later years of their life:

> Do not look at us as examples of faith. Don't look at people; look at God. Meditate on who he is, what he has done for you, and what he has commanded us to do. He doesn't count your mistakes against you. He bore all your sins and made you pure and irreproachable. He sees you through the cross of Christ as his beloved and righteous children. And he gave you the great privilege as his co-workers to be a part of his great love mission to the world.
>
> Do not be casual about your commitment to the Lord. Do not let yourself be contaminated by the world. You cannot have one foot in the world and one foot in the kingdom of God. Quit straddling a fence, dragging the name of Christ down and making yourself unhappy at the same time. Beware of any distraction that keeps you from focusing on the Lord and on his calling on your life. It takes discipline to take time to study the Bible and meet the Lord. Place yourselves at God's complete disposal, without reserve. Then not only will many people be blessed by you but you yourself will also move from blessing to blessing.
>
> Always remember that God is faithful. We have all of God's promises on our side. We only have to take care of the possible. God will take care of the impossible. Miracles are God's department, not ours. Don't try to do the work that only God can do. Do not tell God how to run things. But let God do his work through you. Doing this, be gracious with yourself. Anything doing well takes practice. And remember that God loves you not because of what you do for him or for your fellow people but because you are his beloved child.
>
> Spend a lot of time studying the Bible and talking to the Lord! Rejoice, yes, indulge in the Lord! Tell him how much you love him. Remember: Time spent in prayer and in the study of the Word of God is the secret of successful life. If you neglect this, you neglect the very heart of a fruitful life and ministry for the Lord. Share the Bible as God's authoritative Word, and trust the Holy Spirit to use the Word. Do not be ashamed to stand up and say that God is your life's joy. Make people thirsty for the Water of Life.

Do not focus on your own problems. Instead, shoulder those of others, then God will take care of your problems. If God allows you to go through difficult times of sorrow and disappointments, then do not miss the lessons that go along with them. Instead, feel honored to have served the Lord under difficult circumstances. God is preparing his heroes in the wilderness. And when the time has come, they do appear and everybody is wondering where they are coming from.

If you are in danger of complaining, then look at the cross of Jesus and think what he endured for your sake. Then begin to thank him for this, and peace will flood your soul again. Strive to live closer to Jesus every day of your life. Remember that he has won the victory. It's time to quit being the victim of your circumstances. Instead, rule over your circumstances, focusing on Jesus, the great Victor. And if the Lord blesses your ministry and lets you experience great spiritual victories, never forget to give the glory to the Lord! And remember: The greatest triumph is yet to come!

Epilogue

W hat is Ruth and Billy Graham's message to the people of the twenty-first century?" While writing the book, I often asked myself this question, and I ultimately came to the conclusion that Ruth and Billy have a very important message, indeed, several important messages for us. I believe that their lives and ministry have never been more relevant, instructive, and important as examples and role models than today. To understand this, we first need to take a closer look at the current world and the effects on our Christian testimony.

Today's world has become a global village in which different concepts of life and faith coexist in an ever-changing environment. The world of the twenty-first century is marked by a great complexity and an overwhelming variety of options. There is unlimited freedom of choice, an openness without boundaries. At the same time, there are no longer absolute criteria and therefore no guidelines for decision making. There are no coherent values, no overriding principles, no permanent identity, no overarching goals, no sustaining sense of meaning or purpose in life, no trust in traditional value transmitters like parents, schools, and churches. On the one hand, this new freedom of choice is liberating because tradition or authorities no longer interfere with our personal decisions, and we are able to choose what feels best for us. On the other hand, with the dismissal of the absolute truths of the Christian faith, all kinds of competing "truths" have emerged on the scene, providing people with an even wider range of possibilities and the opportunity to pick the "truths" that best seem to suit a specific personal situation.

The basic value in human relationships is no longer responsibility but tolerance. We value tolerance highly, not necessarily out of compassion for our neighbors but out of our own need to be shown tolerance when defining and living our lives. As personal pleasure and instant gratification have increasingly become the only purpose left in life, the main question has become, "What will I get out of it?" and no longer, "What is right before God and man?" When confronted with the Christian message, postmodern people do not ask, "Is this true?" but "What's in it for me? How will I benefit from it? Does it promote self-awareness and my self-realization? Does it fill my need to belong and feel connected?" In an experience-oriented society, belonging and experiencing come first and believing second. The inflation of mere words has devalued them. People no longer believe our words and constantly question whether we are trustworthy. Although this kind of critical thinking is in itself a good thing, an individual's subjective judgment of the sincerity and trustworthiness of the speaker ends up being the sole determining factor as to whether they listen at all. As a result, an authentic life takes precedence over spoken words or even actions.

Let me start with a personal example that encouraged me tremendously. A Russian TV station invited our evangelistic team to reply to questions posed by people in the studio audience or who called in by telephone. I vividly remember when a man in the studio looked straight into our eyes and said, "I see in your eyes that you are good people." During the communist regime, he had obviously learned not to trust the words without looking into the eyes of the person speaking. Afterward, the whole atmosphere changed and the Russians were very receptive to the gospel. On the other hand, a fellow student once told me frankly, "What you say makes sense. But looking at your face, I feel I already have enough problems myself."

The reaction of the people of today when confronted with the gospel is similar, even if they do not say it out loud, to this Russian man or this Swiss student. In a way, this makes our witness easier, provided we are filled with the love and joy of God's Spirit. Nothing speaks louder than genuine love and joy. People begin to assume that we have a good God and that following our Father in heaven is sheer joy. Ruth was such an attractive person because she kept her joy in the Lord by putting her burdens daily on the Lord. A joyful, loving person is attractive and attracts people to Christ, as everyone looks for more joy and love.

We have to take this into account when approaching people with the gospel. People judge what we say by what they see. They first want to see and experience the relevance of our message in our lives before seriously considering it for themselves. We need to be constantly asking ourselves whether we walk our talk or just produce empty words. Words generated in the head reach the head; words that flow from deep within the heart reach the heart. This could mean praying with people first and explaining what happened when we prayed together later on. This could mean exposing them to loving fellowship by sharing our lives with them before attempting to share the gospel. This could mean showing love in practical ways such as meeting basic needs before expecting people to be open to hearing about the God of love. People do not care what we know until they know that we care.

The Grahams taught us that we have to speak about grace in a gracious way. Paul, the first apostle to the Gentiles, makes this clear in his letter to the Colossians: "Let your conversation be always full of grace, seasoned with salt" (Col. 4:6). The original Greek term is *charis*, which means "grace." The closest English word is *charm*. We should preach the truth charmingly. We should be "charming ambassadors" of Christ. This is especially important in a time when all kinds of religions are increasingly accused of applying truth without grace through abuses of power and the use of cult-like coercion.

Jesus makes it clear that we should love others, even if they do not share our views. However, showing love does not mean sacrificing our convictions. Paul makes it clear that the charming way in which we share the gospel should never be at the expense of proclaiming the truth, regardless of the reaction of the hearers. A combination of love and truth is what is required of a trustworthy messenger of God. In the same way, a balance between words and actions makes all the difference. It is not enough to proclaim a kingdom that is not "a matter of talk but of power" (1 Cor. 4:20); we have to demonstrate this transformational power with our lives. Merely speaking about a God who wants to befriend people cannot convey the complete message. Instead, we have to befriend others and love people unconditionally. At the same time, loving someone as a friend also includes speaking the difficult truth about the need for repentance. The Grahams can again serve as role models in this. People need to acknowledge their sinfulness before the Lord and ask for his forgiveness and grace. The best way for people to fully comprehend and experience God's love is by being closely connected with a friend who stays by them through thick and thin.

Because the people of today increasingly associate Christianity with staid formality and outdated traditions rather than with love and meaningful relationships, they search for substitutes, a group of people to call "friends." The success of virtual communities like Facebook and Twitter are the glaring proof. The more friends one has, even if they are only virtual friends, the more the need for identity and recognition appears to be satisfied. In the long run, though, virtual friends can never fill a deep need for love and acceptance or give the kind of purpose that makes life worth living. Depending on so-called friends, who often do not deserve the name, leads to disconnection and disillusionment. A self-centered lifestyle void of meaningful relationships inevitably leads to frustration and increasing pessimism. If people depend too much on the virtual world, personal values lose all foundation, the individual's personality begins to disintegrate, and all kinds of addictive behaviors develop.

At the same time, the internet, online networks, and virtual communities are great ways to reach people who get most of their information this way. Our staff is currently in contact by email with several thousand people inquiring about faith as a result of our evangelistic websites. Recently, we were privileged to put up an evangelistic website in Japan and trained e-coaches in close cooperation with Japanese churches to give orientation to a bewildered people. In an effort to appeal to most people's general interest in personal stories, we have begun creating personalized testimony websites focusing on the most diverse topics. These websites feature honest and moving stories from people of diverse backgrounds, sharing how they came to faith in Jesus Christ and inviting others to do the same. If there is any valid evangelistic method in the twenty-first century, it is most definitely personal storytelling.

For those readers who think their faith story would never be interesting to anyone else, I want to encourage you to sit down and write out your story in a form that would be easy to share with another person. You will be surprised at what the Lord shows you! Your personal story printed out in a booklet or even put on the internet through MyStory.me will speak directly to the heart. People can question what you believe, but they cannot as easily question what you experienced with the Lord.

Living in a self-focused world, even Christians are no longer immune to the effects of today's experience-oriented society, which lives for self-gratification. A typical twenty-first-century prayer is, "I, mine, me—Lord, bless us three!" Yet God wants us to be a blessing to others. We are in danger of placing our trust in convictions, strategies, and dogmas and not in our Lord. Instead of following the Truth, we follow all kinds of "truths" that promise to provide temporary excitement or relief. When we finally seek the Lord, it is usually just to make a fleeting request. As a result, our works are not built on Jesus as the Truth and the Life but on all kinds of personal views and desires that distract us from depending on Jesus alone. Everything that does not lead to Jesus will lead us to believe in people or temporal concepts rather than the eternal Lord. We can even end up believing in the power of faith as a concept, which is

sheer humanism if not built on faith in Christ. Often, without realizing, we Christians worship our work, our ministry, our movement
or church, our perfect strategy, or our method more than our Lord.

Christians of the twenty-first century, especially in the hedonistic,
performance-oriented West, where there is no or little persecution of
Christians, are not so different from the world around them. They
easily get distracted by a myriad of choices offered by a world that
promises quick results without sacrifice or personal commitment, let
alone pain. *Discipline* has become a foreign word to most disciples
of Christ. As a result, they lack the necessary perseverance and fail
to live up to their God-given potential. Stamina for the long haul is
a dying concept. Today's "instant" mentality has been reinforced by
new technology. In our consumer-oriented society, we jump from one
"special offer" to the next, neglecting both God and our neighbor. Life
has become a multifaceted patchwork quilt that is unraveling before
our eyes. Form has replaced content; aesthetics has replaced ethics;
superficiality has replaced depth. Christianity has become more of a
belief system than a revolutionary lifestyle and radical counterculture
standing in direct opposition to the secular world around us.

Jesus has become more of a "head issue" than a "heart issue."
Fewer and fewer Christians live lives deeply connected to him. We
might still regard Jesus as our Savior but not as our Master. We are
overlooking the aspect of lordship, which requires that our wills be
replaced with God's will and recognizes that God knows best when
it comes to directing our lives. Even if we believe in Christ as Lord
of lords, we might not follow him as our personal Lord and Master.
We prefer to follow our own ideas and deal with the demands and
problems of life in our own strength. As a result, our lives lack deep
roots and do not produce spiritual fruit. Jesus describes this type of
person in the parable of the sower:

> Those on the rocky ground are the ones who receive the word with
> joy when they hear it, but they have no root. They believe for a while,
> but in the time of testing they fall away. (Luke 8:13)

But there are hopeful signs! More and more Christians are realizing that their faith is not strong enough to cope with the challenges of modern life. An increasing number of Christians, churches, and movements are fed up with arguing about nonessentials and are beginning to reach out to their brothers and sisters in faith. All over the world a growing number of believers are uniting to pray and take action across denominational boundaries. Unity in love is a powerful testimony to the world. The minister of religion of a country closed to open missions activities told me that she was willing to make an exception in our case and would support our mission because we collaborated equally with all denominations and churches. She added that equality and unity were values held highly in their socialist constitution.

The twenty-first century is marked by greed and an exaggerated consumer mentality, as well as by an increasing sense of chaos coupled with an existential fear of losing the standard of living to which we have become accustomed. The situation can quickly become uncontrollable for authorities who are unable to restrain the growing number of people who take to the streets to fight for their right to have a better life. These desperate attempts to improve bad situations inevitably end in violent riots. There are no easy solutions.

As Christians, we know that God is in control. Only things that are not eternal will be shaken so that the things that cannot be shaken become more visible. The Bible makes it clear that the coming of the Lord will be preceded by increasing waves of upheaval that are God's call to an estranged world to return to him. Christians who have a deep faith in the Lord and the truth of the Word of God will stand like beacons of righteousness because their faith is rooted in a personal knowledge of the Lord. They know who he is. They know his character. They know he always extends grace before judgment, always. And they know he is fully in control. In the midst of turmoil, they are at peace. Amid increasing discord and hatred, they display unity and harmony. In the shadows of increasing darkness, they reflect the light of Christ. Faced with hopelessness and despair, they are heartened by the assurance that the Lord will never abandon them and that he wants to use them as living testimonies of love and hope. They gladly live as his ambassadors who bring the message of grace, restoration, and eternal life.

In light of what I have described, let us review the lessons we can learn from Ruth and Billy Graham as ambassadors of Christ.

When Billy Graham's oldest daughter, Gigi, is asked to describe her father, she characterizes him as someone who always evaluates things with eternity's perspective in mind. The same was true for her mother, Ruth, who always tried to look at circumstances and people through God's eyes.

Both Ruth and Billy approached life with both feet on earth and their eyes focused on heaven. Biblical promises were just as real to them as the visible world before them. In times of dizzying change and innumerable options that competed for their attention, it was crucial to them to be rooted in unchanging, eternal values. In a day and age when the world seems to be spinning out of control, decisions need to be made from a long-term, eternal perspective. Ruth and Billy teach us to keep our eyes focused on heaven as chaos rages on. They show us how to stay cool as the temperature rises. They exemplify a life not driven by circumstances but by God's eternal values. Their only guide was God's will for their lives. This kind of lifestyle provides great stability, a must for the Christian life and witness in the twenty-first century.

Ruth seldom complained because she felt it was not valid from God's point of view. She chose to trust that he always had everything under control. During her childhood in China and North Korea, she was confronted by constant turmoil and dangers of all kinds as a result of civil war. Through these circumstances, she learned that the fear of the Lord drives away all other fears. She came to know God as utterly reliable, knowing that nothing would be able to thwart his purpose and future for her life. If God wanted her husband to go on preaching, then she would not worry that something could happen that would hinder him from doing so. The same was true for Billy. He was never afraid of something bad happening to him as long as he was carrying out God's will. Interestingly enough, he did not feel the same way about his wife and children. He often worried about them. The family was Ruth's responsibility, but she refused to worry, especially after she learned the power of thanking and praising God in all situations.

Looking at people and things through God's eyes provides stability and hope. In a time of increasing despair, a vision nourished by eternal hope is of great importance. The scope of our vision normally corresponds to the scope of our lives. We can never go further than what we see with our inner eye. Christians need to develop the ability to see things and people not primarily as they are now but as what they can become by God's transformational work. They need to live lives focused on God's promises, not clouded by problems. They need to believe in God's unlimited power to change both circumstances and people. Ruth saw people through the lens of the Holy Spirit's transforming power. She gravitated to broken people and damaged things because she already saw them restored and healed by the grace of Christ.

God recently spoke to me in this respect. As I do from time to time, I was hunting for crystals in the Swiss mountains with a friend who had never accompanied me on an expedition before. We found a cave with brownish rock crystals called smoky quartz. When we found them, they were covered with mud. My friend saw only the muddy surface and was not interested in taking them home. As a crystal hunter with a lifetime of experience, I could already see the beautiful crystals hidden under the layer of mud and was excited about our find. What looked like only dirt and debris was very valuable to me. After being cleaned, the crystals shone so brilliantly that even my friend got excited. I sensed God speaking to me through this experience:

> I want my people to be like crystal hunters, able to see the sparkling crystals that people will be after being washed in the blood of my

Son. I want my people to see beyond the dirty surface of others. I want them to look at sinners with the eyes of crystal hunters.

One person who was able to see beyond the dirty surface to envision the shining crystals underneath was Ruth Graham. This gift helped her when she encountered people with unmistakable flaws, and it was invaluable to her when raising her children. In the years of her sons' rebellion, she saw the hunger for authenticity and purpose in life. She believed that God would finally turn the rebellion around and make them into revolutionaries of love. She encouraged her daughters when they went through times of personal hardship, helping them redirect their focus to the Lord. She learned that nothing is more important than encouraging and praising children, telling them what God can make out of their lives.

This attitude is important not only in helping our children grow and mature but also in making a significant difference in the lives of the people we minister to, especially the broken ones. Both Ruth and Billy ministered to them by infusing them with God's vision for their lives. They were aware how sharing God's unconditional love can build up others' self-esteem and faith. They instilled in them the knowledge that they were perfect and holy in God's eyes and taught them how to bring their brokenness to the Lord by faith. By acting with grace, they personified God's grace to them.

In times when people are driven to high performance and every action is measured in dollars and cents, people need to be constantly reminded that there are deeper, more important values to live by. Our value is not determined by school grades, salary size, physical strength, or our chances of winning a beauty contest. Every individual is beautiful and exceedingly precious in God's eyes. This is the message people of today need to hear. The Grahams give us a blueprint for the way we should treat people.

One of Billy Graham's greatest strengths was always his acceptance of people in spite of their earthly status. He treated the lowly the same way he treated the celebrities, and vice versa. He treated sinners the same way he treated saints. In his company, one felt like a king. My wife and I experienced this loving kindness during our visits in his home. He treated us like we were very important people. Many who met Billy personally later shared that they felt perplexed in his presence, confused about who the "very important person" was, Graham or themselves.

This welcoming attitude toward people irrespective of their importance in the eyes of the world helped Graham when encountering "ordinary" people as well as when he met the important and powerful. When asked how he could be so kind to the American presidents even after an obvious failure, he responded, "I just loved them." This was not a pious platitude but revealed Billy's true feeling for everyone he met. He saw in each person God's wonderful creation, no matter how distorted in some cases. From an eternal perspective, he saw all believers as perfect and beloved children of God and coheirs of God's kingdom. The American presidents in particular needed acceptance that was not based on their earthly status and power. They liked Graham because, in President Clinton's terms, "he was always so kind to us." He could love the biggest sinners because he felt God's deep love for them, which Jesus demonstrated in his willingness to give up his life for them.

Both Ruth and Billy cared for simple people as much as for celebrities because they saw the eternal value of each soul. From eternity's point of view, there was no difference between the successful and the people who were down and out. They all needed God's daily forgiveness and transformation.

Because Ruth and Billy built their own identity on eternal values, they were not overly unsettled by the ups and downs of earthly life. For them, "only what God thinks of it" counted. Billy and Ruth lived by this conviction. Earthly glory did not hold much appeal for them. This attitude allowed them to keep their childlike faith and remain dependent on the Lord both in times of overwhelming acclaim and when faced with harsh criticism. They saw the mighty and powerful as ordinary people who needed the Lord, personal attention, and words of encouragement. The same was true for those beyond the limelight. Billy took as much time to listen to a maid as to the important politician seeking counsel. The same was true for Ruth. When she was on the road with Billy, she liked talking with waiters in restaurants and filling station employees as much as with the celebrities or wannabes who constantly surrounded them.

In a time when a person's worth is defined by economic achievement, we can learn a lot from the Grahams. If we are honest, we can admit to seeing a similar attitude at work in the church today, with people being esteemed according to their ability "to perform." In God's eyes, a slow worker is as respected as a fast one, a person skilled in public speaking is as prized as one who has difficulty communicating at all. We should treat underprivileged people with special kindness because they show us God's loving and gracious character in a way that strong, healthy people cannot. After all, God promises us a special blessing when we care for the poor and disabled.

My father owned a company that manufactured wonderful embroidery, including the fabric used to make the Queen of England's coronation gown in 1953. During my university studies in business administration, I once asked him why he always employed several disabled people who could never produce enough to match the salary they received. I still remember his response: "If we care for the weak and disabled, then God will also care for us and the well-being of our company."

As far as his message is concerned, Billy Graham is a typical evangelical. The cross of Christ is the center of his message. Early in his ministry, he decided never to give an evangelistic message without mentioning the center of Christianity, the cross, where the Son of God gave his life so that anyone who believes in him will not be lost but receive eternal life. He rarely ever spoke in public without extending the invitation to receive Christ as personal Savior and Lord.

He believed in the authority of the Bible as God's Word to humankind. And he preached this Word with great power and urgency. He never compromised his core message but adapted it to the local situation. He always tried to connect with the audience, never missing a chance to bring in a good local angle by referring to a political situation or an event on the minds of his listeners. He tried to make his message relevant without ever changing the core element. In doing this, he relied completely on the work of the Holy Spirit, who uses the Word to convict. He decided to follow the example of the apostle Paul: "For I resolved to know nothing while I was with you except Jesus Christ and him crucified. . . . My message and my preaching were not with wise and persuasive words, but with a demonstration of the Spirit's power" (1 Cor. 2:2, 4).

Billy also emphasized the cost of following Jesus. He often quoted Jesus: "Whoever wants to be my disciple must deny themselves and take up their cross daily and follow me. For whoever wants to save their life will lose it, but whoever loses their life for me will save it" (Luke 9:23–24). He was convinced that the cross that called Jesus to a sacrificial death also calls his followers to a sacrificial life. To some, this would mean direct persecution; to many more, it would involve harassment and ridicule for their testimony of Jesus.

Billy and Ruth always wanted to be a voice of God in the world, but they never wanted to lower their standard to worldly conformity. They were aware of the danger of a faith that glorifies personal gratification and self-realization. Self-denial was a cardinal value for them and a prerequisite for experiencing God's new, abundant life. They never wanted to preach a gospel that accommodated the prevailing tide of superficiality and ego stroking. They separated themselves from the influence of the world but never from world influencers. They took seriously Jesus's prayer to his Father, recounted in John 17, which describes the followers of Jesus as being *in* the world but not *of* the world:

I have given them your word and the world has hated them, for they are not of the world any more than I am of the world. My prayer is

353

not that you take them out of the world but that you protect them from the evil one. They are not of the world, even as I am not of it. Sanctify them by the truth; your word is truth. As you sent me into the world, I have sent them into the world. (vv. 14–18)

Billy felt that Christians far too often built unnecessary walls between one another. As important as separation from the world was to him, he never wanted to separate himself from fellow Christians who held varying viewpoints on certain issues. He sought to cooperate with them as long as it did not require him to let go of his God-given mandate to preach the unabridged gospel of Jesus Christ.

He forged new paths when proclaiming the eternal gospel but never compromised the content of his message. He did not work exclusively with evangelicals but partnered with anyone who professed Christian faith and accepted the focus of the Graham campaigns. As long as he was not asked to alter his message, even theologically liberal Christians were welcome partners in his crusades.

He developed personal friendships with several Catholic leaders, especially Bishop Fulton Sheen, who, like him, was one of the first to use modern media to proclaim Christian truth. He described the late Pope John Paul II in very friendly terms. They met several times and held each other in high esteem. Because of this attitude, more and more Catholic leaders supported his campaigns, realizing that the commonalities outnumbered the points of disagreement. More and more Catholic priests openly confessed that they needed not one but many Billy Grahams for the ministry of (re)evangelization.

Many Protestants who originally held liberal convictions regarding the ministry of Christ and the need for repentance changed their minds through participation in Graham's campaigns and seeing the results of his preaching. It was much easier for them to change their opinions through this process because Graham did not distinguish between evangelicals and those who were less evangelical; he treated everyone with equal respect.

All through his life he·worked tirelessly to tear down needless boundaries and build bridges instead of walls. He did so with the Pentecostals and charismatics. He regarded them as precious brothers and sisters from whom he could learn important lessons. Graham played an important role in bringing staunch evangelicals together with Pentecostals and charismatics, an important act of unification among Protestants. He did this through both his conferences and his evangelistic campaigns.

One of the typical outcomes of his missions was increased Christ-based unity within the local body of Christ following the mission. A shared project provided opportunities for people from different denominations to get to know each other as individual believers, which dispelled false assumptions. This love and unity among Christians made the gospel more acceptable to seekers.

Graham also built bridges between academic theologians and evangelistic practitioners. He emphasized that he himself did not have a formal theological education. He looked to theologians and missiologists as instructors from whom he had much to learn. His gift of biblical discernment even allowed him to engage with theologians whose views on some issues he found to be questionable. His faith was so deeply rooted in the Word of God that he was not spooked by interactions with theologians such as Karl Barth and Reinhold Niebuhr.

Nor was he timid when meeting politicians or other dignitaries. Like Ruth, Billy believed he could learn something from every person, and they both had an insatiable appetite for learning new things. For them, there was always room for improvement. Even the secular world provided positive opportunities to learn. Billy widely used modern media. He was convinced that the best message deserves the best methods and strategies so it could be heard by as many people as possible. He invited well-known Christians to sing or give testimony, thus reaching a much larger audience. Ethel Waters, Johnny Cash, and Cliff Richard were regular guests at his crusades. Nowadays, well-known artists like Michael W. Smith enrich Franklin Graham's

Festivals of Hope with their music, adding to the stadium-filling crowds. At the same time, Billy Graham always emphasized that he did not put his trust in these human methods but solely in the transforming work of the Holy Spirit, who could use all means to glorify Christ and lead people to repentance.

Billy and Ruth chose to look at everything from God's perspective, which was often very different from the human point of view. Seemingly indispensable, nonnegotiable elements were often ultimately the result of human tradition and habit alone. They felt that many traditional barriers were not God-ordained but man-made. They vigorously opposed the segregation of whites and blacks at their events, seeing the separation as unbiblical because the Bible states that all are one in Christ. Billy never preached to segregated audiences, even turning down many invitations to preach in the pre–civil rights United States and in South Africa as long as apartheid was enforced.

Ruth certainly was a very secure person. Because she lived in dependence on the Lord, she was not dependent on the opinions of people. She did not try to fulfill the expectations people had of the wife of the most important evangelist of the time. She was quite opinionated, freely sharing her views with those around her. She wore

Ruth Graham had many artistic skills. Here Gigi Graham holds one of her mother's paintings that depicts God's hand, which is protecting the sheep from the wolves.

lipstick and makeup at a time when many Christians believed it was not appropriate behavior for a Christian woman. She tried riding a Harley Davidson and hang gliding just to experience the adrenaline rush that attracted young people to these kinds of activities.

Ruth was also very nontraditional when it came to homemaking. In fact, she actually built her home using logs from abandoned cabins. Humor was her constant companion, and she placed something to make people laugh in every room of her home, like eyes on the ceiling of one room that appear to follow the astonished guests. My wife and I only became aware of some of these bits of fun in the Graham home when our hosts pointed them out to us. Ruth placed a note on one wall with the following advice: "If you want the best seat in the house, you will have to move the cat." Yes, Ruth Graham was a spunky lady, full of wit and mischievous fun. She did not behave as nice Christian ladies were expected to, nor did she even try. At the same time, she was very sensitive and attentive to people's needs. She always led people to her Lord, who alone could meet their real needs.

Ruth monitored her own behavior constantly, adjusting her approach to suit the person at hand. She was very loving to those who needed an extra portion of love. She was very caring toward people in need. Still, she never tried to put on a pious facade and detested made-up Christianity. When someone's ego got too big, she found a humorous way to tell them so. She felt no sympathy for those who indulged in self-pity, and she let them know it in no uncertain terms. At the same time, she felt that every person had a message for her, even the most broken one who questioned the existence of a loving God. For Ruth, the main problem was not the lack of faith of an unbeliever but the small faith of believers who often put limits on God's transforming power.

Ruth Graham wanted to remain a lifelong learner and always questioned her own opinions and views. For example, she was able to dislike a certain style of music without condemning it. And she was very creative. Not many people know that in later years Ruth used her creative gifts not just to write poems, which she had done since she was very young, but also to create paintings. When Gigi showed me one of Ruth's paintings, I was surprised by its quality in light of the fact that her mother never took lessons.

Because Ruth and Billy were lifelong learners, they were open to new things and situations and could adapt to a quickly changing environment. This quality is essential in today's rapidly changing world. If we do not learn to live daily in the power and presence of the Holy Spirit and discern his leadings, we will no longer be able to meet people's needs. If our Christianity is to stay relevant, we need to be flexible and willing to change as God leads. We need to develop the ability to constantly learn while staying true to the essentials of our faith. Few things are more important in the twenty-first century than the ability to change and acquire new skills while staying true to eternal values.

Let me finish with another personal story, this time about my mother.

My mother was very active in politics. She was the first woman to preside over the parliament in Kanton St. Gallen. My mother's life motto was "Until I am ninety years old, I want to learn something every day of my life." She put this into practice. When she was already eighty years old, she learned to use a personal computer and took piano lessons. Now at over ninety years of age, she has revised her motto to state, "As long as God gives me life, he has a task for me to fulfill. It's exciting to find out what God has in store for me today." Despite her physical frailness, she constantly urges us children to use our God-given talents for the good of others, modeling this attitude for us: "As long as the Lord gives me life, I want to light a small fire in the hearts of people I meet and make them a little bit happier."

Appendix

Ruth Graham's Message to Wives

When Ruth made one of her rare public appearances at the International Conference for Itinerant Evangelists in Amsterdam in 1983, I was unfortunately not able to attend because the question and answer time with Ruth was intended only for evangelists' wives, and I was not brave enough to disturb the women's tranquility by being the only man present. However, I did buy a recording of the session and had it transcribed. I found Ruth's remarks very valuable, particularly those on the identity of a wife at a strong man's side. I would like to summarize her most important points.

Ruth first emphasized what a privilege it was to be able to participate in such a wonderful mission: "I think we have perhaps one of the most difficult and most rewarding jobs in the world, to be married to a traveling evangelist. It's a great responsibility and a great privilege, but we've got to keep our priorities straight."

Ruth considered it a great honor to serve at an evangelist's side, even though it was not always easy. But perhaps God had specifically chosen the women present because he had the confidence that they would manage with his help. Their task was to release their husbands for their evangelistic work so that they could follow their calling. Obviously, this would not work without certain adjustments. Ruth's advice was, "We need to study our husbands carefully and prayerfully and ask the Lord what we can be to our husbands, how we can adapt ourselves to them." She then pointed out that each man is different and requires individual support. "We can ask the Lord to help us minister to each one of our husbands the way they need to be ministered to."

According to Ruth, it was important to give one's full yes to the calling as a wife and a mother, a ministry that is just as important and valuable as the husband's. She emphasized that wives who cannot fully accept their God-given role would eventually become bitter and poison the atmosphere at home so that even the children would no longer wish to have anything to do with their parents' faith. Ruth said, "It's terribly important to have a happy home. There are some Christian homes that are pretty grim places." Ruth then provided a positive and a negative example of this. In one case, the children followed in their parents' footsteps because the whole house was filled with laughter from morning to night. In another case, the children were glad to leave all the pious stuff behind them as quickly as possible.

Ruth felt that the main task as the wife of a spiritual leader was to joyfully stand beside him and support his ministry with all one's strength. As a mother, the task was to raise children with love and biblical guidelines and provide a happy home. This twofold responsibility sometimes meant that one had to put one's own wishes as a wife on the back burner for a certain time so as not to overburden an already heavily laden husband. In such situations, Ruth recommended going to God and handing the matter over to him. "There are times when you can't go to anybody but the Lord. And you can't beat the Bible for good practical advice." Ruth advised the women to reserve a special corner in the house for themselves where they were not distracted by anything. And when God spoke to them, they should write it down. Even in the middle of the day, they should take a break and have a chat with God. That's how they would be able to recharge their batteries and head back to work again spiritually refreshed, just as Elijah had.

"A busy mother doesn't have too much time to spend on her knees, and that's all right. We've been told to pray without ceasing, and if we had to be on our knees all the time we wouldn't be getting anything else done. But you can learn to pray as you are dusting, ironing, shopping, walking. Just keep in constant fellowship with the Lord!"

Then Ruth confessed that in earlier days she had often neglected giving thanks in favor of petitions. With time, she had learned how important it was to thank God for everything and everyone. Then all sorts of worries seemed to disappear on their own.

"I realized that worship and worry cannot abide in the same heart. They are mutually exclusive. Once you start to worship and to thank God for those children he has given you and for the husband he has given you and for the difficulties he sent your way and for the tests—frankly, I've learned more in the difficult times than in the happy times. That's when your Bible comes to life for you, and that's when the Lord Jesus is the most real to you. So in other words, God is faithful, and he won't let you down when you've committed yourself to him." Ruth emphasized that especially evangelists' wives had reasons to thank God and worship him.

Ruth then dealt with the fact that many of the women present also contributed directly to their husbands' ministries, particularly those whose children had left home. She herself supported her husband's ministry by reading for him, doing research for his sermons, and proofreading his books. Ruth saw her role as an assistant to her husband. He came first, carrying the responsibility, and she was set free to do her part too. He allowed her to be herself so she could be truly liberated. She said that with a little wink at the women's liberation movement, which postulated that women needed to liberate themselves from their husbands in order to be truly free.

When asked, "What should the wife of an evangelist do when her ministry seems to conflict with her husband's?" Ruth replied,

"I feel my husband has priority. And I feel that I was called to be a help to him, and if something conflicts with his responsibilities, I look at that twice, and then there's maybe something I can get rid of. But I really feel that if we are to be a help, we have got to give our husbands priority."

Unlike Billy, Ruth was very practical. At home she was the boss.

At home it was the other way around. There she was the boss and Billy her helper at best. When her husband once joked about the fact that he had no say at home, she told him, "Do you want me to come to you every time the septic tank needs cleaning or the gutters need cleaning or something needs repairing? I'd be glad to bring these problems to you, but I'm trying to run the home conveniently and comfortably to free you for more important ministry."

Unlike Billy, Ruth was very practical. She was the head of the household. Her husband very quickly realized that this division of tasks was efficient, at least in their case, and that each of them bore enough responsibility. But Ruth did not believe that it was always the man who preached while his wife stayed at home. If a woman had the gift of teaching before big audiences, she should do it, and her husband should back her up. Ruth always encouraged her daughters to use their gifts of teaching.

Then one of the workshop participants expressed her disappointment that her husband's schedule seemed to pull them apart instead of draw them together. Ruth answered her with the following illustration:

362

If you are both keeping close to the Lord like the spokes of a wheel, there will be closeness. Sometimes we expect too much of marriage. We expect it to be a continual honeymoon. . . . Be a good listener, go out of your way to love your husband. Sometimes if he is preoccupied, just give him a touch on his shoulder, a kiss on the top of his head, little things like that. Don't expect too much from each other. We are in a tough spot. We've been trusted with a lot, so don't expect too much. Just give everything you've got and give it joyfully unto the Lord and love the one he has trusted you with.

At the conclusion of her talk, Ruth again strongly encouraged the women in the audience to go to the source with their problems, to God and his Word. She finished by passing along a word of encouragement from the Bible: "I will pour water upon him that is thirsty and streams upon the dry ground. I will pour my Spirit upon thy seed and my blessing upon your offspring" (Isa. 44:3).

Photographic Credits

Billy Graham Archives, 137, 187

Billy Graham's personal photo, 175

Chicago Daily News, Anderson Jarecki Stiewe, 171, 179

Geschenke der Hoffnung, Berlin, 19, 25

Gigi Graham's personal photos, front and back covers, 17, 33, 36, 61, 64, 65, 68, 70, 71, 75, 113, 122, 129, 149, 150, 173, 210, 221, 288, 292, 310, 316, 362

Gordon-Conwell Libraries, 82

Hanspeter Nüesch, back cover, 37, 45, 79, 105, 119, 213, 286, 324, 356

ICIE Amsterdam 1983, 76, 276

LCWE Lausanne 1974, 242

LCWE Manila 1989, 246

Press Photos, 26, 58, 84, 87, 106, 226, 272, 300

Religion News Service, 20, 28, 35, 38, 39, 47, 50, 52, 55, 60, 66, 78, 85, 90, 91, 93, 99, 130, 132, 142, 146, 154, 166, 168, 194, 204, 217, 218, 220, 240, 265, 266, 283, 284, 287, 298, 306, 307, 308, 328

Schweizer Illustrierte Zeitung, Ringier & Co AG, Zofingen, 133

Tom Sommer, 22, 156

WCE Berlin 1966, 232

World Council of Churches, Geneva, John P. Taylor, 228, 237

World Telegram & Sun, 56

Notes

Chapter 1: Partnership—A Couple's Legacy

1. William Martin, *A Prophet with Honor: The Billy Graham Story* (New York: William Morrow, 1991), 175.

2. Dr. A. Maurer, "Ein Paar Gedanken zum Besuch von Dr. Billy Graham," *Zürcher Kirchenbote*, June 1955.

3. Nancy Gibbs and Richard N. Ostling, "God's Billy Pulpit," *Time*, November 15, 1993, 72.

4. Ibid.

5. Billy Graham, *Calling Youth to Christ* (Grand Rapids: Zondervan, 1947), 7.

6. D. G. Hart, *Deconstructing Evangelicalism* (Grand Rapids: Baker, 2004), 119.

7. Pat Boone, *Thank You, Billy Graham* (Los Angeles: Lamb & Lion Records, 2006), DVD.

8. Russ Busby, *Billy Graham: God's Ambassador* (Nashville: W Publishing Group, 1999), 159.

9. Boone, *Thank You, Billy Graham*.

10. Alan Nichols and Warwick Olson, *Crusading Down Under* (Minneapolis: World Wide Publications, 1970), 140.

11. "Does a Religious Crusade Do Any Good?," *U.S. News & World Report*, September 27, 1957, 74.

12. Billy Graham, foreword to *Pope John Paul II: A Tribute* by Robert Sullivan (Boston: Bulfinch Press, 1999).

13. Charles T. Cook, *The Billy Graham Story* (Wheaton: Van Kampen Press, 1954), 98.

14. James Schaffer and Colleen Todd, *Christian Wives* (Garden City, NY: Doubleday, 1987), 51.

15. Gloria Gaither, "A Divine Appointment," *Homecoming* (May/June 2006): 34.

16. Ruth Bell Graham, *Ruth Bell Graham's Collected Poems* (Grand Rapids: Baker, 1997), 158.

17. John Pollock, *The Billy Graham Story* (Grand Rapids: Zondervan, 2003), 30.

18. Boone, *Thank You, Billy Graham*.

19. http://transcripts.cnn.com/TRANSCRIPTS/0506/16/lkl.01.html.

20. Nancy Gibbs and Michael Duffy, *The Preacher and the Presidents: Billy Graham in the White House* (New York: Center Street, 2007), xi.

21. Vernon McLellan, *Billy Graham: A Tribute from Friends* (New York: Warner Books, 2002), 39.

22. "George W. Bush Reflects on the Rev. Billy Graham," *FCX News*, December 21, 2010.

23. Thom S. Rainer, *Evangelism in the Twenty-First Century* (Wheaton: Harold Shaw, 1989), 173.

24. Patricia Cornwell, *Ruth, a Portrait* (New York: Bantam Doubleday Dell Publishing Group, 1997), 282.

25. http://www.msnbc.msn.com/id/8326362/.

26. Michael G. Long, *The Legacy of Billy Graham: Critical Reflections on America's Greatest Evangelist* (Louisville: Westminster John Knox, 2008), 128ff.

27. Billy Graham, *Angels: God's Secret Agents* (Nashville: Thomas Nelson, 1995).

Chapter 2: Authenticity—Genuine Living

1. Grady Wilson, *Count It All Joy* (Nashville: Broadman, 1984), 287ff.

2. Betty Frist, *My Neighbors, the Billy Grahams* (Nashville: Broadman, 1983), 22.

3. A personal meeting with the author.

4. Billy Graham, *Living in God's Love: The New York Crusade* (New York: G. P. Putman's Sons, 2005), 37ff.

5. Livingstone Corporation, *Thoughts and Reflections on Billy Graham's Life Principles* (Grand Rapids: Zondervan, 2005), 86.

6. Charles Templeton, *Charles Templeton: An Anecdotal Memoir* (Toronto: McClelland and Stewart Limited, 1983), 54.

7. "Billy Graham, the New Evangelist," *Time*, October 25, 1954.

8. "Billy Graham, the Crusade for Britain," *Time*, March 8, 1954, 73.

9. Gloria Gaither, "God's Ambassador," *Homecoming* (May/June 2006): 24.

10. David Aikman, *Billy Graham: His Life and Influence* (Nashville: Thomas Nelson, 2007), 299.

11. "Billy Graham's Invasion: His Mission—Save New York," *Newsweek*, May 20, 1957, 66.

12. *Christianity Today*, September 16, 1957, 32.

13. Stuart Barton Babbage and Ian Siggins, *Light beneath the Cross* (Garden City, NY: Doubleday, 1960), 56.

14. Ibid., 39.

15. Norman S. Rohrer, *Leighton Ford: A Life Surprised* (Wheaton: Tyndale, 1981), 166.

16. Ruth Graham, *A Legacy of Love* (Grand Rapids: Zondervan, 2005), 131ff.

17. Ibid., 132.

18. "Remembering Ruth Graham," *Reflection, a Magazine for Alumni and Friends of Montreat College* 10, no. 2 (Fall 2007).

19. Guy Kawasaki, *Hindsights: The Wisdom and Breakthroughs of Remarkable People* (Hillsboro, OR: Beyond Words Publishing, 1993), 196.

20. *Time*, July 11, 1969, 65.

21. Patricia Daniels Cornwell, *A Time for Remembering: The Ruth Graham Story* (San Francisco: Harper & Row, 1983), 62f.

22. Anne Graham Lotz, *Heaven: My Father's House* (Nashville: W Publishing Group, 2001), 98.

23. Helen W. Kooiman, *Transformed: Behind the Scenes with Billy Graham* (Wheaton: Tyndale, 1970), 98f.

24. Barbara Hootman, "Ruth Graham Remembered by Her Friends," *Black Mountain News* 62, no. 43 (June 21–28, 2007).

25. Ibid.

26. *Time*, June 7, 1954, 44.

27. Elizabeth R. Skoglund, *Wounded Heroes* (Grand Rapids: Baker, 1992), 200.

28. Deborah Hart Strober and Gerald S. Strober, *Billy Graham: An Oral and Narrative Biography* (San Francisco: Jossey-Bass, 2006), 145.

29. Ruth Bell Graham, *Legacy of a Pack Rat* (Nashville: Oliver-Nelson Books, 1989), 197.

30. Kooiman, *Transformed*, 100f.

Chapter 3: Humility—Dependent Living

1. *Billy Graham: Ambassador of Salvation*, DVD, AIM International Television, Dist. by Vision Video, Worcester.

2. David Poling, *Why Billy Graham?* (Santa Fe, NM: Sunstone Press, 2008), 154.

3. Helen Kooiman Hosier, *100 Christian Women Who Changed the Twentieth Century* (Grand Rapids: Revell, 2000), 355.

4. Leighton Ford, *Transforming Leadership: Jesus' Way of Creating Vision, Shaping Values, and Empowering Change* (Downers Grove, IL: InterVarsity, 1991), 233.

5. C. H. Spurgeon, a sermon delivered on August 17, 1856, New Park Street Chapel, Southwark.

6. Betty Frist, *My Neighbors, the Billy Grahams* (Nashville: Broadman, 1983), 190.

7. Vernon McLellan, *Billy Graham: A Tribute from Friends* (New York: Warner Books, 2002), 137ff.

8. Livingstone Corporation, *Thoughts and Reflections on Billy Graham's Life Principles* (Grand Rapids: Zondervan, 2005), 123.

9. Bill Bright, ed., *The Greatest Lesson I've Ever Learned* (San Bernardino, CA: Here's Life Publishers, 1991), 93ff.

10. Harold J. Ockenga, *Power through Pentecost* (Grand Rapids: Eerdmans, 1959), 125ff.

11. Ibid., 119f.

12. Ibid.

13. David Frost, *Billy Graham Talks with David Frost* (Philadelphia: A. J. Holman, 1971), 26.

14. Ibid., 26f.

15. McLellan, *Billy Graham*, 73f.

16. John Corry, "God, Country, and Billy Graham," *Harper's*, 238, no. 1425 (February 1969): 36.

17. Livingstone Corporation, *Thoughts and Reflections on Billy Graham's Life Principles*, 66.

18. Ruth Graham, *A Legacy of Faith: Things I Learned from My Father* (Grand Rapids: Zondervan, 2006), 66.

19. George Burnham, *To the Far Corners: With Billy Graham in Asia* (Westwood, NJ: Revell, 1956), 124ff.

20. "Billy and His Beacon," *Newsweek*, May 1, 1950, 66.

21. "Billy Graham: Young Thunderer of Revival," *Newsweek*, February 1, 1954, 42.

22. "Billy Graham, the New Evangelist," *Time*, October 25, 1954, 54ff.

23. Ibid.

24. Ibid., 56, 59.

25. "Billy Graham's Invasion: His Mission—Save New York," *Newsweek*, May 20, 1957, 66.

26. Jon Meacham, "Pilgrim's Progress," *Newsweek*, August 14, 2006, 37ff.

27. Ibid., 43.

28. Charles T. Cook, *London Hears Billy Graham* (London: Marshall, Morgan & Scott, 1954), 7.

29. Frist, *My Neighbors*, 39.

30. *Christian Life Magazine*, May 1972.

31. Patricia Daniels Cornwell, *A Time for Remembering: The Ruth Graham Story* (San Francisco: Harper & Row, 1983), 60.

32. Guy Kawasaki, *Hindsights: The Wisdom and Breakthroughs of Remarkable People* (Hillsboro, OR: Beyond Words Publishing, 1993), 193f.

33. Ruth Bell Graham, *Prodigals and Those Who Love Them* (Colorado Springs: Focus on the Family, 1991), 46.

34. Ruth Bell Graham, *Ruth Bell Graham's Collected Poems* (Grand Rapids: Baker, 1997), 275.

35. Ned Graham, "True Righteousness," *Decision*, Billy Graham Evangelistic Association, 2007, 31.

36. Graham, *Legacy of Faith*, 80.

37. John Calvin, *Commentary on the Book of Psalms*, Psalm 9.

38. Andrew Murray, *Humility* (New Kensington: Whitaker House, 1982), 27, 117.

39. Graham, *Ruth Bell Graham's Collected Poems*, 72.

40. Billy Graham, *Calling Youth to Christ* (Grand Rapids: Zondervan, 1947), 34f.

41. Morrow Coffey Graham, *They Call Me Mother Graham* (Nashville: Thomas Nelson, 1982), 70f.

Chapter 4: Intimacy—Living in God's Presence

1. Ruth Graham, *A Legacy of Love* (Grand Rapids: Zondervan, 2005), 59.

2. George Burnham, *To the Far Corners: With Billy Graham in Asia* (Westwood, NJ: Revell, 1956), 156.

3. Betty Frist, *My Neighbors, the Billy Grahams* (Nashville: Broadman, 1983), 49.

4. "Billy in Dixie," *Life*, March 27, 1950.

5. Patricia Daniels Cornwell, *A Time for Remembering: The Ruth Graham Story* (San Francisco: Harper & Row, 1983), 88.

6. Anne Graham Lotz, "A Godly Example," *Decision*, Billy Graham Evangelistic Association, 2007, 30.

7. Ibid.

8. Elizabeth R. Skoglund, *Wounded Heroes* (Grand Rapids: Baker, 1992), 194f.

9. Helen Kooiman Hosier, *100 Christian Women Who Changed the Twentieth Century* (Grand Rapids: Revell, 2000), 350f.

10. Julie Nixon Eisenhower, *Special People* (New York: Simon & Schuster, 1977), 65.

11. Ibid., 47.

12. "Remembering Ruth Graham," *Reflection, a Magazine for Alumni and Friends of Montreat College* 10, no. 2 (Fall 2007).

13. Ibid.

14. Stephen Griffith, *Ruth Bell Graham: Celebrating an Extraordinary Life* (Nashville: W Publishing Group, 2003), 43.

15. John Charles Pollock, *A Foreign Devil in China: The Story of Dr. L. Nelson Bell* (Minneapolis: World Wide Publications, 1988).

16. Brother Lawrence, *The Practice of the Presence of God*, rev. ed. (New Kensington: Whitaker House, 1982), 67ff.

17. Tullian Tchividjian, *Do I Know God? Finding Certainty in Life's Most Important Relationship* (Colorado Springs: Multnomah, 2007), 103f.

18. Jon Meacham, "Pilgrim's Progress," *Newsweek*, August 14, 2006, 43.

19. Vernon McLellan, *Billy Graham: A Tribute from Friends* (New York: Warner Books, 2002), 113f.

20. Harold Myra and Marshall Shelley, *The Leadership Secrets of Billy Graham* (Grand Rapids: Zondervan, 2008), 293.

21. George Burnham and Lee Fisher, *Billy Graham and the New York Crusade* (Grand Rapids: Zondervan, 1957), 168f., 62.

Chapter 5: Focus—Disciplined Living

1. Vernon McLellan, *Billy Graham: A Tribute from Friends* (New York: Warner Books, 2002), 15.

2. Stephen Griffith, *Ruth Bell Graham: Celebrating an Extraordinary Life* (Nashville: W Publishing Group, 2003), 65.

3. David Poling, *Why Billy Graham?* (Santa Fe, NM: Sunstone Press, 2008), 142.

4. William Martin, *A Prophet with Honor: The Billy Graham Story* (New York: William Morrow, 1991), 595.

5. Raymond V. Edman, *Das ausgetauschte Leben* (Wuppertal: R. Brockhaus Verlag, 1974).

6. Deborah Hart Strober and Gerald S. Strober, *Billy Graham: An Oral and Narrative Biography* (San Francisco: Jossey-Bass, 2006), 144.

7. Ibid., 133f.

8. James Schaffer and Colleen Todd, *Christian Wives* (Garden City, NY: Doubleday, 1987), 56.

9. "Dr. Billy Graham in Zurich," *St. Galler Tagblatt*, June 20, 1955.

10. *Der Stern*, June 27, 1954.

11. Billy Graham, *Just As I Am: The Autobiography of Billy Graham*, rev. ed. (New York: HarperCollins, 2007), 692.

12. Helen W. Kooiman, *Transformed: Behind the Scenes with Billy Graham* (Wheaton: Tyndale, 1970), 97.

13. Billy Graham, *Nearing Home: Life, Faith, and Finishing Well* (Nashville: Thomas Nelson, 2011), 90.

14. "Billy and His Beacon," *Newsweek*, May 1, 1950, 67.

15. "Billy Graham's Invasion: His Mission—Save New York," *Newsweek*, May 20, 1957, 67.

16. Graham, *Just As I Am*, 243.

17. Poling, *Why Billy Graham?*, 142f.

18. Karl Barth, "Evil Is Nothingness," *Time*, October 17, 1949, 65.

19. Luis Palau, *Scottish Fires of Revival* (Cupertino: Dime Publishers, 1980), 89.

20. J. D. Douglas, *Let the Earth Hear His Voice* (Minneapolis: World Wide Publications, 1975), 28.

21. Ibid., 29.

22. Robert O. Ferm, *Cooperative Evangelism: Is Billy Graham Right or Wrong?* (Grand Rapids: Zondervan, 1958), 23.

23. Morrow Coffey Graham, *They Call Me Mother Graham* (Charlotte, NC: Billy Graham Evangelistic Association, 2007).

24. Billy Graham, *Billy Graham Talks to Teenagers* (Wheaton: Miracle Books, 1958), 14ff., 33, 35.

25. Billy Graham, *The Holy Spirit* (Waco: Word, 1980), 55.

26. Cort R. Flint, *The Quotable Billy Graham* (Anderson, SC: Droke House, 1966), 61.

27. "Billy and His Beacon," *Newsweek*, May 1, 1950, 67.

28. *Time*, June 24, 1957, 74.

29. Wilhelm Brauer, *Billy Graham: Ein Evangelist der Neuen Welt* (Giessen: Brunnen-Verlag, 1955), 32.

30. Duncan Campbell, *God's Standard* (Fort Washington, PA: Christian Literature Crusade, 1964), 15.

31. Palau, *Scottish Fires of Revival*, 88.

32. Harold Myra and Marshall Shelley, *The Leadership Secrets of Billy Graham* (Grand Rapids: Zondervan, 2008), 45.

33. Martin, *Prophet with Honor*, 109.

34. "Remembering Ruth Graham," *Reflection, a Magazine for Alumni and Friends of Montreat College* 10, no. 2 (Fall 2007): 27.

35. Schaffer and Todd, *Christian Wives*, xiv.

36. Ruth Bell Graham, *It's My Turn* (Old Tappan, NJ: Revell, 1982), 75.

37. Guy Kawasaki, *Hindsights: The Wisdom and Breakthroughs of Remarkable People* (Hillsboro, OR: Beyond Words Publishing, 1993), 194f.

38. J. Lee Grady, "An Anchor of Integrity," *Charisma & Christian Life*, July 2005, 6.

39. Ruth Bell Graham, *Legacy of a Pack Rat* (Nashville: Oliver-Nelson Books, 1989), 97.

40. http://www.billygraham.org/articlepage.asp?articleid=113.

41. Ibid.

42. http://www.annegrahamlotz.com/static/uploads/Media-Coverage/Early_Show_9-13-01.pdf.

43. Ibid.

44. Anne Graham Lotz, *Expecting to See Jesus: A Wake-Up Call for God's People* (Grand Rapids: Zondervan, 2011), 45ff.

Chapter 6: Integrity—Responsible Living

1. Richard Neuhaus in *Billy Graham: Ambassador of Salvation*, DVD, AIM International Television, Dist. by Vision Video, Worcester.

2. Billy Graham, *A Biblical Standard for Evangelists* (Minneapolis: World Wide Publications, 1984), 131.

3. Harold Myra and Marshall Shelley, *The Leadership Secrets of Billy Graham* (Grand Rapids: Zondervan, 2008), 58.

4. Charles Templeton, *Charles Templeton: An Anecdotal Memoir* (Toronto: McClelland and Stewart, 1983), 61–63.

5. Ibid.

6. Ibid.

7. Ibid.

8. William Martin, *A Prophet with Honor: The Billy Graham Story* (New York: William Morrow, 1991), 603.

9. Henry and Richard Blackaby, *Spiritual Leadership: Moving People on to God's Agenda* (Nashville: Broadman & Holman, 2001), 107.

10. Ibid., 239.

11. Billy Graham, *Just As I Am: The Autobiography of Billy Graham*, rev. ed. (New York: HarperCollins, 2007), 27f.

12. Ibid., 29f.

13. Ibid., 106f.

14. Ibid., 128.

15. Myra and Shelley, *Leadership Secrets of Billy Graham*, 57.

16. Graham, *Just As I Am*, 128f.

17. "The Religion Issue," *Time*, September 19, 1960, 14.

18. Billy Graham, "Billy on Religion and Politics," *Time*, September 19, 1960, 6.

19. William Thomas, *An Assessment of Mass Meetings as a Method of Evangelism: Case Study of Eurofest '75 and the Billy Graham Crusade in Brussels* (Rodopi: Vrije Universiteit Amsterdam, 1977), 61.

20. www.beliefnet.com/News/2002/10/Billy-Graham-Organization.

21. http://www.accessmylibrary.com/coms2/summary_0286-8767760_ITM.

22. Martin, *Prophet with Honor*, 73.

23. Graham, *Just As I Am*, 59.

24. Martin, *Prophet with Honor*, 566.

25. *Billy Graham: Ambassador of Salvation*, DVD.

26. "Billy Graham Answers His Critics," *Look* 20, no. 3 (February 7, 1956): 47ff.

27. Thom S. Rainer, *Evangelism in the Twenty-First Century* (Wheaton: Harold Shaw, 1989), 173.

28. Ibid.

29. Ibid.

30. Ibid.

31. Ibid.

32. Jay Dennis, *Leading with Billy Graham: The Leadership Principles and Life of T. W. Wilson* (Grand Rapids: Baker, 2005), 148.

33. Grady Wilson, *Count It All Joy* (Nashville: Broadman, 1984).

Chapter 7: Faith—Living by God's Word

1. Ruth Graham, *A Legacy of Love* (Grand Rapids: Zondervan, 2005), 53f.

2. Julie Nixon Eisenhower, *Special People* (New York: Simon & Schuster, 1977), 75.

3. Billy Graham, "Biblical Authority in Evangelism," *Christianity Today*, October 15, 1956, 6.

4. Mel Larson, *Youth for Christ: Twentieth-Century Wonder* (Grand Rapids: Zondervan, 1947), 135.

5. Lewis W. Gillenson, *Billy Graham: The Man and His Message* (Greenwich, CT: Fawcett Publications, 1954), 14.

6. Ruth Bell Graham, *Christianity Today*, March 4, 1983.

7. http://www.christianitytoday.com/tc/storiesofhope/powerofprayer/9r4043.html.

8. Ibid.

9. Guy Kawasaki, *Hindsights: The Wisdom and Breakthroughs of Remarkable People* (Hillsboro, OR: Beyond Words Publishing, 1993), 199.

10. *Ich betrachte das Leben als Vorrecht und nicht so sehr als Problem*, interview with Ruth Graham, *Lydia*, ICI (International Correspondence Institute), Darmstadt, 2nd quarter, 1987.

11. Ibid.

12. Ruth Bell Graham, *Legacy of a Pack Rat* (Nashville: Oliver-Nelson Books, 1989), 59, 80f.

13. Helen W. Kooiman, *Transformed: Behind the Scenes with Billy Graham* (Wheaton: Tyndale, 1970), 94.

14. Vonette Zachary Bright, *The Greatest Lesson I've Ever Learned: Inspirational Stories from Prominent Christian Women* (San Bernadino, CA: Here's Life Publishers, 1990), 96f.

15. Graham, *Legacy of Love*, 13.

16. Graham, *Legacy of a Pack Rat*, 81.

17. Patricia Daniels Cornwell, *A Time for Remembering: The Ruth Graham Story* (San Francisco: Harper & Row Publishers, 1983), 149.

18. Jennifer Briggs Kaski, *Quotable Billy Graham* (Nashville: Towle House, 2002), 39.

19. Grady Wilson, *Count It All Joy* (Nashville: Broadman, 1984), 289.

20. Stephen Griffith, *Ruth Bell Graham: Celebrating an Extraordinary Life* (Nashville: W Publishing Group, 2003), 37.

21. Ruth Bell Graham, *Ruth Bell Graham's Collected Poems* (Grand Rapids: Baker, 1997), 187.

22. Ibid., 259.

23. Ibid., 255.

24. Ruth Bell Graham, *Footprints of a Pilgrim* (Nashville: W Publishing Group, 2001), 110.

25. Billy Graham, *Just As I Am: The Autobiography of Billy Graham*, rev. ed. (New York: HarperCollins, 2007), 135ff.

26. Ibid.

27. Ibid.

28. Ibid.

29. Ibid.

30. Charles Templeton, *Farewell to God: My Reasons for Rejecting the Christian Faith* (Toronto: McClelland & Steward, 1999), 9.

31. Ibid.

32. Cort R. Flint, *The Quotable Billy Graham* (Anderson, SC: Droke House, 1966), 74.

33. Ibid., 30.

34. Graham, "Biblical Authority in Evangelism," 7.

35. J. D. Douglas, *Let the Earth Hear His Voice* (Minneapolis: World Wide Publications, 1975), 24.

36. Ibid., 25f.

37. Ibid., 28, 31.

38. Billy Graham, "Why Lausanne?" *Christianity Today*, September 13, 1974, 5.

Chapter 8: Global Responsibility—Committed Living

1. Billy Graham, *Billy Graham Talks to Teenagers* (Wheaton: Miracle Books, 1958), 59.

2. Stephen Griffith, *Ruth Bell Graham: Celebrating an Extraordinary Life* (Nashville: W Publishing Group, 2003), 66f.

3. Billy Graham, *The Hour of Decision*, October 1964.

4. Melvin Cheatham, *Make a Difference: Responding to God's Call to Love the World* (Nashville: Thomas Nelson, 2004), 134.

5. Ibid., 139.

6. Franklin Graham, *Rebel with a Cause* (Nashville: Thomas Nelson, 1995).

7. Russ Busby, *Billy Graham: God's Ambassador* (Del Mar, CA: Tehabi Books, 1999), 236.

8. Ruth Bell Graham and Gigi Graham Tchividjian, *Mothers Together* (Grand Rapids: Baker, 1998), 15f.

9. George Burnham, *To the Far Corners: With Billy Graham in Asia* (Westwood, NJ: Revell, 1956), 81.

10. "Remembering Ruth Graham," *Reflection, a Magazine for Alumni and Friends of Montreat College* 10, no. 2 (Fall 2007): 5.

11. Garth M. Rosell, *The Surprising Work of God: Harold John Ockenga, Billy Graham, and the Rebirth of Evangelicalism* (Grand Rapids: Baker Academic, 2008), 15.

12. William Martin, *A Prophet with Honor: The Billy Graham Story* (New York: William Morrow, 1991).

13. John Harold Ockenga, "America's Revival Is Breaking," Sermon 1577, Ockenga Papers.

14. Ibid.

15. Sunday morning sermon, World Council of Churches North American Study Conference, September 3–10, 1957, Oberlin College, quoted in *Christianity Today*, September 30, 1957.

16. George Burnham, *Billy Graham: A Mission Accomplished* (Westwood, NJ: Revell, 1955), 143ff.

17. *Billy Graham: A Prophet with Honor*, DVD, Tullstar Productions, 1989, Vision Video, Worcester.

18. "Billy Graham Makes Plea for an End to Intolerance," *Life*, October 1, 1956, 138ff.

19. Ibid.

20. Ibid.

21. Michael G. Long, *The Legacy of Billy Graham: Critical Reflections on America's Greatest Evangelist* (Louisville: Westminster John Knox, 2008), 228f.

22. H. Richard Niebuhr, *The Kingdom of God in America* (New York: Harper & Row, 1959), 193.

23. Brian Stanley, *The World Missionary Conference, Edinburgh 1910* (Grand Rapids: Eerdmans, 2009), 88.

24. C. Howard Hopkins, *John R. Mott, 1865–1955: A Biography* (Grand Rapids: Eerdmans, 1989), 363.

25. Billy Graham, *Just As I Am: The Autobiography of Billy Graham*, rev. ed. (New York: HarperCollins, 2007), 559.

26. Ibid., 561.

27. Quoted in ibid.

28. Carl F. H. Henry, *God, Revelation, and Authority*, 6 vols. (Wheaton: Crossway, 1999).

29. Graham, *Just As I Am*, 563.

30. Billy Graham, "What God Is Doing," *Decision*, Billy Graham Evangelistic Association, January 1967, 13.

31. Graham, *Just As I Am*, 566.

32. Graham, "What God Is Doing," 14.

33. Ibid.

34. Ibid., 15.

35. Ibid.

36. Curtis Mitchell, *The All-Britain Crusade of 1967: A Pictorial Report* (Minneapolis: World Wide Publications, 1967), 124.

37. Erhard Berneburg, *Das Verhältnis von Verkündigung und sozialer Aktion in der evangelistischen Missionstheorie* (Witten: SCM R.Brockhaus, 1997), 58.

38. *Christianity Today*, September 30, 1957.

39. Graham, *Just As I Am*, 568.

40. Peter Beyerhaus, *Krise und Neuaufbruch der Weltmission* (Bad Liebenzell: Verlag der Liebenzeller Mission, 1987), 57.

41. "A Challenge from Evangelicals," *Time*, August 5, 1974, 48f.

42. Ibid., 48f.

43. Graham, *Just As I Am*, 568f.

44. J. D. Douglas, *Let the Earth Hear His Voice* (Minneapolis: World Wide Publications, 1975), 29f.

45. Martin, *Prophet with Honor*, 454.

46. Horst Marquardt, *25 Jahre Lausanner Bewegung*, DEA, Stuttgart, 1999.

47. Douglas, *Let the Earth Hear His Voice*, 1448.

48. Marquardt, *25 Jahre Lausanner Bewegung*.

49. Tom Houston, *Good News for the Poor II*, transcript of video presentation, Congress of World Evangelization, Manila, 1989.

50. Communications@capetown2010.com, October 5, 2010.

Chapter 9: Empowerment—Spirit-Led Living

1. Billy Graham, opening prayer, Evangelistic Crusade, Melbourne, Australia, 1959.

2. Personal conversation, Tallinn, Estonia, June 2009.

3. Ruth Graham, *A Legacy of Love* (Grand Rapids: Zondervan, 2005), 68.

4. www.quotationspage.com/quoter.

5. Earle E. Cairns, *V. Raymond Edman: In the Presence of the King* (Chicago: Moody, 1972), 5ff.

6. Ruth Bell Graham, *Legacy of a Pack Rat* (Nashville: Oliver-Nelson Books, 1989), 183.

7. Ibid., 98f.

8. Ruth Bell Graham, *It's My Turn* (Old Tappan, NJ: Revell, 1982), 170f.

9. Ibid., 171.

10. Helen W. Kooiman, *Transformed: Behind the Scenes with Billy Graham* (Wheaton: Tyndale, 1970), 94.

11. Ibid.

12. *Charisma*, May 2007.

13. "Billy Graham, the New Evangelist," *Time*, October 25, 1954, 60.

14. "Billy Graham's Invasion: His Mission—Save New York," *Newsweek*, May 20, 1957, 67.

15. Ibid., 70.

16. Basyle Tchividjian and Aram Tchividjian, *Invitation: Billy Graham and the Lives God Touched* (Colorado Springs: Multnomah, 2008).

17. Wilhelm Bauer, *Billy Graham: Ein Evangelist der neuen Welt* (Giessen: Brunnen Verlag, 1955), 56.

18. Charles T. Cook, *The Billy Graham Story* (Wheaton: Van Kampen Press, 1954), 95.

19. Ibid., 97.

20. Ibid., 100f.

21. Stanley High, *The Personal Story of the Man* (New York: McGraw-Hill, 1956), 17.

22. Harold Myra and Marshall Shelley, *The Leadership Secrets of Billy Graham* (Grand Rapids: Zondervan, 2008), 22ff.

23. Billy Graham, *Calling Youth to Christ* (Grand Rapids: Zondervan, 1947), 41f.

24. Billy Graham, *Revival in Our Time: The Story of the Billy Graham Evangelistic Campaigns—Including Six of His Sermons* (Wheaton: Van Kampen Press, 1950), 82, 93.

25. From a printed transcript of the radio broadcast *The Hour of Decision*, "The Fruit of the Spirit," 1957.

26. Billy Graham, "The Spirit of Pentecost," *Decision*, Billy Graham Evangelistic Association, May 1961, 3ff.

27. Billy Graham, "Why Lausanne?" *Christianity Today*, September 13, 1974, 14.

28. J. D. Douglas, *Let the Earth Hear His Voice* (Minneapolis: World Wide Publications, 1975), 1466.

29. J. D. Douglas, *The Work of an Evangelist* (Minneapolis: World Wide Publications, 1984), 8.

30. Ibid., 41.

31. Vernon McLellan, *Billy Graham: A Tribute from Friends* (New York: Warner Books, 2002), 36.

32. Ibid.,149.

33. Manila Manifesto, closing message of the International Missions Congress of Lausanne, July 11–20, 1989, Manila.

Chapter 10: Grace—Compassionate Living

1. Jim Bakker, *I Was Wrong* (Nashville: Thomas Nelson, 1996), 610.

2. Guy Kawasaki, *Hindsights: The Wisdom and Breakthroughs of Remarkable People* (Hillsboro, OR: Beyond Words Publishing, 1993), 192.

3. Grady Wilson, *Count It All Joy* (Nashville: Broadman, 1984), 296.

4. Ruth Graham, *A Legacy of Faith: Things I Learned from My Father* (Grand Rapids: Zondervan, 2006), 186ff.

5. Bakker, *I Was Wrong*, 265, 610.

6. Ibid., 367f.

7. Ibid.

8. Ruth Bell Graham, *It's My Turn* (Old Tappan, NJ: Revell, 1982), 130.

9. Betty Frist, *My Neighbors, the Billy Grahams* (Nashville: Broadman, 1983), 170.

10. Ibid., 163.

11. Ibid., 149f.

12. Wilson, *Count It All Joy*, 295f.

13. David Frost, *Billy Graham: Personal Thoughts of a Public Man* (Colorado Springs: Chariot Victor Publishing, 1997), 116f.

14. Jhan Robbins, *Marriage Made in Heaven* (New York: G. P. Putman's Sons, 1983), 129f.

15. Philip Yancey, *What's So Amazing about Grace?* (Grand Rapids: Zondervan, 1997), 262.

16. *Look*, February 7, 1956.

17. *Guideposts*, November 1977.

18. Ibid.

19. Russ Rusby, *Billy Graham: God's Ambassador* (New York: HarperCollins, 2007), 190.

20. Ruth Graham, *A Legacy of Love* (Grand Rapids: Zondervan, 2005), 106.

21. Armstrong Freed, "Ruth," *Wheaton College Alumni* 10, no. 4 (Autumn 2007): 29.

22. Richard Wrightman Fox, *Reinhold Niebuhr: A Biography* (New York: Pantheon Books, 1985).

23. *Newsweek*, April 20, 2009.

24. Nancy Gibbs and Michael Duffy, *The Preacher and the Presidents* (New York: Center Street, 2007), 303ff.

25. *Fox News*, December 21, 2010.

26. Ibid.

27. YouTube, Johnny Cash 1989 talks about PT 4 Billy Graham and Waylon Jennings, part 4.

28. Barbara McQueen with Terrill Marshall, *Steve McQueen: The Last Mile* (Deerfield, IL: Dalten Watson Fine Books, 2006), 233.

29. Grady Ragsdale Jr., *Steve McQueen: The Final Chapter* (Ventura, CA: Vision House, 1983), 10.

30. www.christianitytoday.com, January 2011.

31. Ibid.

32. Stephen Griffith, *Ruth Bell Graham: Celebrating an Extraordinary Life* (Nashville: W Publishing Group, 2003), 66.

33. Billy Graham, *Friede mit Gott* (Witten: SCM R.Brockhaus, 1974), 6.

34. Ibid.

35. Helmut Thielicke, *Zu Gast auf einem schönen Stern* (Hamburg: Hoffmann und Campe Verlag, 1984), 380.

36. http://thinkexist.com and http://womenshistory.about.com.

37. Ibid.

Conclusion

1. Billy Graham, *Nearing Home: Life, Faith, and Finishing Well* (Nashville: Thomas Nelson, 2011), 90.

2. Hans R. Flachsmeier, *Geschichte der Evangelischen Weltmission* (Geissen und Basel: Brunnen-Verlag, 1963), 320.

3. Graham, *Nearing Home*, 91.

4. Ibid., 156.

5. Ibid., 157.

6. Rose Adams, *Treasured Moments with Mother Graham* (Nashville: B & H Publishing, 2012), 163.

7. J. Edwin Orr, *Full Surrender* (London: Purnell and Sons, 1951), 5.

8. A. J. Appasamy, *Write the Vision! Edwin Orr's Thirty Years of Adventurous Service* (London: C. Tingling, 1964), 119f.

9. Orr, *Full Surrender*, 125.

10. Tony Campolo, *Stories That Feed Your Soul* (Ventura, CA: Regal, 2010), 142.

11. Ruth Bell Graham, *It's My Turn* (Old Tappan, NJ: Revell, 1982), 53.